Sex Tourism and Prostitution: Aspects of Leisure, Recreation, and Work

Edited By

Martin Oppermann
Griffith University
Gold Coast Campus

Sex Tourism and Prostitution:
Aspects of Leisure, Recreation, and Work

Cognizant Communication Offices:

U.S.A.   3 Hartsdale Road, Elmsford, New York 10523-3701
Australia   P.O. Box 352 Cammeray, NWS, 2062
Japan   c/o OBS T's Bldg. 3F, 1-38-11 Matsubara, Setagaya-ku, Tokyo

Library of Congress Cataloging-in-Publication Data

Sex tourism and Prostitution: aspects of leisure, recreation, and work
   / by Martin Oppermann, editor.
        p.   cm. — (Tourism dynamics)
     Includes bibliographical references (p.) and index.
     ISBN 1-882345-14-2 (hard). — ISBN 1-882345-15-0 (soft)
      1. Sex tourism. 2. Prostitution. 3. Sex oriented businesses.
   I. Oppermann, Martin. 1964-   . II. Series.
   HQ117.S47   1998
   308.74—dc21   98-4404
                                            CIP

Printed in the United States of America

Printing: 1 2 3 4 5 6 7 8 9 10 Year: 1 2 3 4 5 6 7 8 9 10

Cover designed by Lynn Carano

Contents

Chapter 1

Introduction

Martin Oppermann

The term sex tourism invariably evokes the image of (white) men, usually older and in less than perfect shape, traveling to developing countries, may they be in Asia, Africa, Latin America, or the Caribbean, for sexual pleasures generally not available, at least not for the same price, in their home country. Commonly it is considered to be an economic (return) flow from the economic prosperous to the less well-off nations. The health scare of AIDS has not halted or even hampered this flow of money and sperm but only modified the age composition of the female supply. Yet this nomen-cliche is only part-truth. Part-truth because it overshadows many other forms of sex tourism that currently exist and that may be of similar importance, and locally of greater eminence. For example, female sex tourists are reputedly more prominent in destinations such as Kenya, The Gambia, and several Caribbean islands (e.g., Aparicio, 1993; Beckmann & Elzer, 1995; Brown, 1992; Meisch, 1995; Pruitt & LaFont, 1995). In addition, in the Asia-Pacific region, demand by Japanese and other Asian visitors generally exceeds demand by Western tourists (e.g., Leheny, 1995; Mackie, 1992; Mings & Chulikpongse, 1994). Furthermore, a considerable number of sex tourists are pedophiles. And gay sex tourism is reputedly also quite prominent (Holcomb & Luongo, 1996).

Sex tourism is inseparably linked with prostitution but they are two different entities that just happen to share a lot of commonalities. One may consider their relationship similar to that of tourism and leisure: 70% the same but 30% different. Both terms—prostitution and sex tourism—are easily understood but very difficult to define in their fullness of meaning. Commonly, prostitution is considered as the exchange of sexual activity for payment. Yet, such a meaning exclusively relates to sexual–monetary exchanges where one persons sells his or her body to receive a financial benefit. What about a worker or secretary who sleeps with the boss? What about other than financial rewards? And what about those persons who are selling their persons to work on farms or factories for a minimum wage with the sole hope of surviving (see Chapter 5 and Chapter 15)? Or on a more intellectual level, how about the person who gives up his/her ideals in order to get and keep a

1

job? Is not that person also prostituting—selling out to somebody for monetary rewards?

The term sex tourism is conceivably even more complex and difficult to define. Obviously a major component is tourism, which, if one uses the World Tourism Organization's (WTO) definition, requires a person to be 24 hours away from home to be termed a tourist and less than that to be an excursionist. Hence, are there sex tourists and sex excursionists? For example, what about all the prostitutes in Mexican border cities who serve a largely "international excursionist" clientele (Roebuck & McNamara, 1973). And need sex to be the major component of the journey or a motive for the journey? Or can it be a side activity, convenient because of the circumstances and actively sought but not crucial to the trip? Is the intention to have sex already enough or does there need to be a "sexual act"? Does it have to be an unknown sexual partner on a trip to be counted as sex tourism, as one obviously excludes the usual partner? Surely, the wedding certificate alone cannot be a determining factor either, as too many cases are known where people temporarily got married simply for sexually exploitive motives and/or to circumvent legal barriers to work (Launer, 1991; Schmitz, 1987a). And what about "repeat visits" to the same prostitute in the same destination, which apparently is not too uncommon among sex tourists to Thailand (Cohen, 1986, 1993; Odzer, 1994) or elsewhere (Kleiber & Wilke, 1995; Symanski, 1981). And just as trips to "second homes" are included within the tourism domain, are trips to "second wives" or concubines also considered within the domain of sex tourism? And what exactly is considered "sex"? Does it have to be vaginal in heterosexual relationships or can it be anal, oral, hand jobs, or watching others perform either live or in video or per Internet with or without masturbation? How about the virtual reality sex tourist, or was it excursionist as the cyberspace stay is usually less than 24 hours, especially on one site? And who has to travel? The demand to the supply as in traditional tourist interactions? Or supply to demand as in modern tourist settings where tourist attractions are reinvented in closer proximity to the demand location for convenience?

This range of questions, which undoubtedly could be extended considerably, reveals the wide isthmus that needs to be crossed before one can truly understand and position sex tourism as a concept. The reduction of sex tourism to "tourism whose main or major motivation is to consummate commercial sexual relations" (e.g., Graburn, 1983; Hall, 1992) would mean an oversimplification of the whole concept and, as the following discussion will demonstrate, an exclusion of the majority of sex tourism cases and settings. Or as Kruhse-MountBurton (1995) phrased it, it "masks the complex process by which individuals choose to seek sexual gratification, first within prostitution, and secondly as a part of the tourist experience" (p. 192). The remainder of this chapter intends to provide a framework for inquiry into the arena of sex tourism and prostitution in order to facilitate a more ordered, directed, and balanced analysis of these topics instead of the one-sided representation so common in the contemporary sex tourism literature. It is the consequent development of ideas suggested by the author previously

(Oppermann, 1996). Although this book generally refers to sex tourism, one needs to realize that a considerable amount of demand is usually generated locally, as, for example, shown by Cooper and Hanson in Chapter 15. Also dance bars are often considered as "recreational" settings (see Chapters 11 and 12) where only a small proportion of the customers are tourists in its strictest sense.

Sex Tourism and Prostitution

> With a few notable exceptions the topic [prostitution] has not been seen as one for serious intellectual inquiry until relatively recent times. For all the touted liberalism one is supposed to find in universities, academics have been amazingly provincial toward the topic. (Symanski, 1981: xii)

Although the situation has improved somewhat over the last 15 years, a literature review quickly reveals the narrow scope of the majority of studies that might be considered as falling into the domain of sex tourism research. On one side are those books and studies that intend to reveal the male sex tourist flows from the developed to the developing countries with all their associated effects, very often highlighting the child exploitation issue (e.g., Ackermann & Filter, 1994; Bugnicourt, 1977; Latza, 1987; Maurer, 1991; Launer, 1993; O'Grady, 1992; Renschler, 1987a; Thiemann, 1989). At least geographically and conceptually falling into the same category are more academic studies that report on the phenomenon of sex tourism in, predominantly, Southeast and East Asia (e.g., Hall, 1992, 1994a; Leheny, 1995). Interestingly enough, the fact that a majority of sex tourists in infamous Thailand are from neighboring developing countries is generally ignored in these studies, but it was highlighted by Mings and Chulikpongse (1994) and mentioned by Renschler (1987b). Also, there seems to exist an emerging interest in gay (sex) tourism with its recognized monetary value in excess of US$10 billion worth of travel spending per year (Holcomb & Luongo, 1996).

An increasing number of studies devote their attention to female tourists seeking romance or other sexual encounters, again tourists being from the developed and the "conquered" from the developing world (e.g., Brown, 1992; Meisch, 1995; Pruitt & LaFont, 1995). Günther argues (Chapter 7) that the difference between male sex tourism and female romance tourism is minimal, contrary to the argument by Pruitt and LaFont (1995). Male sex tourists also often want more than simple physical release and view the exchange of money for sex as unimportant. Kleiber and Wilke's (1995) data indicate, however, that female sex tourists do seem to have a somewhat different approach to sexual encounters in the destination country. Unfortunately, their limited data set on female sex tourists ($n = 12$) does not allow the drawing of irrefutable conclusions on the differences and similarities between male and female sex tourists. In the same study, the authors also revealed that the interviewed sex tourists usually do not consider themselves as such, despite having preplanned to have sex with locals and often reimbursing the prostitutes with money.

In contrast to the sex tourists traveling to the destinations, very little is known about prostitutes traveling to their workplace, although a large number of "internationals" are working in strip joints, massage parlors, brothels, and walking the streets in most countries (e.g., Leheny, 1995; Maurer, 1991; Schmitz, 1987b). Not always are these women working there because of their own free will. But it is not or has not always been women from the developing countries who are traded around the globe. As Hanson points out (Chapter 5), white slavery was quite common well into this century, and Dietrich (1989) provided a historical account of how women from Europe and especially Germany were sold into brothels overseas. The current focus on sex tourism destinations in the Third World ignores the fact there is an international market for prostitutes that often replicates the sex tourism routes (Schöning-Kalendar, 1989), sometimes in the disguise of marriage trade (Ackermann & Filter, 1994; Launer, 1991; Tübinger Projektgruppe Frauenhandel, 1989). As Schöning-Kalendar (1989) put it, the "resource woman" is either imported from the Third World or consumed at the place of production just as many other resources. Yet she also recognized that prostitution is a survival strategy for many women in the Third World who lack other avenues of gaining sufficient income.

Little attention has been paid to homosexual sex tourism, with most studies having discussed heterosexual encounters. Interdeveloping countries' and interdeveloped countries' sex tourism have also received very limited attention, perhaps as a result of the inability to place them into a dependence and thus exploitation perspective. Several authors have pointed out the fact, however, that domestic sex demand in developing countries, including Thailand (and most likely also in the developed world), is of similar if not greater importance than the highly publicized international sex tourism part (e.g., Chapter 15; AGISRA, 1990; Wilkinson & Pratiwi, 1995).

When studies have looked at the individual person level, the focus has mostly been at the prostitutes or supply personal and not at the customers and their thoughts and motivations. Günther (Chapter 7) closes a crucial gap here with his presentation on the reasoning of a sex tourist. Kleiber and Wilke's (1995) study on the motives and activities of German sex tourists on overseas trips and Kleiber and Velten's (1994) study of customers of prostitutes in Germany are other recent valuable contributions to this much neglected area.

An area yet to be fully covered is tourism where sex tourism settings and sex tourists constitute the attraction for other voyeurists. Latza (1987) mentioned in passing that many Western women can be seen in Gogo-bars and other establishments in Thailand, obviously in a voyeuristic role observing the male sex tourist behavior. Then again, at least massage parlors are not strangers to female customers as the same author pointed out and there may be a number of female tourists testing out their lesbian nature. Moreover, many red light districts around the world constitute major tourist attractions for tourists who are not going to pay for sexual services but rather visiting those places for voyeuristic reasons (e.g., Ashworth, White, & Winchester, 1988).

The Sex Tourist

Due to the prevalent double moral standard in most societies, the customers of prostitutes, in contrast to the prostitutes themselves, are rarely ever stigmatized or, where prostitution is illegal, seldom prosecuted for their usage of prostitute services (Cottingham, 1981). It is and has always been the prostitutes who had and still have to bear the brunt of society's moral attitudes and the ensuing social and legal pressures. Much too often, it seems, it is argued that supply causes demand and not vice versa. As a result, however, a clear data bias exists towards the prostitutes in the form of police arrest records, health records (in many countries prostitutes are required to undergo regular health checks whereas the customers are not), and employee records of brothels, massage parlors, etc. (Symanski, 1981). It even appears easier to survey and interview prostitutes as they tend to be present in one location for an extended period of time whereas the customer may make only a brief visit to the red light district. In addition, it has been thought that the customers would not like to be interviewed as it increases their "exposure" and might reveal their double standards. Kleiber and Wilke's (1995) study of German sex tourists in a number of different destination countries (Thailand, Philippines, Kenya, Brazil, Dominican Republic) showed, however, that to successfully interview sex tourists is not an impossible feat as their sample size included 661 heterosexual male, 122 homosexual male, and 24 heterosexual female sex tourists. The latter category was very small, making comparisons between male and female sex tourists impractical. Deficiencies in the survey strategy were a major reason for the small sample. For example, the authors only tried to contact female sex tourists in Kenya and not the other destination countries. For practical purposes, the authors defined a sex tourist as somebody who engaged in sex with a prostitute, knowingly excluding many other forms of sex tourism, and potential respondents were approached in the destination countries in typical settings for sexual activities or encounters (e.g., bars, beach). As a result, the sample is not necessarily representative, but it provides some very valuable quantitative insights into the data-deficient aspect of sex tourists.

Kleiber and Velten's (1994) study of the customers of prostitutes in Germany included a sample of 598 respondents who answered to one of many advertisements in newspapers and magazines that asked for female prostitute customers to come forward and share their experiences for a research project. This self-identification approach resulted in a biased sample towards the younger and more well-educated spectrum of the population.

Kleiber and Wilke (1995) also reported on the results of an add-on section to the annual representative nationwide tourism survey in Germany, which was answered by about 60% of all the respondents who had traveled in 1992. The survey revealed that 8.5% of all those who answered the add-on questionnaire had engaged in sex with a person whom they only met during the holidays. This compares favorably with a 7% result in a similar survey in Switzerland (Kleiber & Wilke, 1995). If one draws the inference from this 8.5% to the whole population of German travelers, it means that in that year 2.2 million German tourists had sex with a previously

Table 1.1. Number of Local Sexual Partners and Number of Sexual Contacts

No. of Locals	% (n = 653)	No. of Sexual Contacts	% (n = 634)
1	36.9	1	12.5
2–4	40.4	2–5	38.2
5 and more	22.2	6–10	18.9
		More than 10	27.8
Median 2		Median 5	
Mean 3.8		Mean 11.9	

Source: adapted from Kleiber and Wilke (1995).

unknown person, may that have been a fellow traveler, a local, or a prostitute. Approximately one third or 800,000 of these were with a non-German partner, and some 11% of these were in the form of sex for money. Hence, if one was to use a very narrow definition of sex tourists as being those who pay for their services, there would have been about 100,000 German sex tourists in 1992. Because one might expect a certain underreporting, especially in respect to the financial reimbursement, this figure should be taken as the absolute minimum.

Not surprisingly, sex tourists often have multiple sex partners during their travel (Table 1.1). Contrary to popular belief, however, they do not seem to have different women every day or even several on each day but often spend a lot of time with one prostitute. Their sexual encounters were not limited to prostitutes either. On average, some 15% of the respondents in that survey also had sexual contacts with fellow holiday makers of either German (6%) or other nationality (9%). Interesting also was the fact that most respondents (77%) had not made use of prostitutes at home during the previous year, but had been in one or more regular relationships.

Rowbottom (1991) reported that Australian sex tourists to Southeast Asia also had sex with multiple partners, both with prostitutes and casual contacts besides their regular partners if they traveled with the latter. Indeed, the majority of those sex tourists traveling with their spouse or regular partner also had sex with others. The incidence of having engaged in sexual actvities was the highest among those who had traveled to Thailand (94%) and the Philippines (96%). As several authors (e.g., De Schryver & Meheus, 1989; Mulhall et al., 1993; Rowbottom, 1991) have pointed out, this active sexual behavior of travelers, often without using condoms, facilitates the spread of sexually transmitted diseases, including AIDS, to and from countries of origin and destination.

The Prostitutes

Many authors (e.g., Launer, 1993; Renschler, 1987b) recognize that there are different types of prostitution, ranging from women forced into the trade to those making a conscious decision to enter the trade. Launer (1993) distinguishes a three-tier system of prostitution in Southeast Asia, namely high-class prostitution, tourism services, and poverty prostitution; similar class differences have been observed by other authors (e.g., Almeida, 1988; Latza, 1987; Naibavu & Schutz, 1974) in other countries. High-class prostitutes serve the domestic elite and foreign businessmen and are generally from a middle- or upper-class background who actually could enter other well-paying carreers or indeed may do prostitution just as a sideline. These prostitutes often retain a large share, if not all, of their earnings. Prostitutes working in the tourism service are also often independent workers or are attached to a bar, which the customer has to pay to release the prostitute. They are able to negotiate their own price with the customer directly and, therefore, are able to retain most of their income as well. The worst off are the prostitutes in the brothels where they are often kept as slaves who have to pay off their original acquisition fee first (Renschler, 1987b). Generally they serve an exclusively domestic clientele (Latza, 1987; Launer, 1993). However, in contrast to many developed countries, pimps are rare in Southeast Asia (Latza, 1987).

Prostitutes in developed countries can also be distinguished into different categories according to their working environment and especially their money-retaining potential. There are also high-class prostitutes who often work independently or are attached to exclusive escort agencies. Then there are prostitutes working in the better brothels or bars who have to pay a higher share to the owner, but who usually can determine their working hours and do not have to worry too much about police harassment if they are licenced. At the bottom of the scale are the street workers, who are often not able to obtain a licence even if it were available (see Chapter 10; Symanski, 1981). Because streetwalking is illegal in many countries, or at least frowned upon, these prostitutes are more often arrested and are generally subject to more police harassment. In addition, to survive in the streets they often have a pimp, which reduces their money-retaining ability even further (Symanski, 1981).

Reasons to Become a Prostitute

Although there are often social and personal reasons that make certain women likely candidates for prostitution, many simply discover that working in an illegal or immoral market makes good economic sense. Throughout history prostitution has provided a solution to the problem of economic hardship. Simply put, men are willing to pay more for sexual access than for almost all other forms of female labor. (Symanski, 1981, p. 3)

There are several reasons to become prostitute, many of them related to social factors. Poverty is often mentioned as the primary reason for women in developing countries being involved in prostitution (e.g., Ackermann & Filter, 1994; Cottingham, 1981; Häusler, 1993; Launer, 1993; Senftleben, 1986). In Thailand, according to Launer (1993), increasingly parents are selling their daughters to brothels in order to obtain money for the purchase of luxury goods. But loss of face in Asian (and also Western) societies, out-of-wedlock childbirth, or rape are other frequent reasons why women leave for the anonymity of large cities and eventually enter into prostitution as means to survive.

Senftleben (1986) suggested that in Taiwan the reasons for entering prostitution have changed as the society and wealth of the country have changed. Whereas in former times it was mostly extreme poverty or escape from prearranged marriages, in modern Taiwan it is often the free choice of the women lured by the good pay and relatively attractive working conditions compared to factory work. Similar arguments have also been mentioned for other developing countries, with consumerism seemingly becoming an increasingly more important reason to enter the trade (e.g., Häusler, 1993). These reasons resemble those in Western societies, at least for those working in the middle and higher parts of the prostitution spectrum (e.g., Scott, 1994; Symanski, 1981; Thompson & Harred, 1992). "There are two kinds of prostitutes . . .: those who work from need, and those who work from greed. The first are likely to be lower-class women, those in the second category have bought the myth of consumerism" (Symanski, 1981, p. 63).

Numbers of Prostitutes

On discussions about sex tourism destinations, the fact is often ignored that a large number of prostitutes are also active in less typical sex tourism destinations such as Germany or The Netherlands. The Hamburg Reeperbahn, the Berlin Kurfürstendamm, or the red light districts of Amsterdam and Rotterdam are world-famous sex destinations, attracting both international and domestic sex tourists. In Germany estimates include 50,000–400,000 female prostitutes (Kleiber & Velten, 1994) serving 1.2 million customers daily (Ackermann & Filter, 1994). Many of the prostitutes in developed countries are foreigners. For example, Ackermann and Filter (1994) stated that one third of the prostitutes in Germany are foreigners. Moreover, Schmitz (1987a) reported that 40% of all prostitutes in Zürich (Switzerland) were from developing countries alone.

Symanski (1981) reported that there were about 250,000–350,000 prostitutes in the United States and more than 200,000 in Poland. Launer (1993) reported that there were 140,000–300,000 in South Korea. Yet, in most countries nobody really knows how many there are. Even in countries such as Germany, where prostitution is generally legal, a large number of prostitutes do not register, perhaps because they fear to be stigmatized or because they only work part-time. Especially women who are housewives or students often fear that through registration their side-work may become known to their husbands, friends, or future employers (see Chapter 11).

In many developing countries where prostitution is illegal, it is even more difficult to obtain accurate figures and consequently the estimates vary considerably, perhaps depending on the motives of the authors. In Thailand, for example, the numbers provided range from 700,000 to 2 million with up to 800,000 of the latter estimate being under the age of 16 (e.g., Ackermann & Filter, 1994; Launer, 1993). Considering that approximately 25% of the 6 million international tourist arrivals to Thailand in recent years were sex tourists and that only 25% of the prostitutes work for international tourists, this would mean that for these 1.5 million international sex tourists there was contact with 200,000–500,000 prostitutes, or only three to eight tourists per prostitute. Given that each sex tourist makes use of an average of four prostitutes during his visit, thus bringing the number of tourists per prostitute to 12-30, it would seem as though the prostitutes are severely underworked and most would be starving to death. Hence, this simple calculation suggests that many estimates are just that, namely estimates with little or no foundation in reality. This is not to say that there are not many prostitutes in countries such as Thailand, but that the numbers of prostitutes are probably lower than some sources suggest and many authors unquestioningly repeat.

The Place

> Besides the solitary pavement, prostitutes hustle in bars, cafes, "grindie" theaters, and around shipping docks and trucking stops. They get business through the telephone, referrals from colleagues, and CB radios. (Symanski, 1981, p. 169)

Sex tourism and prostitution take place just about everywhere. It is not restricted to certain countries, areas, cities, or seedy parts of a city. It is only more apparent in some places than in others, either because it is in fact more prevalent or because it is in a form that attracts more public and police attention. Symanski (1981) argued convincingly that there is an obvious police bias against certain types of prostitution and prostitutes. As a result, some prostitutes are picked up more often than others, giving certain parts of town a reputation that they may not deserve. Particularly streetwalkers are prone to frequent arrest, whereas call girls and especially mistresses face few such hassles. Symanski also suggested that many streetwalkers work in the same area day after day as the regularity of work place provides them with regular customers and, therefore, regular sources of income, to the extent that they establish territorial claims.

> Working the same stroll infuses much needed predictability into an illegal, sometimes dangerous, environment. Knowledge of place means that prostitutes become familiar with the quirks, prejudices, and demands of hotel owners, bellhops, and elevator boys, good, bad, and indifferent types of potential customers who come to the area and—most important of all—the policemen who patrol. (Symanski, 1981, p. 176)

Where prostitution is legal, as for example in most of Nevada but not in Las Vegas (Clark County), there are few reasons to hide the activity behind different fronts; as a result, brothels are often called as such. Where the activity is illegal, more or less elaborate fronts are established in order to pacify the public eye. The massage parlor is but one typical approach (see Chapter 8 and Chapter 10). At some point, no one will be fooled into believing that, for example, massage parlors are anything but brothels. And yet, by some twisted social logic, the fact that they are called massage parlors rather than brothels ensures their continuing existence (Symanski, 1981, p. 215). But prostitution or sexual gratification for money can take place virtually everywhere: in cars, parks, streets, hotels and motels, private homes, bars, dance places, etc. As Senftleben (1986) suggested, it is often not easy to ascertain that such activities are taking place except for those in the know.

Can use for Explanation of sex tourism

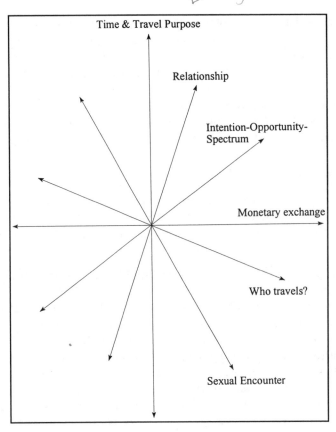

Figure 1.1. The dimensions of sex tourism and prostitution.

A Framework for Sex Tourism

Figure 1.1 presents a framework of the major issues identified in sex tourism that
are central to the concepts of sex tourism and prostitution. Most of the included
variables are represented within sex tourism in an axis form rather than as
uniquely defined points and issues. For example, monetary exchange or reimbursement is only one end of the spectrum. At the other end are forms of open-ended
prostitution where little or no monetary exchange takes place, at least not in the
short run. Intentions and the actual act are another two end points of a spectrum.
Similarly, the tourist may shift his/her location on the spectrum as the journey
progresses through its time–space dimension. Obviously traveling is a key characteristic of the definition and occurrence of sex tourism, but the issue of who is
doing the traveling is much less well-defined: either the demand is the tourist or
the supply is the tourist, or both. The individual aspects of the framework are
discussed below.

Table 1.2. Intention to Engage in Sex With Local Women at Destination Before Departure

	Thailand (n = 99)	Philippines (n = 78)	Kenya (n = 136)	Brazil (n = 112)	Dom. Rep. (n = 236)
Yes, intended	72.4%	71.8%	69.1%	70.9%	55.5%

Source: adapted from Kleiber and Wilke (1995).

Intention–Opportunity Spectrum

Many tourists experience sexual encounters simply because the opportunity arises or because they meet like-minded individuals. In other cases, they just feel lonely and sexually deprived (e.g., people on conference travel) and use the opportunity of being an "unknown stranger" to buy sexual services. If these persons were confronted with the question "Are you a sex tourist?", none would answer "Yes." To what extent does intention to enter into a sexual encounter while traveling need to be present to classify somebody as a sex tourist? In other words, does it need to be planned sexual behavior? Or is openness to such a possibility sufficient? What about those travelers who were lured by insinuated potential sexual encounters in advertisements to book a holiday (Chapter 2)? For example, in a discussion of the "Spring Break Phenomenon" in the United States, Gerlach (1989) suggests the students' travel motives are "to drink, raise hell, and ultimately involve themselves in sexual activities" (p. 15). Are all the more than 1 million Spring Break travelers each year in the United States sex tourists? Or do both intention and the actual "act" need to be present to qualify one to be classified as sex tourist?

Kleiber and Wilke's (1995) interviews with German sex tourists are helpful here. They asked two questions of particular relevance to this issue: if the tourists intended to engage in sex with local women before their departure (Table 1.2), and if they would call themselves sex tourists (Table 1.3). In four out of five countries, some 70% of the interviewed tourists answered the first question positively and even in the fifth country, the Dominican Republic, it was still the majority. Because the interviewed persons had already had contact with prostitutes to be included in the survey, one could qualify these 55–70% for all practical purposes as sex tourists because both intention and actual sexual involvement

Table 1.3. Would You Call Yourself a Sex Tourist?

	Thailand (n = 99)	Philippines (n = 78)	Kenya (n = 136)	Brazil (n = 112)	Dom. Rep. (n = 236)	Total (n = 661)
Yes	25.3%	17.9%	24.3%	18.8%	17.8%	20.4%
No	73.7%	79.5%	75.7%	76.8%	81.4%	78.1%
No response	1.0%	2.6%	—	4.5%	0.8%	1.5%

Source: adapted from Kleiber and Wilke (1995).

Table 1.4. Australian Thailand Tourists' Intentions for Sexual Contacts

	Men	Women
Intend to have sexual contact while in Thailand		
Yes	23.7%	6.3%
No	21.4%	55.0%
Depends	46.6%	28.8%
Don't know	8.4%	10.0%
Type of potential partner		
Australian traveler	46	56
Non-Australian traveler	61	56
Thai national	42	18
Bar girl	14	0
Other	17	11

Source: adapted from Mulhall et al. (1993).

with a prostitute were present. Yet, only a minority of around 20% considered themselves as being sex tourists (Table 1.3). This phenomenon of not seeing oneself as a sex tourists when all obvious signs of being such are present is an interesting sociopsychological phenomenon that Günther (Chapter 7) analyzes in more detail.

Mulhall et al. (1993) examined the planned sexual activities of Australian tourists to Thailand (Table 1.4). More than 20% of the responding men indicated that they planned to have sex while in Thailand, but only 6% of the women responded so positively. However, another 47% and 29%, respectively, said it depends on the situation. As to the type of sexual partner they would or could themselves with, fellow Australian or non-Australian travelers were clearly favored over locals.

Monetary Exchange

Monetary exchange is commonly considered as the most important characteristic of prostitute–customer relationships. Yet the field of sex tourism goes beyond the traditional norm of prostitution, as was elaborated above and vividly illustrated by

Table 1.5. Have You Paid Your Sexual Partner(s) With Money?

	Thailand ($n = 99$)	Philippines ($n = 78$)	Kenya ($n = 136$)	Brazil ($n = 112$)	Dom. Rep. ($n = 236$)	Total ($n = 661$)
Yes	79.8%	50.0%	66.2%	37.5%	77.1%	65.4%
No	18.2%	50.0%	30.9%	58.0%	19.5%	31.8%
No response	2.0%	—	2.9%	4.5%	3.4%	2.9%

Source: adapted from Kleiber and Wilke (1995).

Table 1.6. Length of Time With Last Prostitute in the Destination

	German Sex Tourists (n = 661)	Customers of Prostitutes in Germany (n = 530)
Less than 1 hour	5.9%	78.8%
1–2 hours	13.8%	21.2%
2 hours to less than 1 day	21.3%	—
1 day	12.9%	—
Several days	44.6%	—
No response	1.5%	—

Source: adapted from Kleiber and Wilke (1995).

authors such as Cohen (1986), Odzer (1994), Dahles (Chapter 3), and Phillip and Dann (Chapter 6). Hence, one may need to give monetary exchange a wider meaning than simply the immediate exchange of money. In the case of mistresses, the "customer" may provide the accommodation, clothing, travel, etc. (Chapter 14). And even in typical sex tourism settings, quite a number of sexual encounters seem to be taking place without direct sex-for-money exchange (Table 1.5). Pruitt and LaFont (1995) argued that, in the case of female sex tourists to Jamaica, "neither actor considers their interaction to be prostitution, even while others may label it so. The actors place an emphasis on courtship rather than the exchange of sex for money" (p. 423). Although Pruitt and LaFont used that argument to support their thesis that female sex tourism to Jamaica is not sex but romance tourism, many male sex tourists also see the monetary exchange as peripheral to the relationship, especially in developing countries where they often tend to stay with one prostitute for several weeks or even on repeat visits (e.g., Chapter 7; Ackermann & Filter, 1994; Latza, 1987).

In developing countries, there seems to exist an interesting phenomenon whereby tourists not only hire prostitutes on an hourly basis but may be with them for weeks on end. It appears not uncommon for such relationships to extend for several days or even weeks (Chapter 3 and Chapter 7; AGISRA, 1990; Ackermann & Filter 1994; Latza, 1989). Table 1.6 indicates the difference between some developing countries and, in this instance, Germany. Whereby the interaction between customer and prostitute lasted in almost 80% of the cases less than 1 hour in Germany, close to 50% of the sex tourists interviewed in a range of developing countries indicated that they had been together with the same prostitute for several days. This extended time spent with one prostitute is obviously also a contributing factor to the self-perception of the tourists. The prostitutes are not reimbursed after or before each sexual act when spending day after day together. Undoubtedly, the prostitutes also get their customers to pay, but payment is packaged in different forms, for example, as support for the education of their siblings or paying for the hospital visit of their mother (e.g., Odzer, 1994). This helps to give the tourists the illusion that they are together with a "friend" ra than with a prostitute, something they can hardly get in Germany or other developed countries where the prostitute–customer encounter is very much dominated by sex–monetary exchange (Chapter 7; Kruhse-Mountburton, 1995; Symanski, 1981). The "soft-selling techniques" adopted by prostitutes in developing countries leave a lot of room for the interpretation of the relationship on both sides. As Günther (Chapter 7) vividly illustrates, the sex tourist can see himself as being in love or just being with a woman friend. The prostitute could arguably see herself as having a string of individual relationships with men who just happen to pay her bills and support her family.

Comparing Table 1.5 with Table 1.3, one immediately recognizes that whereas many men did pay their prostitute with money, that was no reason for them to see themselves as sex tourists.

Travel Purpose

Very often travelers are classified according to their primary activity. Hence, a business traveler is somebody whose primary purpose of travel is, for example, to attend a meeting. However, that same person may also use the opportunity to stroll around downtown and do some shopping, add a couple nights of vacation, and rent a car to visit interesting places. Or a traveler visiting friends and relatives (VFR) may also tour the destination just like any other pleasure traveler would do. As Naibavu and Schutz (1974) noted, sexual activity in most cases is incidental to other travel motives:

> Visitors do not mainly come to Fiji in search of sex, whether in the form of prostitution or otherwise. . . . The primary motive for travel may be to experience a different physical or social environment or to enjoy the prestige of foreign travel. Sex, like food, is often incidental to these things. (p. 66)

If primary activity or amount of time is a deciding factor, then there might not exist very many sex tourists. After all, the amount of time spent on sexual activities is probably relatively small compared to other activities. If travel purpose is the deciding factor, then only those people who set out with "sex" in their mind are sex tourists. Yet, as was discussed above, this number may also be fairly small compared to the full range of what might be classified as sex tourists.

Another category of travelers quite renowned for their usage of prostitutes are military persons. The military presence of the United States during the Vietnam War is generally attributed with the rapid increase in prostitution in Thailand, the Philippines and, while they were still there, in Vietnam. The "rest & relaxation" program for soldiers resulted in a strong male bias in the "R&R" areas with the resulting influx of prostitutes (Cottingham, 1981). Latza (1989) reported that whenever the U.S. navy was in Pattaya (Thailand), prices for almost everything tripled or quadrupled, a result of the sudden increase in demand and the limited time available to the sailors. Yet, obviously these sailors' main travel purpose was not sex.

Table 1.7. Intention to Revisit Same Sex Partner

	German Sex Tourists (*n* = 661)
Most certainly	19.1%
Probably	8.5%
Perhaps	26.5%
Probably not	21.6%
Definitely not	23.1%
No response	1.2%

Source: adapted from Kleiber and Wilke (1995).

Relationship Between "Customer" and "Prostitute"

> Since prostitution and courtship exists as a continuum, the vast majority of copulatory opportunities involve costs to males in terms of time and/or material goods. In the male perspective, prostitution realistically may represent nothing other than a relatively explicit sexual transaction. (Symanski, 1981, p. 251)

Symanski suggested that prostitution and a "normal" relationship are parts of a relationship continuum. This notion was supported by Cohen (1986, 1993), who revealed that not everything is black and white in customer–prostitute relationships. Prostitutes often start straightforward sexual service–monetary exchange relationships that then, over time as the customer stays for an extended period of time in the destination, may evolve into a relationship of "travel companion" and eventually perhaps even marriage (Thiemann, 1989). Similar to the regularity of client–prostitute "business relationships" in the Western world (Symanski, 1981), sex tourists often return to the same prostitute on repeat holidays (e.g., Ackermann & Filter, 1994; Latza, 1987; Launer, 1993), keeping the contact through writing letters. Among the interviewed sex tourists, some 20% had very firm intentions to be reunited with the same prostitute on future visits and another 35% mentioned perhaps or probably (Table 1.7). The repeat customer relationship appears beneficial on both sides as it reduces the "risk taking" for both.

> Though initially men paid outright for sex, prostitution in Thailand differed from the West in the way women used poverty and the Third World conditions of Thailand to turn the customer/prostitute relationship into a savior/damsel-in-distress relationship. It was hard for men to leave the country where they played the role of hero so completely. . . . Many men eventually married the women they met in a Patpong bar. (Odzer, 1994, p. 15)

Marriage is certainly an aspiration on the side of some prostitutes involved in open-ended prostitution. When does the prostitute, in such a development, stop being a prostitute? Certainly not with the signing of the marriage certificate.

What is the case with mistresses or second wives who do not live at one's usual place of residence? Hobson and Heung (Chapter 14) reveal that this is not uncommon in the Hong Kong–China border area where quite a number of Hong Kong residents support a second wife. A similar situation exists at the Thailand–Malaysia border and may indeed be present at many different borders, not only those between countries with drastic economic disparities. It is not unheard of that sailors or traveling salesmen have more than one wife, conveniently located in different parts of the country or world.

With the increase in female executives, the reversed sex roles may also become more common. As was reported in a popular New Zealand female magazine, the number of male prostitutes or callboys is on the increase and at least one had been offered to be set up in his own apartment paid by a female executive frequently being in town (Wane, 1996). Indeed, Pruitt and LaFont (1995) also mentioned that some women enjoy the power that money gives them over men.

> The economic and social status the women enjoy provides them with a security and independence that translates into power and control in the relationship. Some of the women enjoy the control they have in these relationships and express a preference for keeping a man dependent on them. (p. 427)

Hence, as women increase their economic and social standing around the world, one might expect more and more female sex tourists and consequently more male prostitutes serving females.

Another issue is sex with colleagues or friends while traveling who are not one's usual sexual partner. These examples may suffice to show that, once one moves out of the "usual sexual relationship," a whole range of complex relationships exists that are traditionally not considered as falling into the area of sex tourism but that could easily be constructed as such.

Sexual Encounter

In terms of the "sexual encounter" itself, a range of questions and issues can be raised. Traditionally, a sexual act was considered to be penetrative, vaginal intercourse (in heterosexual relationships), which, as a definition, does not apply to homosexual encounters. If one spins the net wider, what would be considered as being included? Oral or hand jobs? Or is watching already enough to qualify? Obviously, there are many places that offer peep-shows and where customers commonly masturbate. Some customers would simply travel to such facilities for that purpose. In Thailand and the Philippines, many places offer sex shows and, although prostitutes are also available, the primary purpose of those watching is simple voyeurism (Latza, 1987).

Other encounters involve topless bars and shows, with some offering table-dancing and lap-dancing (Chapter 11 and Chapter 12; Thompson & Harred, 1992) where customers receive merely sexual stimuli at one end of the spectrum and perhaps masturbation through lap-dancing at the other end (Schmitz, 1987a). What

Table 1.8. Sexual Practices Engaged in by Heterosexual Male Tourists and Customers of Prostitutes in Germany (Multiple Choice Permitted)

	Sex Tourists With Prostitutes[a]	With Prostitutes in Germany[b]	With Usual Female Partners[b]
Intercourse	96.4%	78.1%	87.4%
Petting	46.7%	60.0%	64.4%
Oral (female active)	73.2%	70.9%	48.1%
Oral (male active)	35.1%	29.9%	55.9%
Hand/body massage	29.4%	n/a	n/a
Sex with multiple partners	9.2%	8.5%	1.8%
Anal	8.9%	9.6%	2.9%
Bondage & discipline	1.2%	17.6%	2.5%
Other	1.6%	n/a	n/a

Sources: [a]Kleiber and Wilke (1995); [b]Kleiber and Velten (1994).

happens after the shows is yet another issue, with at least the dancers and/or waitresses sometimes also being available for "real" sexual activities after working hours off premises (Chapter 16; Schmitz, 1987a; Symanski, 1981). Thompson and Harred (1992) reported that dancers have even coined the term "parking lot duty" to describe sexual encounters that supposedly occurred in the parking lots outside the clubs because soliciting and prostitution were strictly prohibited in the clubs.

The Internet opens up a whole range of new questions in that area as the "customer" is not physically traveling any longer, but nonetheless may be considered a "cyberspace tourist" or even a "cyberspace sex tourist" (Chapter 13; Durkin & Bryant, 1995). Perhaps it is not unlike the "phone sex lines" where customers also remain at home but the prostitute may be on the other side of the world, providing sexual arousal and helping the customer to masturbate. Just as with brothels, peepshows, or porn magazines, the cybersex tourist also has to pay his or her way into these sites with sexual content, generally conveniently made easy by payment through a credit card.

If one compares the various sexual practices that German sex tourists or customers of prostitutes are engaging in with the prostitutes or with their usual partner, one notes that intercourse is by far the most common form, followed by oral sex where the female is the active partner (Table 1.8). However, the latter seemed to be less prevalent at home with the usual partner, where the men themselves seem to be taking more the active role when it comes to oral sex. Other activities that are more prevalent with prostitutes are "sex with multiple partners," "anal," and, in the case of German prostitutes, "bondage & discipline."

Who Travels

As addressed above, it is not always the tourists who are traveling to the prostitutes; sometimes it is the prostitute who is the tourist serving the locals; or sometimes both are foreigners to the actual place where the sexual encounter takes place. In Limbang (Sarawak, Malaysia), for example, most male demand originates from Brunei, which is only 30 minutes down the river. However, much of this demand is not from Brunei citizens but temporary workers or business travelers working in Brunei and looking for sexual experience and release in the slightly more relaxed environment of the cities in neighboring Sarawak. Yet, most of the prostitutes in these towns are also not locals, but rather migrants or immigrants. One may also recall the colonial times in Malaysia when the male immigrant workers in the tin mines and rubber plantages were served by an immigrant prostitute population brought into the country solely for that purpose. Similar circumstances prevailed in many other countries (e.g., in the United States and its Chinese railroad workers). And in Thailand, the majority of the prostitutes until the 1930s were of Chinese origin largely serving a Chinese immigrant population (Leheny, 1995; von Krause, 1993). In more modern settings, Launer (1993) reported that a considerable number of South Koreans work as Kisaeng women in Japan, and Leheny (1995) also suggested that quite a number of women from other Asian countries work in Japan as prostitutes. It is also frequently reported that women from Laos, Myanmar, and even Southern China are working as prostitutes in Thailand and that most of the prostitutes in Bangkok and Pattaya are from Thailand's poor Northeast.

International travel of prostitutes is only one aspect; many prostitutes work away from their home in their own country, especially for big events such as the navy coming to port (Launer, 1993). Such a pattern has a long history. For example, Symanski (1981) reported that prostitutes traveled with the Roman legion and other armies, traveled to army bases for payday, solicited while traveling in trains such as the Winnipeg–Vancouver or Leningrad–Moscow lines, traveled from city to city on planned prostitution circuits, followed the "snowbirds" to the warmer parts of Europe for the winter, or simply commuted for the weekend to Las Vegas from Southern California. Similarly, Aparicio (1993) related how prostitutes in the Dominican Republic engage in seasonal migration to the respective tourist hubs during different times of the year. In addition, most of the prostitutes are women from the inland rural areas who have migrated to the coast but who return home frequently. Häusler (1993) reported that Indian prostitutes flock to Goa during the high season around Carnival and Christmas. She also noted that some of the upper-class tourists bring their prostitutes with them. In Pangandaran, Indonesia, the majority of both tourists and prostitutes are Indonesian; the latter are outsiders to that particular tourist resort, although some local women and men are also involved in prostitution (Wilkinson & Pratiwi, 1995).

Summary

This chapter provided an overview of what might constitute sex tourism and prostitution and discussed many of the pertinent aspects of both. The framework of sex tourism and prostitution (Figure 1.1) is useful for understanding the range of activities and the multifaceted nature of customer–prostitute relationships. The overview of the literature on sex tourism and prostitution also revealed that, whereas a number of recent studies have added insights into the phenomenon, there are still many areas that require more attention and research. Unfortunately, these topics are highly charged with emotions, social prejustice, sociocultural and political bias, and economic interests—often resulting in at least questionnable data provided by authorities and organizations. The problem of data accuracy seems to be a major hurdle in this particular field of inquiry, even more so than in the wider field of tourism. Few authors have actually collected primary data; most rely on data provided by others, sometimes without realizing that those authors also derived their data from elsewhere, or used estimates of estimates of estimates.

The following chapter discusses the usage of nudity and sexual innuendo in picture and language in tourism marketing and specifically destination marketing. The wide range of different forms that sex tourism and prostitution might take and the associated problems, issues, and opportunities are presented in Chapters 3 through 15. They range from discussions of beachboys available for female and male customers (Chapters 3 and 4) to child prostitution (Chapters 4 and 5); from topless or exotic dancing (Chapters 11 and 12) to concubines (Chapter 14); from sex in cyberspace (Chapter 13) to female prostitutes (Chapters 6 and 10); and from legal issues (Chapters 8 and 9) to the sex tourists themselves (Chapter 7). The final chapter will then return to a more general perspective on who actually benefits and who is exploited in sex tourism and prostitution. This collection is not intended to be yet another book that decries sex tourism. Instead, it intends to provide a well-balanced and diverse overview of the different forms that sex tourism and prostitution take.

Chapter 2

Marketing Sex and Tourism Destinations

Martin Oppermann, Shawna McKinley, and Kye-Sung Chon

Marketing has long made use of idealized sexual images and information to sell products. Over the last few decades the general use of sexual imagery to advertise many types of products has greatly increased (Kerin, Lundstrom, & Sciglimpaglia, 1979; Soley & Reid, 1988). Nowhere is this more evident than in the tourism industry. A glance through most tourism brochures will soon reveal not only an obvious gender bias, but also a preponderance of naked skin, especially among the portrayed female models. Bikini-clad tourists lounging at pool sides, exotic locals in grass skirts, and happy couples strolling on the beach have long been used as images in travel and tourism promotion. "The romance, mystique and eroticism of the South Pacific" has been identified as a promotional option for a regional South Pacific tourism strategy (Yacoumis, 1989). In addition, the smiling faces of flight attendants and the promise of subservient service have also been used in airline promotions. It cannot be denied that the use of sexual imagery and sexual innuendo is widespread in tourism marketing. Yet, few studies have examined the effect of such advertising on the actual travel decision. In a more general view, Smith (1983) questioned advertising's effect on changing travel patterns, citing a lack of supportive reliable data. This chapter will deliberate on why, how, and to what extent sex images and sexual imagery are used in tourism destination marketing.

Tourism Destination Images

For more than 20 years, images and perceptions of tourism destinations have been a major area of tourism research (e.g., Chon, 1990; Echtner & Ritchie, 1993; Gartner, 1993; Hunt, 1975; Woodside & Lysonski, 1989). Essentially, most authors have argued that tourist visitation patterns are greatly influenced by tourists' images and perceptions of destinations. Studies have also examined advertising's ability to influence tourists' perceptions and behavior, concluding that marketing plays an important role in creating tourism destination images (Dilley, 1986). Tourism promotions can therefore be very powerful economic tools as "image is the most important aspect of tourist attraction" (Lew, 1987).

Images of tourism destinations are the sum of ideas and beliefs about a destination. Thus, they are highly individualistic in nature and may change at any time. Unfortunately, the term "image" has been used in four different ways with similar, yet distinct, meanings. Hence, one needs to distinguish among the "presented," "organic," and "perceived" images. The first are the images presented by the destinations, operators, travel agencies, etc.—what Gunn (1988) and Gartner (1993) termed "induced images." The second are formed from sources not directly related to the destination area, such as movies, documentaries, word-of-mouth, and news. These two types of images are the "input" into the individual's perceived image formation process. These inputs are filtered, with the "filter" being affected by the individual's own experiences, desires, background, etc. At the end of this process emerges a perceived or cognitive image of a tourism destination, a specific holiday package, a travel agency, an airline, etc.

The sum of all individuals' images of a destination in a specific market may be termed the "market's image" of that particular destination—the fourth type of image. This gives recognition to the fact that the very same destination is usually perceived quite differently in different markets (Crompton, 1979) and that marketing strategies need to be tailored to these differences (Dilley, 1986). Destinations need to be very aware, however, that once a negative image is established in a market, it may take a long time to recover from such an image as it tends to linger around (Lucas, 1994).

Today's media is a powerful agent in the formation of destination images, especially of distant places that the viewers and/or readers are not familiar with (Butler, 1990). The murders of tourist in Florida, California, and Egypt made world headlines, as do military coups and volcano eruptions. Any such event has an almost instantaneous impact on tourist flows. As Richter (1993) noted, the four "Ss"—sun, sand, sea, and sex—need to be expanded to five "Ss," by adding "safety," which is arguably as powerful an agent in directing and redirecting tourist flows as the others.

Despite the large number of studies that have investigated tourism destination image, none has explicitly included "sex" as a variable. Typically, destination image studies have investigated the importance of a range of physical, historical, and cultural destination attributes, such as climate, coastline, historical buildings, and friendliness of the people. Yet, for a long time, it has been implicitly recognized that, besides all the natural, cultural, and historical beauty, holiday destination promotion emphasizes sex.

Nudity and Innuendo in Advertising

Nudity and sexual innuendo have been increasing in advertising (LaTour & Henthorne, 1993). Sexual innuendo is implied in the language of tourism advertising (Dann, 1996) and it usually takes one of two forms. First, the promotional language describes the destination and its people in sexually permissive terms, thus actually locating erotic feelings in the tourist himself or herself (Dann, 1996). An example is a tourism advertisement that describes a destination in explicit and direct terms such as "vacation in the land of most beautiful women in the world, accessible and sensible. . . ." The second form is "sexual mythology" as shown in an advertisement for Phuket, Thailand: "the island of incredible lushness and ready to delight your every taste. . . ." The reasons for the use of sex in marketing are "that sexuality is a persuasive motivator in consumer behavior" (Gould, 1995, p. 395) and "that travel may be readily compared to the phenomenon of love in terms of its varieties, approaches, games, and conquests; travel is a disorienting process in which one abandons the familiarity of home for exciting new amorous experiences elsewhere where the destination becomes a woman" (Cassou, 1967, as in Dann, 1996, p. 127). This "destination being a woman" perspective also surfaces in the feminist literature on sex tourism and tourism destinations (see Chapter 16). Gould (1995) further observed that there has been little systematic effort in studying the relationship between sexuality and consumption patterns.

Although nudity and sexual content usually increase the attention directed towards that advertisement, this does not translate into positive feelings about that advertisement or the product promoted. To the contrary, it is often perceived as offensive (Alexander & Judd, 1979; LaTour & Henthorne, 1993; Mitchell, 1986). The Austrian airline, Lauda Air, had to withdraw the advertisements it had placed for Thailand in Germany, after objections that the provocative youthful looking girl on the advertisements would encourage underage sex (Hobson & Dietrich, 1994). Further, Peterson and Kerin (1977) argued that the actual outcome may be largely influenced by the congruence of product and the sexual content of the advertisement.

In looking at print advertisement, LaTour and Henthorne (1993) argued that sexual or erotic advertising uses two approaches: amount of nudity and degree of suggestiveness. Suggestiveness is often achieved by using more than one model in an ad, whose respective positions may suggest anything from romanticism to very close intimacy (Lowry, 1993). The typical tourism destination advertisement, however, consists of more than just a picture. Thus, these two approaches are complemented by a third: the language used. Commonly, sexual innuendo in language goes hand in hand with the actual imagery. In some cases, both obtain their sexual meaning only by being combined in an advertisement.

"Advertising presents an unrealistic or idealized picture of people and their lives" (Richins, 1991, p. 71). By using attractive models, advertisements invite a social comparison of the viewers with these models, which may result in lower self-satisfaction among viewers, despite being aware of the unrealistic nature of the advertisements. Joseph (1982) showed that advertisements with attractive models are generally more effective, thus supporting the implicit or explicit promise of advertisements that one's life will more closely approach the ideal by product use even though this promise is imperfectly, if at all, fulfilled (Richins, 1991).

Gould (1995) has forwarded the notion of "product sexualization." He postulated "that just about anything may become a conditioned sexual stimulus when paired with an unconditioned one. Thus, a product . . . becomes sexually conditioned when it is associated with an unconditioned sexual stimulus, such as an attractive model in an ad or a sexually attractive person in an actual consumption situation" (p. 396). Furthermore, he argued that such a sexualization approach may be used for positioning products among competitors. Where better to use product sexualization than in promoting the exotic as erotic tourism destinations?

Sexual Imagery and Tourism Marketing

In tourism marketing, product sexualization is very prominent. In fact, it is so flagrant that commentators have called such advertisements "body shots" (Heatwole, 1989) to denote the conspicuous emphasis on the sexualization approach. Having noted the existence and preponderance of such imagery in tourism destination advertising, Heatwole proposed a number of reasons why body shots of women might be used to promote tourism destinations. His "Climatic Hypothesis" that body shots inferred warm climates is countered by the fact these photographs are primarily of women and are emphasized year-round. The "Heterosexual Hypothesis" argues that "what you see is what you get," indicating the attraction of sexual fantasy. This hypothesis is not supported by statistical evidence and the dominance of female body shots would indicate tourists are primarily male, which is not the case. The "Female Fantasy Hypothesis" argues female body shots encourage women to live out their fantasies to be as beautiful as the women pictured in advertisements. This view is countered by studies that suggest that women are more attracted to pictures of couples and actually identify female body shots in advertising as methods of exploitation. Another hypothesis suggests that the emphasis on women's bodies would allow the promotion of an unphotogenetic destination. In a sense, by providing body shots and other generic imagery, the destination may be able to provide a photogenic stimulus to potential customers that otherwise might not exist. Finally, the "Hedonistic Hypothesis" argues that body shots suggest a destination of rest, relaxation, and indulgence, because bathing suits are the most popular apparel, the model's pose almost always projects leisure, and the settings generally connote leisure environments. In conclusion, Heatwole (1989) argued that whereas body shots are successful in attracting attention to the advertisement, some are offended by them: "To most people a body shot suggests that a pleasant vacation awaits in a pleasant place. And that is what tourism-related advertising is all about" (p. 11).

Uzzell (1984) identified three levels at which tourism brochures try to relay a message. The first is the prototypical "sun, sand, sea, and sex" image. On the second level, destinations are trying to sell place attributes that act as enhancement to the customer's self-image. The simultaneous neglect of actual destination features themselves ties in with Heatwole's (1989) observation that very little of the actual destination is shown. The third dimension is destinations trying to sell the image of ourselves in a reality and fantasy world of meaning. Thus, Uzzell believed that many of these advertisements intimate consumer involvement in the pictured scene. When sexual imagery is used, this suggests tourists' realization of the sexual fantasy portrayed by buying the advertised product.

R. A. Britton (1979) argued that sexual images in tourism promotion can cover up reality, mystifying and inaccurately representing destinations as sensuous and unspoiled remnants of Paradise. According to Britton (1979), marketing of Third World tourism destinations makes little if any reference to the locals and the actual reality in such countries: "Locals are generally absent from illustrations; . . . when references to the local society cannot be avoided, it is rationalized or romanticized" (p. 323). Sexual liaison with non-whites is another theme in which locals may be used in advertisements.

Yet, it is important to recognize that the perception of sexual material in tourism promotion is a very subjective process. What one person might see as a sexual image will depend on that individual's perceptions and frame of reference. This frame of reference may vary depending on age, culture, education, gender, and numerous other factors. Unfortunately, comparative investigations of what is perceived as sexual innuendo, erotic, or blatant sexual imagery are still lacking.

Sex and Marketing of Tourism Destinations

Tourism marketing uses both information and image-based advertising (Laskey, Seaton, & Nicholls, 1994). The information and images provided by these advertisements may be as diverse as the people, climate, and history of the destinations they promote. Despite these differences, however, it is possible to identify certain themes that are commonly presented in tourism marketing. Marketing information and images may be based on landscapes, culture, or services (Soley & Reid, 1988). Uzzell (1984) identified the most superficial emphasis of holiday destination promotions to be sun, sea, sand, and sex. Such emphasis, especially sexual imagery, are common mediums for marketing tourism destinations.

Using content analysis, Dilley (1986) compared destination brochures from a wide range of different countries. He disclosed differences in the positioning of the destinations. Although he did not categorize sex as an individual category, the category "recreation," a primary category for most Caribbean Islands, included mostly nudity and sexual innuendo: "Island vacation spots from Bermuda to Trinidad and Tobago not surprisingly concentrate on projecting themselves as paradises for wearing or watching bikinis" (p. 64). The four "Ss" dominate the Caribbean-area literature.

Lowry (1993), in a study on how sexual imagery in tourism advertising might be interpreted given individual frames of reference, argued that the use of female body shots in tourism advertising causes different responses in males and females. Whereas males tend to respond positively to such advertisements, many women believe these marketing methods objectify and exploit women. The attraction to women who responded positively was based on the possibility of becoming like the women pictured in these advertisements by traveling to the featured destination. Hence, these women wanted to become attractive to men. Both sexes agreed that sexual imagery grabbed their attention, but did not ensure purchase of the promoted product.

The Case of Marketing Pacific Tourism Destinations

The remainder of this chapter surveys, analyzes, and interprets the sexual images used to promote Pacific tourism destinations. It aims to identify what sexual images and information are used in advertisements and to uncover trends in the use of such images and information. It also attempts to identify any contrasts in the use of sex in tourism marketing between different countries in this region, in order to reveal how commonly sex is used in tourism promotion.

Material was solicited from South Pacific Islands, American, and Asian sources. National and government tourism offices for countries within this area were sent letters designed as general tourist inquiries. Letters requested that any information or promotional material be sent in order to explore tourism opportunities at a given destination. These inquiries were very general in nature, emphasizing open and flexible holiday plans, although the inquirer was stated as being female and resident in New Zealand. Brochures and travel booklets on Pacific Rim destinations were also collected from local travel and tourism agencies. These were generally produced by airline companies, including Air New Zealand and Singapore Airlines, or by organized tour groups, such as Contiki and Integrity Tours.

The response rate from the inquiries sent was very good as approximately 75% of requests were accommodated. Replies were received from offices in Tahiti, Singapore, Vanuatu, Australia, New Zealand, Canada, Thailand, Hawaii, and the Cook Islands. The packages collected included numerous brochures and booklets providing information about these destinations as well as maps, airfare, and transportation information and numerous advertisements for tourism services provided in the area. Sex is a common theme present throughout much of this material. The manner in which sex is used in these promotions fits into three general categories. Along the lines of previous studies, they are termed body shots, suggestive postures, and sexual innuendo in language.

The first two of these categories address the pictorial content that is used in tourism promotions. The most common and direct of these images involves body shots of locals and visitors, whether they are male or female. The female body shots that are the subject of Heatwole's study fit into this category. Allusive postures refer to how individuals are arranged in space, indicating an attraction or special relationship between them. In certain circumstances, how individuals are arranged within images and in relationship to the audience may cause these images to be interpreted in a sexual manner. Suggestive language can also provide sexual references in tourism promotion, especially in circumstances where connotative language is linked with potentially evocative pictures.

Body Shots

Although tourism promotion for destinations in the Pacific makes use of both image- and information-based marketing, it is image-based marketing that makes the most use of sex to promote a destination. Body shots of locals most commonly—and in many cases most blatantly—portrayed these people in a sexual manner. Body shots of indigenous peoples usually clothe them in a traditional manner—conveniently showing a great deal of bare skin. Indigenous people pictured in such a manner are generally young, beautiful or handsome, and curvaceous or muscular. The dark skin and more primitive clothing of these people combine to present them as exotic symbols of cultures, still living a wilder, simpler, and unspoiled life in paradise. It would not be unreasonable to imagine a tourist's feelings of desire and attraction toward these people and their life-style as a result of such portrayals. Picturing locals as exotic symbols of a destination has the effect of objectifying these individuals. Locals are also "put on display" for visitors by demonstrating their crafts and talents.

The material also contained body shots of individuals who are presumably visitors to these destinations. In most cases, the visitors are delineated from locals by their fair skin and Western dress and are commonly as young and attractive as their local counterparts. Body shots of visitors may not be as common as those of locals, but are nonetheless present in tourism promotion. Tourists, both male and female, are commonly relaxing at pool sides, lying in the tropical sun, or strolling along on the beach, clothed in little more than bathing suits. Such situations appear to be designed to create feelings of desire not only for the situation that is portrayed, but often for the individual that is pictured as well.

Body shots promoting a destination are most commonly females. Both women of indigenous cultures and those who appear to be visitors were the subject of such advertisements. Bathing suit-clad poolside shots of women were the most frequent example, although photographs of local women in traditional costume were also frequent. Female body shots appeared to be a staple for the promotion of accommodation services throughout the Pacific. Couples were also used, lying on hotel room beds or sharing drinks at cocktail bars. Body shots of men were far less common than those of women, with photographs of local males being much more frequent than those of male tourists. Bare-chested and muscular indigenous men were pictured both on their own and with other local women, whereas body shots of male tourists generally accompanied female tourists or locals.

Suggestive Postures

Visitors and locals are portrayed as both single and in couples. Either way the message is that travel to this destination provides romance. This is indicated by relational references present in the promotional images studied, such as in the position of bodies and the prevalence and types of touch between individuals or facial expressions. Certain individuals may appear closer together than others, touching or looking at each other in a way that may indicate more than basic friendship.

In the case of couples, there are many images that may indicate the presence of intimate relationships. Common images show couples strolling along beaches, reclining on beds in their hotel rooms, chatting intimately over meals, or reflecting romantically at tropical sunsets. Although the majority of such images picture individuals who are probably tourists, the opportunity to develop sexual relationships between locals and visitors is also suggested by some promotional material. Of all the material studied only one publication made reference to homosexuality; most concentrated on heterosexual attraction within groups and between couples. Some tourism promotions also indicate many opportunities for those unattached or traveling independently to develop relationships and have loads of fun with members of the opposite sex. For example, Trekset and Contiki Tours publications indicate that their companies provide opportunities for young people to meet numerous members of the opposite sex, and do not rule out the opportunity of developing intimate relationships within tour groups.

Sexual Innuendo in Language

Sex is suggested much less frequently, although still evident, in information-based promotion of Pacific tourism destinations. When promoting their holiday packages to Tahiti, Air New Zealand labels the country "one of the Pacific's most alluring and romantic destinations." In other cases, the sexual use of language in tourism is much less obvious. The connotative value of language can often give dual meanings to phrases that are written on tourism promotions and in many cases these vague meanings could be used to make reference to sex. For example, Singapore Airlines promotes their

> Gentle Singapore Girls, in their distinctive sarong kebayas, [who] will serve you delicious three-course meals with an outstanding selection of wines and drinks, as you recline in comfort. . . .

The meaning of such information is supplemented by smiling and complacent beautiful young women, who appear eager and happy to serve every need of passengers who purchase the airlines' "Asian Affair" holiday packages. Another example is the advertisement for the Rarotongan Resort Hotel, where photos of men dancing with traditionally dressed female dancers complement invitations to satisfy your hunger "for the taste of Paradise" in the hotel's "exciting, pulsating traditional floor shows." The accompaniment of such invitations can cause images to be interpreted in a sexual manner.

Differences Among Destinations

It has been argued that sex is present in tourism promotion and that there are trends in its presentation, yet how common is its use in tourism marketing? The predominance of sexual imagery and information in tourism advertisements appears to vary among the destinations that are promoted. For example, in a 139-page booklet from Tahiti Tourisme, approximately 28% of the pages had at least one sexual image as described in the previous section. In contrast, a similar 117-

page booklet filled with photographs received from the Australian Tourist Commission contained only 10 images that could be considered sexual in nature.

The frequency of sexual images and information in destination promotion varies between three subregions within the Pacific area studied: the Pacific Islands, excluding New Zealand; Asia; and the developed states. Each of these regions used differing types and amounts of sexual imagery and information in their tourism promotions.

Pacific Island nations were the destinations most likely to use sex as a means of tourism promotion. Body shots of attractive and youthful tourists and locals predominated the booklets and brochures that were received and collected from destinations such as Hawaii, Tahiti, Vanuatu, and the Cook Islands. Both men and women were the subject of sexual images, although women were most likely to make bathing-suited appearances in hotel and resort advertisements. Sexual images of indigenous people also tended to be far more common than those of visitors in South Pacific tourism promotions.

The other extreme was demonstrated by more developed countries. Advertisements for Australian, New Zealand, Canadian, and American destinations made the least use of sex in their promotions. Similar to the Australian example above, Air New Zealand's booklet advertising Swing Away packages to Canada and America makes use of only seven sexual images and contains just one instance of sexually connoted language. All of the sexual images included in this booklet advertised accommodation services, rather than displaying the exotic appearance of locals, and were rather small and inconspicuous. These destinations tended to place far more emphasis on family and senior's holidays, special attractions, and scenic and historic values over sexual attraction.

Asian destinations occupy the middle ground in this spectrum. Booklets and brochures that were collected promoting Singapore, Thailand, India, and Singapore Airlines Asian Affair Holidays employed very few seminude body shots of visitors and locals. Visitors were very rarely pictured in these promotions at all, as most images showed locals. Unlike South Pacific advertisements, Asian promotions were far less likely to include men in these images, with women being more commonly pictured in advertisements for restaurants, shops, hotels, and other tourist services. Again locals were traditionally dressed, but national costumes revealed much less bare skin than in the South Pacific examples. Even so, the facial expressions given by women in traditional dress had the potential to create feelings of attraction. The manner in which Asians were portrayed still indicated the entertainment value that these people might have to the tourism industry, further objectifing them and their culture.

The promotional material provided by the Tourism Authority of Thailand must be singled out for its publication of unique images. Unlike all of the other material collected, this information appeared to be the most accurate and realistic representation of tourism in that destination. The majority of images presented in these brochures and booklets presented visitors and locals in realistic and modest dress and their actual less-than-perfect appearance. The photographs included seemed less staged and artificial as well as more spontaneous than the other publications studied. Sunbathing tourists were not as physically perfect or attractive as the models used in other promotions. Sexual imagery was still present in Thailand's promotions; however, it was portrayed in a more natural and less blatant way than many other advertisements. Photographs of city nightlife showed many young people interacting with Thai natives at clubs and restaurants. One can only speculate if a more natural appearance of sexual images is because such opportunities to pursue sexual relationships actually exist as a tourism opportunity in Thailand; however, that is another study entirely.

Conclusion

There is little literature identifying how sex is used in tourism promotions and less proposing that there are any trends in its representation. Many questions remain. How common is sexual imagery in tourism marketing? Are certain images more common than others? Do tourism promotions give equal representation to both sexes or are different gender roles evident? Are certain destinations more likely to employ sex as a means of promoting themselves than others? It is important to identify how sex is used in tourism marketing and whether or not these usages contain any trends or similarities before identifying the effect that such promotions have on tourist behavior.

There is no doubt that sex is a common subject in tourism marketing. Body shots, relational references, and connotative language can all indicate the presence of sex in tourism advertising. Although some Pacific destinations may employ sexual images and information more frequently than others, all of the destinations studied used this type of advertising in some way or another. Whether using sex in advertising contributes to an "embarrassing abstraction" of a destination's image is a topic of study beyond this chapter; however, if promotion is such a strong factor in creating a destination's image and image is the most important part of tourist attraction, then the effect of sexual images and information in such advertisements cannot go unnoticed because sex in tourism marketing is so very widespread.

Chapter 3

Of Birds and Fish: Street Guides, Tourists, and Sexual Encounters in Yogyakarta, Indonesia

Heidi Dahles

"Hello Miss, how are you today?"
"Hello Misses, you look happy today!"
"Hello Miss, you nice sunglasses, where you buy?"
"I like your shoes, Miss, where you go?"
"This is Kraton, Miss, you see Kraton? I will show you, I'm your friend."
"Excuse me Miss, where you stay? Are you married? Have boy-friend? Want boy-friend? I be your boy-friend. Have many girl-friends from Europe, America, all very happy."
"I love you, Miss, where you go?"
"Want banana, Miss? Indonesia banana small but hot!"

These and other related modes of address are typical of the way young men, hanging out in the streets of Yogyakarta, approach individually traveling female tourists. It is the mode of behavior that is typical for self-employed tourist guides—street guides—to attract the tourists' attention. As Crick (1992) observed in Sri Lanka and as I was able to experience in Yogyakarta, street guides are rather skilled in catching the eye of tourists and engaging in tactics talks. Their purpose is to make tourists buy souvenirs, as they largely depend on a commissioned income. However, there is another dimension to approaching tourists: the sexual dimension, which is omnipresent wherever female tourists appear without male company.

The literature suggests that tourism is closely related to increases in prostitution. In many exotic destination areas, female prostitution is common (e.g., Graburn, 1983; Hall, 1992; Kruhse-MountBurton, 1995; Shaw & Williams, 1994). Knowledge of tourism-related male prostitution, however, is rather limited. One of the best-documented cases is the tiny West African country of The Gambia, which has been successfully marketed in Scandinavia causing middle-aged Scandinavian women to openly solicit sex from local males (Harrell-Bond, 1978; Lea, 1988; Wagner, 1977). More recently attention has been drawn to the Caribbean area where one of the main attractions for white female tourists is the Rasta men (Van Schaardenburgh, 1996). And Cohen (1971) examined the motives of Arab boys making sexual overtures to female tourists as early as the 1960s.

Cohen's work (1982, 1986, 1993) on the prostitutes of Bangkok indicates that their dealings fit in with established Thai and Western cultural norms: weak young woman depends on older and more powerful man. As far as the sexual involvement of local males with Western female tourists is concerned, the Thai model is reversed: poor local young men prostitute themselves to rich white women who often are considerably older than themselves. Referring to the Gambian case, Wagner (1977) noted that this "inversion" is perverting the norms ruling gender relations in many societies, including ours. Wagner detected a destructive potential in these relationships: "what to the tourist is a pleasant and refreshing interlude where the disregarding of norms in no way threatens the structures pervading in their home society, could result in the destruction of one of the very foundations of local social structure, that of ordering social life according to age and generation differences." What remains unclear is whether this diagnosis is based on an analysis of local power relations or rather on the author's bias. The fact that the local boys "sleep with women of their mothers' generation"—as Wagner lamented—may bother a Western female academic, but may have a rather different meaning in the lives of the men involved.

A different perspective is offered by an Australian journalist commenting on the subculture of male youth in Bali—the so-called "bad boys," "Kuta cowboys," "gigolos" (by other people), or "guides" (their own term), "whose peripheral yet lasting flirtation with the West has left them with a taste for drugs, alcohol, and one night/ one month relationships with tourist girls. . . . Maybe a life of shallow, temporary relationships, on the fringes of the tourists' largesse is better than the alternatives" (Wolf, 1993). These alternatives entail leading the life of a rice-cultivating peasant, a factory worker, and the head of a large family in a situation of dire poverty. The "Kuta cowboys" emerged with surfing, the sport that created a new life-style for tourists and new livelihoods for Balinese youngsters from the 1970s onwards. Besides becoming excellent surfers themselves, young Balinese men come to Kuta to make money accepting casual work in the tourism industry, collecting commissions by selling jewellery, carvings, or paintings, and picking up tourist girls "who would pay for everything" (Mabbett, 1987).

Instead of looking at the sexual overtures of local males toward female tourists in terms of prostitution and the supposed detrimental impacts on social life, this study analyzes this behavior from the perspective of the everyday life of these men. To understand why young local males desire sexual relationships with female tourists, it is argued that these sexual advances have to be understood within the context of small-scale peddling that is characteristic among street guides. It is a *pasar* style of making a living that has been characterized by Geertz (1963) as highly competitive, individualistic, and ad hoc acts of exchange. The street being his domain, the street guide is grasping occasions for gain as they fitfully and spontaneously arise, benefiting in every possible way from the diffuse flow of individual tourists passing by. This chapter will raise the question in which ways the growth of international tourism poses a challenge to the vast number of young people on a marginal or near-marginal level of living. With tourists in town, the chances of making a quick windfall are bigger, but the stakes are higher—not only economically speaking. Doing business with tourists involves selling goods and strategically exploiting personal networks—as is characteristic of the classical *pasar* mode of making a living, described by Geertz.

After a short description of the working space of the street guides (i.e., the tourist area of Yogyakarta), the following aspects of their life will be analyzed: the way they approach and cater to tourists in general and female tourists in particular; the way they operate within the city's tourist industry, relating to the local shopkeepers and artisans and to other street guides; the way they make a living and spend their income; and their future prospects and perspectives.

This chapter is based on anthropological fieldwork during the tourist seasons of 1994, 1995, and 1996. For about a total of 1 year, the author lived in the main tourist area of the city of Yogyakarta, observing and informally interviewing street guides. The ethnographic nature of the research restricted the author to focus on heterosexual relations. Incidental observations give rise to the assumption that homosexual tourist–guide relations show a similar pattern. However, more research is needed to confirm or disconfirm this observation.

Tourism Development in Indonesia and Yogyakarta

The tourist industries of the Association of South East Asian Nations (ASEAN) countries have grown dramatically since the 1980s. Though numbers of foreign tourist arrivals in Indonesia are still low by ASEAN standards, they have increased particularly rapidly in Indonesia, growing by about 11% throughout the 1980s—the highest growth rate in the ASEAN area (Booth, 1990). Although Indonesia has benefited from the general tourist boom throughout the region, there have been a number of special factors that have led to the dramatic acceleration in foreign tourist arrivals: the abolition of visa requirements for Organization for Economic Cooperation and Development (OECD) and ASEAN nationals staying less than 2 months; the granting of additional landing rights to foreign airlines in the major ports of entry (Jakarta, Medan, and Bali); the opening of new airline ports of entry (e.g., Menado, Surabaya); the reduction in the number of licenses required to build new hotels; and the opening of the Islands of Bantam and Bintan for Singaporean tourists. The growth of numbers of arrivals since 1980 has been due to increasing numbers from Indonesia's main markets: Singapore, Australia, and Japan. Among the West-European countries there has been a considerable growth from the United Kingdom, the Benelux, and Germany (Booth, 1990). The average tourist stays longer in Indonesia than elsewhere in the ASEAN region, and thus has ample opportunity to spend money. There is a rapid growth in earnings from tourism, meaning that the sector has become a major source of foreign exchange for the economy. It is not impossible that tourism could emerge as the country's largest export industry in the 21st century.

The city of Yogyakarta in Central Java, with 500,000 inhabitants, seems almost unaffected by the pressing problems that modern mass tourism brings about in urban tourist centers all over the world. Although the city had approximately 350,000 foreign and 830,000 domestic visitors in 1995 (Department Pariwisata, Pos and Telekomunikasi [DPPT], 1995), life-styles are unhurried and relaxed, life is inexpensive and relatively crime free, and the people remain courteous and proudly conscious of their artistic traditions, the wealth of fine arts, and refined behavior. The core of Yogyakarta, spreading over an area of about 3 square kilometers, can easily be covered on foot. Many tourists taking a 1- or 2-day break in Yogya during an extended round trip through Indonesia explore the city by taking a walk along the major attractions: the Palace complex (Kraton [Sultan's palace], birdmarket, watercastle); Jalan Malioboro as the major shopping area with its daytime market and nighttime street entertainment; the arts and crafts (wayang kulit [puppet theater], classical dance, gamelan orchestra, batik, leather and metal work). Only a short bus trip away are the ancient monuments of Borobudur and Prambanan (both designated World Heritage Sites by the United Nations in 1991), the Grave Sites of Kota Gede and Imogiri, and the coast (Parangtritis) and the mountains (Mount Merapi) (Smithies, 1986).

The impact of a foreign-oriented consumer culture, of which international tourism is an exponent, is already visible in the inner city (i.e., Mulder, 1994): budget accommodations, restaurants offering fast food, shops with screaming pop music and flashing neon lights, catering mainly to young backpackers from Europe, America, Japan, and Australia. In the major tourist areas, alcohol and drugs are as easily available as international tourist menus. At the same time, the number of star-rated hotels has increased considerably. Once, the Grand Hotel—at present better known as the Garuda Hotel—on Jalan Malioboro was the only hotel with allure in the inner city. In the meantime, the Garuda has to share its position with the new high-storeyd Melia Purosani, which belongs to an international chain financed by Spanish investors. Other hotel chains—Holiday Inn, Hyatt, and Sheraton—have started to build new hotels, to accommodate what the authorities prefer to call "quality" tourism. On Jalan Malioboro, a fancy shopping mall with trendy boutiques, a large supermarket in the basement and a McDonald's Restaurant, frequented by trendily dressed local youth, is offering Western amenities. Impressive bank buildings of glass and steel, more fast-food restaurants, big department stores and supermarkets, and another air-conditioned shopping mall are adding allure to Jalan Solo. In Yogyakarta, all ingredients of a "global village" are available. A fascinating street life, tokens of high culture and history, World Heritage Sites, along with everyday encounters of the "Hello Mister"-type go hand in hand with the pleasures of shopping, nightclubs, ice-cold Cokes, Big Macs, and Magnums sold by a street vendor playing the Lambada tune.

Street Guides in Yogyakarta

Jalan Malioboro and the streets in the Kraton area swarm with young men offering their services to passing tourists. Most of the young men belong to the unqualified, unorganized, and permanently unemployed categories forming the informal sector of the tourist industry. They call themselves *friends;* but the authorities and representatives of the official tourism sector use to call them *unlicensed guides, informal guides,* or *wild guides,* or a *nuisance* to be removed from the tourist area by occasional "sweepings." Along the streets, there are a number of hangouts from where street guides approach passing tourists. Popular hangouts are the major meeting points of tourists: the doorsteps of shops, cafes, and restaurants, the streetcorners of Jalan Malioboro, the low walls surrounding the flower beds on the shopping street, the *wartel* (the telecommunication office visited by tourists who want to phone or fax home), the main post office, the market, the lounges of many budget accommodations, the central station, and the *alun-alun* (the big square) in front of the Sultan's palace.

Some street guides operate in small, loosely structured groups of friends sharing and controlling a hangout, but many operate on their own, only sharing the hangout with colleagues. The hangouts may be organized according to a shared ethnical and/or geographical background, having visited the same school or university, or being relatives. The best hangouts—the ones along Jalan Malioboro—are controlled by men from Yogya families, their relatives, or in-laws. Being engaged or married to a girl working as a shop assistant or being related to the security or parking lot man enhances one's opportunities to be tolerated at the doorstep. A newcomer requires the introduction of an already-established friend or relative; otherwise, he will not be accepted at a hangout. It is obvious that being of Yogya origin facilitates the access to these hangouts. Men from outside of town are given a hard time of being admitted into such a group.

Within a group there is a loosely structured division of tasks. Success in the "tourist hunt" largely depends on communicative abilities, outward appearance, and mastery of foreign languages. Group members scoring high on these criteria usually take the initiative of approaching tourists. If they are successful, they receive the biggest share of the profit. If they fail, other group members try to take over. Although the tourist experiences a series of approaches by different young men during his city walk, these men often belong to the same group. If one of the group "has a bite," the others follow him and his guest at a distance, observing which restaurants or shops are visited, what souvenirs are bought, and how much money is spent. After the tourist and the "guide" have left, group members enter the shop or restaurant to collect the commission, which will be divided among the group. The smart and handsome guides break away from the group when they turn out to be successful, preferring to work for themselves.

The street guides present themselves as friends, as someone who wants to help. As street guides told me over and over again, their foremost aim is to make tourists *senang*—happy. If the tourist is happy, then he or she is in the mood of spending money, which makes the guide happy. To keep the tourist in a happy mood, the guide takes a rather flexible and sympathetic position. Never would he take the lead; rather, he tries to find out what the tourist wants. Seeing a specific attraction? The guides shows the way. Peeping into backyards? The guide takes tourists to a *kampong*. Buying batic paintings or silverwork or puppets? The guide knows to find a shop or local factory. Finding an unexpensive place to eat where the locals meet? Drinking excessively? Buying joints? A prostitute? The guides knows the right place and the right person.

In Cohen's (1985a) terms, street guides are "pathfinders" rather than "mentors." They make arrangements of different kinds, they do not offer explanations. Their assets consist of wits and time. They have to seize the opportunities as and when they occur. To cater to the tourists' needs, they apply knowledge of a pragmatic kind: where to shop for souvenirs, where to stay or to eat, how much to pay. And they dispose of an understanding of human nature, their ability to read a social situation and turning it to their advantage. They have general conceptions about tourist motivation, national stereotypes, and tourist types. To understand the tourists' needs, the street guides have to study their background. Tourists find themselves being interviewed by these guides: a reversal of the more common pattern of tourists asking questions and the guide answering them. It is quite common that, after the first "hello friend," the guide continues to ask questions of a personal kind—personal in the eyes of Western tourists: Where are you from? Where do you stay? Are you married? Do you have a boy/girlfriend? Do you have children? What's your profession? How much you earn? This interviewing renders information that enables the guide to classify the tourist: Is she rich? Will she spend a lot of money on souvenirs? What kind of souvenirs? Is she traveling alone? Is she available as a sexual partner?

What is striking about the behavior of the street guides who frequent the streets during the day is their being extremely busy, always doing business or looking for a job. From the tourist's perspective, they seem to bump into a visitor purely by coincidence, actually being on their way to some important appointment. This impression is carefully staged. The truth is, however, that these young men do have to attend to several other jobs all the time. They usually combine the guiding of tourists with different kinds of economic activities. Some run a (souvenir) shop, a boutique, or a small workshop where batik, masks, wajang puppets, or other souvenirs are manufactured. They always work as touts for several shops in town on a commission basis. Some sell toys, ice cream, or cold drinks on the street; others work incidentally as barkeeper, waiter, security man, or bellboy in a hotel. Sometimes they invest money in bulk buying goods to sell with a profit. At other times they walk the streets with samples of fake Rolex watches or perfume, trying to sell these products on a commission basis. Most of the time they do all these things alongside each other.

There are street guides who combine a job in the Sultan's palace—being a gamelan player, dancer, singer, security man, cleaning man, or formal guide—with incidental street guiding. This applies to young men from Yogya families who enjoy the privilege of living in the Kraton area and are counted among the personnel of the sultan. Working for the sultan is not paid in money but in kind, and the employees can walk away from their task whenever required by other obligations.

Other street guides are migrants from less prosperous and less touristic areas of Java and from other islands of the archipelago. Attracted by the city as an economic and cultural center, these men try to find a niche in the petty trade. They make a living as street vendor, pedicab man, taxi driver, or street guide. Due to their different ethnic background, they belong to the marginal people in Yogya, where being of Javanese origin still is a precondition for access to networks that provide a successful business career. This also applies to a "career" in petty trade, as even the access to small-scale peddling is controlled by Javanese people. Among the marginals, one can find young men with an excellent education, with diplomas from polytechnics and universities, who cannot succeed in finding appropriate work. To make a living, they collaborate with other young men of a similar ethnic background to benefit from tourism.

Working as a street guide is popular with schoolboys, students, truants, and drop-outs. Yogyakarta is reknown as the "city of education" with about 70, mostly private, universities and countless institutions for vocational and professional training. In the afternoon, after the lectures and lessons are finished, the number of street guides increases significantly in the streets of Yogya. Many students and those who claim to be students try to make some extra money by taking tourists to shops and restaurants. Some are so attracted by the money and glamour associated with tourism that they discontinue their studies to focus completely on some petty jobs in the tourism sector.

The most marked aspect of the street guides' work (accompanying tourists) is only a strategy to earn money. The guiding as such does not provide a substantial income. They have to be satisfied with a tip that tourists give them voluntarily, a meal, a drink, or cigarettes. If they are lucky they receive gifts of some value: Western consumer goods such as wrist watches, walkmans, radios, leather jackets. Street guides do not dare ask for money straightaway. If a tourist is reluctant to buy souvenirs, the guide starts talking about "problems": his poor family being unable to pay for his expensive education, his old mother requiring medical treatment, his young children going hungry, his being an orphan. If the tourist does not or pretends not to understand, then the street guide has no other choice than turn and walk away, as he has no right to ask for a fee. The street guides' income consists substantially of the commission they receive for taking customers to the small hotels, the souvenir shops, and restaurants that the city has in abundance. The commission is a percentage of the selling price of the products and services purchased by tourists. In Yogya, small business proprietors usually hand over about 10% (but sometimes even 50–60%) of the selling price to intermediaries, street guides and other touts (Soedarso, 1992). This applies to the innumerous small enterprises and budget accommodations in the narrow alleys of the tourist areas and the shops and factories at the outskirts of the city; it does not apply to the big stores and star-rated hotels in the main shopping area.

One of the most important motifs for young men to operate as a street guide—an aspect that adds glamour to this "profession"—is the ever-present chance to enter into a sexual relationship with a tourist. Offering sexual services is an important ingredient of the guide–tourist relationship. Regarding the strict cultural codes for the public behavior of women—Indonesia is a Muslim country, after all—females offering their services as guides or friends are immediately associated with prostitutes. Only a small number of the street guides are female, and most of the women working as street guides actually are prostitutes. On the other hand, offering sexual services to female (and male) travelers is quite common among male guides. It is not surprising that one of the first questions upon addressing a female tourist is: "Are you married? Have boyfriend?"A negative answer almost immediately encourages the young man to make romantic overtures.

These overtures may consist of soliciting openly and directly: "Want boyfriend, Miss?" Or in a more indirect way: "Hi, I'm Mike from Bali. I'm new in town, have no friends here, feel lonely just like you, Miss."There is a big chance that this "Mike from Bali" is "Aziz from Yogya," who likes to adopt popular English names, as many street guides prefer pseudonyms that sound more familiar in the tourists' ear. Often the street guide produces business cards or letters he received from tourists originating from the same country as the woman he is approaching. He usually claims that he has many friends in her country to make her feel more comfortable with him. "Where you stay?" is the next step to get closer to the tourist, followed by the announcement: "I come see you tonight"—and the tourist might find her new suitor sitting in the lounge (if he is admitted) or waiting for her in front of the hotel. It is mostly in cafes, restaurants, and hotel lounges that the first romantic overtures are made, and these overtures do not originate exclusively from street guides. Waiters, receptionists, bellboys, and other personnel actually hold the best position to approach female tourists, and do take advantage of this privileged position. However, many street guides hang around in these places, cultivating friendly relations with the personnel to share their access to the constant flow of newly arrived tourists.

The street guide who is becoming friendly with a female tourist will take her to the Watercastle, the remains of the pleasure mansion of the royal family, to tell stories about the virility of previous sultans (who kept 40 wifes and made love with two of them each night—so the story goes), and to praise the virility of Yogya men in general. He will try to take her to the tombs of Imogiri or to Parangtritis beach: both well known but quiet attractions, as they are situated away from the main tourist routes, allowing for a romantic interlude. As Budi (22 years old), one of my informants, recalls:

> My most beautiful experience with a woman happened when I met this Italian girl. Her name was Carmen. If I think of her, I see her body, as beautiful as a Spanish guitar. She had white skin and her hands and legs were covered with soft hair. We went to Parangtritis and on the beach we made love like husband and wife. . . .

If such a romantic interlude leads to a relationship, the street guide might leave his various jobs for a while, make travel arrangements for the remaining days or weeks the tourist will spend in Indonesia, and accompany her on her trip. The tourist is supposed to pay for all his expenses.

Although a relationship emerging from these arrangements is of a transitory and instrumental nature, it can acquire other than purely financial characteristics (see Chapter 1). The relationship can become rather intense, as tourists serve to the guides as an entry to the good life. Tourists give gifts of both money and kind to their young friends, take them along on excursions, visits to nightclubs, and other leisure activities. It is understandable that the chances of acquiring money and gifts, of having a good time, and—for the very lucky ones—of receiving a free ticket and an invitation to stay in Europe/America/Australia or other country are an enormous attraction. This is not only valid for the unemployed youths, but also for those on low wages, because what can be made from the tourists usually far exceeds their wage earnings (e.g., Chapter 6; Wagner, 1977; Wolf, 1993).

Although picking up an endless stream of girlfriends seems to be part of the business routine, street guides make a qualitative difference between such relationships and business arrangements (Crick, 1992). Many have a great desire to find a girlfriend who takes them to her country—which occasionally does occur. Some have a long list of "true loves" who return each year (see Chapter 1 and Chapter 6). The guides would tell their prospective partners that, unlike all the other boys in town, they were after a one-and-only "true love." Though the boys prefer girls of their own age, they do understand that older women often find themselves in a more secure economic position and of a better purchasing power, which makes them highly attractive as sexual partners promising a ticket to a better life in the West or other more developed country. Female tourists in their thirties, fourties, and older find themselves "courted" by boys in their teens and early twenties. "I do prefer older women," one of my informants (24 years of age) used to say; "they are more mature and patient, they understand how my heart feels." The boys know exactly how to entertain, amuse, and attract older women. They even cultivate different styles to cater to specific target groups. Some play up to the younger tourists with calculated cuteness, dance, and sway seductively to the reggae and disco tunes, sing, giggle, and flirt outrageously. They affect a particular style of dress. Some prefer "cool and deadly": tight black jeans clinging to skinny legs, loose shirts unbuttoned to the belly, cascades of long black hair to the shoulder, looking like a hybrid of Prince and Michael Jackson. Others, targeting middle-aged tourists, prefer a sophisticated appearance: short, neatly cut hair, pinstripe trouser, white shirt, "pilot-style" sunglasses, ballpoint in breast pocket and some papers in their hand, apparently on their way to some very important business or sipping coffee in an expensive cafe and only by coincidence bumping into some lost tourists.

Street guides spend part of their income on maintaining their social network. Especially those operating in groups are obliged to share windfalls with their friends from the street and the tourism industry. At night, the pubs in the back-packer areas of Pasar Kembang, Sosrowijayan, and Prawirotaman are crowded with the "wild" guides, drinking beer, smoking weed, and flirting with female tourists. Their life-style is an imitation—not of Western tourists but—of the Kuta *cowboys*, the infamous Balinese *beachboys*, who lead the fashion in the world of guides. Many street guides in Yogya boast of having visited Kuta in Bali to see both, the "bare breasts" on the beach as well as the Kuta beachboys. Young men inspired by their Bali counterparts aspire to a career as musician in a local (reggae) band.

The "sophisticated" type of street guide does not visit the pubs downtown. As they are targeting the middle-aged "quality" tourists, they prefer to associate with the more stylish places of entertainment—although the expences often exceed their possibilities and each drink they have to pay for themselves lasts an hour. They, too, imitate a Western life-style and like to display consumer goods they received as a gift from their tourist friends.

Whatever role model a street guide is associating with, there is one desire all of them are cherishing. They all share the dream of acquiring a ticket to one of the "promised lands" where their ever-changing "true loves" come from: America, Europe, Japan, or Australia. This is basically their future perspective. Meeting individually traveling female tourists, they do not beat about the bush: they offer their services as a lover, servant, housekeeper, or cook—and they want to fulfil these tasks without any payment, just for board and lodging in the tourist's home country. Some street guides succeed in being invited to follow their tourist friends to their home country. However, for many life in the "promised country" turns out to be disappointing. Whereas they expect to lead a prosperous and leisurely life, they experience soon that working life is exhausting and boring, jobs are hard to find, and life-styles are different. Their relationship breaks up and they get incurably homesick. Provided with some savings, they finally return to Yogya, to play the big spender for a short while, buying drinks all round and throwing parties. When all the money is spent, they are back on the street again.

Having gone through a disillusioning experience in the "promised land" or just growing older without being able to realize their dream, most street guides change their tune. They start dreaming of accumulating enough money to start their own enterprise: a shop, cafe, restaurant, *losmen* (inexpensive hotel), boutique, or atelier to become a "boss" in the backpacker area of the city—preferably through marrying a "rich" tourist.

Prostitution, the *Pasar* Economy, and Tourism

"Ask a local in a third world tourist destination [what tourism means to them], and they may well tell you that it's about selling: selling their environment, their culture and their services to the guest," commented the earlier-quoted Australian journalist (Wolf, 1993). One may argue that this attitude characterizes what sociologists have defined in terms of prostitution: emotionally neutral, indiscriminate, specifically remunerated sexual services (Cohen, 1993). As Cohen (1971, 1982, 1986, 1993) and Crick (1992) have observed in various cultural contexts, the concept of prostitution does not adequately convey the meaning of the relationships emerging from sexual encounters between tourists and locals as described here. Cohen (1993) suggested applying the concept of "open-ended" prostitution to characterize a kind of relationship between a prostitute and her [sic!] customer, which, though it may start as a specific neutral service, rendered more or less indiscriminately to any customer, may be extended into a more protracted, diffused, and personalized liaison, involving both emotional attachment and economic interest. The same applies to the street guides of Yogyakarta. The term *gigolo* (male prostitute) is not quite a literal one here. These boys are not paid for their services as such, but relationships with tourists entail an improved degree of financial security.

If prostitution is not the right concept to characterize these relationships, love is not the right concept either. It is true that the young man underplays the commercial side of the relationship from the beginning, stages affection, changes his identity, and—if necessary—hides other emotional or even marital obligations. But different from Cohen's (1993) continuum of "open-ended" prostitution that is characterized by a shift from a "mercenary" through a "staged" to an "emotional" phase, the relationships of Yogya's street guides are not characterized by such a phasing. These young men are risk-taking, small-scale entrepreneurs who have to seize their opportunity under pressing limits of time. Tourists visiting Yogya usually stay in town for only one or two nights. There is no time to "develop" a relationship. Within this short span of time the young man strives to benefit as much as possible from this relationship and, as long as it remains beneficial, he is willing to continue for weeks, months, and, perhaps, even years. But when the profit drops, he breaks off the relationship easily and enters into another one without hesitation when the opportunity arises. He has no problems keeping a number of relationships going simultaneously.

His approach to relationships with female tourists is essentially the approach of a *pasar* trader to business that is of an economical as well as emotional nature. As Geertz (1963) has shown, the *pasar* trader focuses on the individual two-person transaction to get as much as possible out of the deal immediately at hand. He is perpetually looking for a chance to make a smaller or larger killing, not attempting to build up a stable clientele or a steadily growing business. He sees his activities as a set of unrelated exchanges with a wide variety of trading partners and customers, which form no overall pattern and build toward no cumulative end. Petty traders tend to think of their business career as a series of cycles in which one oscillates, more or less rapidly, between being ahead of the game and being behind it, between being well off and being bankrupt (Geertz, 1963). This attitude is reflected in the spending pattern of street guides: being generous for their pals until they are broke, then returning to their hangout to look for the next tourist to get involved with. *Pasar* traders are emotionally involved with their trade: failing to make customers buy and failing to get female tourists involved makes them feel depressed; they feel that they have had their chance and have failed to capitalize on it (Geertz, 1963). This emotional aspect of their trade may explain why street guides feign affection and even love for the female right from the start: they try to maximize their chances, not unlike the reverse gender situation (see Chapter 6).

The guides' position is insecure, their income is irregular—mostly commission based or depending on tips and gifts received from their tourist friends. Windfalls are made, but they may go for days without business. They spend a lot of money, partly on the tourist life-style in which they must to some extent participate, partly because of their social obligations in the guides' world. Having money entails the obligation to share it, to spend it on parties, drinks, and drugs with other guides. They do not save money and they do not invest in any long-term scheme to improve their situation permanently. They perceive any obligation—such as a steady job or a marriage that ties them down—as a loss of freedom. As one of my informants used to say: they want to be free like birds in the sky, not captured like fish in a pond. Street guides decline any obligations and ties that are difficult to combine with the innumerous activities, incidental jobs, and businesses that they are engaged in. As *pasar* traders, they spread themselves thin over a wide range of deals rather than plunge deeply on any one (Geertz, 1963). In the tourism sector, being a very precarious trade, it would be foolish to put all of one's eggs in a single basket. Small-scale peddling and guiding tourists are flexible jobs that allow for a strategic use fitting in with busy tourist seasons and calm off-season trade.

As Yogya is designated as the second tourism area (after Bali) in Indonesia by recent government planning (Tjokrosudarmo, 1991), it may be clear that the dependence of the city on global tourism will increase over the next few years. More than ever, global economy and culture will have an impact on the street life, consumption patterns, and life-styles and the ambitions of local people. The phenomenon of street guiding has to be understood against the background of the increasing dependence on global developments. Street guiding is a specific economic and social niche within the informal sector that is generated and sustained because of the growing influx of international tourists. The young men in Yogyakarta—as young men in other Third World cities characterized by a high unemployment rate and a high birth rate, combined with immigration from rural areas—are attracted to consumer culture. Tourists enact the dream of consumerism and hold the promise of a ticket to a better life.

Chapter 4

Beachboys and Tourists: Links in the Chain of Child Prostitution in Sri Lanka

Christine Beddoe

Tourist behavior in Sri Lanka has provided a myth of a life-style so Utopian that children are being sold to tourists in the belief that at least one member of the family can share in the wealth. Pedophiles and child molesters from industrialized countries have used their knowledge of this to introduce a "children for sex" subculture into the fringes of the informal tourism sector. Child prostitution—the trade in children for the purpose of engaging them in sexual activities—also includes the filming of these acts for the production of pornographic material. More recently, these activities have become known as the commercial sexual exploitation of children, a practice replete with inequalities of wealth and power.

In the face of economic austerity, rising unemployment, inflation, and growing poverty, Sri Lankan *beachboys* convince families to give up their young children in exchange for cash or kind so that the child can have a "good life" with the tourists and maybe even get a ticket out of the country. But the beachboy is not necessarily a deviant. Information collected from research interviews by the author in 1993 and 1994 shows that the motivation is one of providing a tourist service, just as beachboys sold marijuana to the hippies in the 1970s and batiks and gems to the mass tourists in the 1980s. The outcome is the same—economic gain and acceptance into the tourist domain. Acting as *culture brokers*, they gain access to tourist space and time.

Tourism and Child Prostitution

Tourism does not cause child prostitution, but it does provide a vehicle for easy access to vulnerable children. Child prostitution has flourished in developing countries embracing mass tourism as a means of economic growth, particularly in the Asian region. The anonymity and freedom of movement provide an ideal situation for child sex tourists to use relative wealth and power to exploit children and their families (see Chapter 16). The boundaries of child–adult relationships are stretched as children become part of the tourist product. This is especially so as tourism development encroaches upon village communities. Tourism provides an outlet for those individuals with a predisposition for child sex that cannot be met as easily in their own home country and community. It is the phenomenon of child prostitution as a tourist service that provokes further analysis. The term "child sex tourist" is used to describe any person engaging in sexual acts with children in any country other than his/her own. Child sex tourists are not always pedophiles. A pedophile is an adult who derives sexual satisfaction from (usually) prepubescent children. Pedophiles do not always act on these desires.

Culture Contact and Culture Change: Theory and Context

Tourism involves a relationship between strangers where the tourist is free of primary obligations while the hosts, having to serve them, are not (Nash, 1981). The objectification of each player in this relationship is magnified when one or both stand to gain financially. The interaction between tourist and host can produce a *demonstration effect*. Nash claimed that a possible result of this may be a growing dissatisfaction with the old and frustration in one's attempt to realize the new. As it suggests, the demonstration effect encourages one party to emulate the behavior of the other.

The demonstration effect is stronger when the gap between the more and less developed is wider and the extent and awareness of that gap is greater. Although not the only agent communicating this gap, tourism is the most immediate and tangible (Cater, 1987). Cater cited tourism as influencing the breaking up of traditional community and kinship bonds and disruptive to moral conduct. An example of this is the way that certain tourist behaviors such as sex tourism, in particular child sex tourism, has influenced patterns of behavior and attitudes in children and young people. In countries with a history of sex tourism, some children and young people believe that this is a normal tourist practice. Becoming a part of this is, therefore, seen as becoming involved in something advantageous. After all, tourism is perceived as being synonymous with economic, material, and social gain.

Tourism, claimed Graburn (1989), involves for the participants a separation from normal life and offers entry into another kind of moral state in which mental, expressive, and cultural needs come to the fore. Central to the work of Graburn and others (e.g., Cohen, 1988a; Urry, 1990) in the anthropology of tourism is the concept of liminality, which has emerged from theories surrounding pilgrimage and rites of passage ritual. Turner (1974) claimed that liminal entities are neither here nor there; they are betwixt and between the positions assigned and arrayed by law, custom, convention, and ceremony. Cohen (1988a) spoke of the individual being "torn out" of the ordinary social, economic, and political structures of profane life. And Graburn (1989) said that "the rewards of modern tourism are phrased in terms of values we now hold up for worship: mental and physical health, social status and diverse exotic experiences" (p. 24). If, as Urry (1990) claimed, "tourists find themselves in anti-structure—out of time and place—where social ties are suspended," how does this impact upon the local community? Children and young people in developing countries who are witness to this *out of time and place* behavior have nothing to compare it with except their own lives, which are often constrained by family obligation, moral conservatism, and poverty. In wanting to break free from this, they are often lured into the informal tourism sector, which seems so appealing. Others see it as an opportunity to exploit for financial gain.

Crick (1989) described the tourist–local relationship as odd. One member is "at play" and one is "at work." One has economic assets and little cultural knowledge; the other has "cultural capital," but little money. According to Crick, culture broker-age involves the activities of middlemen, entrepreneurs, and cultural transformers who try to structure to their own advantage transactions between the two systems brought together by international tourism.

Nunez (1989) believed that culture brokers are marginalized individuals with a flair for entrepreneurship—individuals who differ from one or more cultural norms and who, by being innovative, are likely to adapt to the stresses and changes brought about by tourism. The culture broker uses his/her ethnic identity as part of the encounter representing the host culture to the tourist and frequently controls the amount and quality of communication between the two groups (Evans, 1976).

Culture brokers in child prostitution are the mediators who use their local knowl-edge and their close association with tourists to facilitate the transaction and sale of children for sexual purposes. They adopt patterns of dress and behavior that allow them the access to tourist space and time. They do not appear out of place in the tourist environment because they have successfully adapted to the many other demands of foreign visitors. They have witnessed the out of time and place behavior of tourists and read it as normal tourist demeanor. So, too, demand children for sex is one more step along the continuum of self-indulgence. In Sri Lanka the culture brokers are often the adolescent beachboys.

Who Are the Beachboys?

There have been several studies of adolescents and young men in The Gambia, Barbados, and other destinations that identified similar patterns of behavior and motives to that of the Sri Lankan beachboys (e.g., Chapter 3; Brown, 1992; Karsh & Dann, 1981; Wagner, 1977). According to Karsh and Dann (1981), a beachboy is a young member of the host community who, as the name suggests, initiates his trade on those beaches frequented by tourists. In this case, the beachboy's "trade" involves the selling of sexual services to tourists in exchange for cash or kind.

Karsh and Dann's study of beachboys in Barbados focused on the interaction between Barbadian beachboys and white female tourists. Just as in Sri Lanka, the Barbadian beachboy is not a boy at all but rather a young man. The context in which age is discussed is relevant to the society and, therefore, the gray area between childhood, adolescence, and adulthood is much more than a legal concept. It could be explored more in the context of postcolonialism, *boy* reflecting the subservient relationship between host and guest.

In her research on mass tourism and charter trips in The Gambia, Wagner (1977) identified liminal behavior shown by Swedish tourists and links it to the often incorrect perceptions of typical Swedish culture by local youths. As Wagner pointed out, the activities of the tourist and experiences taking place during the vacation are not necessarily those of the pervading structures at home. An example of this is the sexual behavior of many older European men and women who openly cross the boundaries of generation and sexuality to engage in relationships with local youth.

The beachboy phenomenon is almost unheard of in Western culture. Karsh and Dann (1981) proposed that the beachboy comes from a neocolonial society where color is still regarded in terms of interassociated variables of class and socioeconomic status. In the tourism setting, access to the white tourist represents a breakthrough to the world which she (or he) is associated. The mere presence of a beachboy on tourist premises represents a personal triumph in overstepping racial boundaries. The conquest of the white female (or male) is perceived in terms of acceptance and integration into the society that she (or he) represents.

Tourism in Sri Lanka

Sri Lanka, or Ceylon as it was then known, gained its independence from Britain in 1948. But it was not until 1966 that Sri Lanka's policy-making interest in tourism began. In 1969, The Association for the Promotion of Tourism in Ceylon held a seminar on tourism and identified such forward-thinking issues as the importance of planning, private and public cooperation, and social and cultural impacts. Up to that time, Sri Lanka had followed the model tourism case study, doing everything right. From 1970 to 1980 tourism increased at 21% annually and in 1978 a 6-year tourism plan was adopted to sustain the impressive growth figures (Richter, 1989). But in 1978 at a conference entitled *The Role of Tourism in Social and Economic Development of Sri Lanka*, Perera presented a case study of the west coast beach resort of Hikkaduwa. Hikkaduwa had fallen outside of the precisely planned tourist infrastructure. The influx of "hippy" and budget travelers over the past decade had converted Hikkaduwa into an example of the unplanned development that the Tourist Board had hoped to avoid. Hikkaduwa later became synonymous with child sex tourism.

The growth of tourism and decrease in fishing opportunities had led to a rise in informal employment and dependence upon tourist dollars and charity. Children began to engage in begging on the beaches and touts provided services including drug dealing and prostitution. Mendis (1981) illustrated a clear picture of the type of tourism that was facing Sri Lanka in the early 1980s. He identified weaknesses in traditional tourism benefits and claimed that the high consumption patterns of tourists and the images they projected had a profound impact on local communities. This demonstration effect had caused dissension and community concern. Mendis claimed that the adjective "tourist" had become synonymous with "fashionable" and "glamorous" and is frequently employed as a sales gimmick to attract local clients.

In Sri Lanka, the 1983 insurgence and persistent civil war devastated tourism revenues. In the following years, tourism declined sharply and was compounded by worldwide recession. Arrivals declined from 407,000 in 1982 to 185,000 in 1989 and a decrease in tourism revenue from US$147 million to US$76 million. By 1992, racial upheaval had abated, tourists started to return, and the government once again had begun to hail tourism as a panacea for economic growth. Tourist arrivals in 1994 were the highest ever recorded in Sri Lanka. Statistics from the Ceylon Tourist Board show that 407,511 people visited during 1994 and in response to this Tourism Minister Dharmasiri Senanayake said that "the government would accord high priority for tourism in its overall programme for National Development and would encourage foreign investment in this sector."

Tourism and Structural Adjustment

The collapse of the extreme left-wing Sri Lankan Freedom Party (SLFP) government in 1977 represented a major change in economic orientation. The inward-looking policies of the SLFP had increased health, welfare, and education standards, but had decimated the Sri Lankan economy. The International Monetary Fund (IMF) and the World Bank, supporters of the newly elected United National Party (UNP), were substantially involved in what became far-reaching changes to Sri Lanka's economic policies, which included liberalization of imports and removal of controls and subsidies; immediate currency devaluation and increasing the price of flour; and increases in interest rates (Jayawardena, Maaslans, & Radhakrishnan, 1988). Sri Lanka embarked on what is known as a Structural Adjustment Program, the payment of major IMF/World Bank loans in return for a rigid austerity program. Social welfare spending was slashed and, against a backdrop of civil unrest, unemployment and inflation continued to grow.

By 1989, a fiscal crisis was imminent and, with civil unrest once again at a peak, the government was forced into dramatic stabilization efforts. The rupee was devalued against the US dollar resulting in a 20% fall since December 1988, subsidies on wheat and fertilizer were curtailed, and public investment was reduced by almost 30% (Adams, 1992). A slump in traditional agricultural export markets coupled with spiraling foreign debt forced the Sri Lankan government to offer foreign investors a lucrative package of incentives to invest in manufacturing and tourism. By the early 1990s, with decreased ethnic violence, privatization had been established as an important element in macroeconomic policy. Foreign tourism investors were able to import equipment and personnel tax free and to repatriate almost 100% of profits (Board of Investment, 1993). The continuing devaluation of the rupee had made Sri Lanka a very cheap holiday destination and many individual foreign investors began to set up small and medium-sized guest house operations. However, it also had the adverse effect of marginalizing the local community, who could not afford to enjoy the benefits of the new tourist establishments. Beach-side development continued to displace fishing communities and create tourist ghettos.

Tourism and Children

Children play a significant role in the informal tourism sector in Sri Lanka. As guides and touts (e.g., Crick, 1992; Samarasuriya, 1982), they offer the tourist a chance to see or obtain something unique, perhaps cheaper than they would get on their own. They prey on tourist needs for authenticity and bring them home to meet their family in the hope of receiving material gains. Friendship in tourism is just a "tactic" or "business" to many of the young guides (Crick, 1992).

Mendis (1981) claimed that children are lured into begging by the throw-away easy money of tourists. Using bits and pieces of language skills, the children extract pens, t-shirts, and chewing gum. Perera (1978) noted the ignorance of low-income parents toward the youth and young children hanging around the tourists and bringing home imported articles. In contrast with this, families surveyed from the middle-income groups were sending their children away, to relatives or boarding schools outside Hikkaduwa.

In their desire to continue in a type of dream world, the children of the villages surrounding the tourist enclaves increasingly frequent the tourist centers and, little by little, abandon their family obligations to the point where eventually the relationships within the family network deteriorate. One of the major attractions that influences boys of 13 years and older to turn to prostitution is the hope of being adopted by foreigners and being taken abroad by them.

Those who work or live in the tourist enclaves, especially the youths, imitate certain types of tourist behavior, particularly the use of drugs and alcohol. If the visitors' behavior does not conform to the social and moral norms of the country, the young try to copy them, especially in dress and male–female relations. The result is disorientation from their own values, which in turn leads to tensions within the family and social group.

The Beachboys and Child Prostitution in Sri Lanka

Beachboys are a familiar sight along the coastal tourist resort areas in Sri Lanka. The beachboys of Sri Lanka exhibit the same entrepreneurial spirit as those in The Gambia or Barbados and are mostly 14 to 26 years old. There are no strict boundaries surrounding the definition of these beachboys. Some are younger, some older. They may just be guides or touts for guest houses and restaurants. Some are dealers in drugs, batiks, or curios. Others are prostitutes or agents for prostitution.

Of those involved with the prostitution of younger children, it is probable they too have been involved in prostituting themselves, either in the past as a younger child or concurrent with their touting activities (Bond, 1980; Seneviratne, 1994).

Unlike Thailand or the Philippines, there is no "red light" district in Sri Lanka. Activists from the Sri Lankan campaign to end child prostitution (PEACE) report that the sale of children occurs mostly in the west coast beach resort areas of Negombo, Mount Lavinia, and Hikkaduwa and now in the inland tourist areas of Kandy and Nuwara Eliya. The mediators are often the beachboys who frequent the tourist areas.

Central to the ideology of beachboys is the desire to emulate tourist behavior and consumption patterns. In a survey conducted in Hikkaduwa in 1986 and 1987 it was found that what lures boys at very tender ages into participation in sex acts and drug-taking was the lure of the "good money" they earned. The income of these boys was very high by local standards and they ate in tourist resorts even when the tourist did not pay (Seneviratne, 1994).

The first international report of child prostitution in Sri Lanka was conducted in 1980 (Bond, 1980). The report, commissioned by *Terres des Hommes*, claimed Sri Lanka to be a major center for international pedophile activities. Although the report was accepted by the Sri Lankan government, little action followed on what was seen to be a "delicate" topic. In 1983 a committee was appointed by the government to inquire into social problems connected with tourism. Although the report denounced that there were problems associated with tourism they did concede that tourist hotels, guest houses, and private rooms were being used in organized operations to sell young girls and boys for the purpose of prostitution (Goonesekere & Abeyratne, cited in Ireland, 1993).

Obtaining statistics of the number of young children engaged in prostitution in Sri Lanka is almost impossible. Some reports claim up to 30,000, whereas other claims are as low as 5,000. The official government figure in 1992 was 30,000 children under 18 in prostitution, 75% of them boys (Seneviratne, 1994).

The only report to have clearly identified patterns of behavior among prostituted children is a 1993 survey of child prostitution in the Kalutara district. Weeramunda (1993) challenged the notion that it is through pure economic necessity that only the poorest of the poor children are forced into prostitution. The survey of sexually active children in this tourist area proved that the majority of children involved in prostitution came from an economic and social mainstream. Some had multiple partners, some had just one but stayed with that partner on repeat visits, others had just the one encounter.

Interviews conducted with beachboys by the author in 1993 and 1994 clearly indicated that their desire was to be with tourists in tourist space. They used their foreign language skills to initiate fellowship and used their newly developed friendship for economic gain. Some banter would occur first. "What is your name?" "What country are you from?" "Let us have a drink." In several cases the beachboy offered to pay for the drinks, expensive in comparison to local wages. But a wad of money would be produced in order to show their status as peer and then from there the negotiations would begin. A series of testing questions was used to see what service or product was in demand. "Would you like to have some ganja (marijuana)?" If the answer was no, then the response would go on to a list of other drugs, including heroin. The questions would persist to include massage—a euphemism for sex—and eventually lead to "do you want a young boy?" Or, in a few cases, a girl. This latter option was much more expensive and obviously not as easy to arrange. All throughout the questioning, the beachboy would present the options as if he was doing a friend a favor. On several occasions, the beachboys would ask if I would like to come home and meet the family, thus bridging the gap between entrepreneur and friend, reinforcing the theory that beachboys use their culture and community as part of the tools of their trade.

One former beachboy, who admitted to having sex with male foreigners when he was younger, claimed that the beachboys themselves were not homosexual, but that it was to please the foreigners. He claimed that the male tourists came with the story that by drinking the milk (semen) of the foreigner it would make the young boys strong and help the tourist stay young. It appears that this myth has been used widely by beachboys to socialize younger children into oral sex. Sometimes the beachboy will instruct the younger child by performing oral and anal sex acts with him, just to prove that it is OK. The younger children, mostly boys, are easily lured by the thought of pleasing foreigners and getting some money for their family. As mediator or culture broker, the beachboy's task is almost fulfilled. Finally, the success of the beachboy is measured by what he wears, where he goes, and who his friends are—in most instances, all relate to tourist space and time. This image is used to convince low-income families to give up their children in the hope that they can achieve such success.

A 1996 Ministry of Health research report revealed that Western women also come to Sri Lanka to engage in commercial sexual activities with Sri Lanka's beachboys. The Ministry of Health study concentrated on the lives of 18 beachboys in an attempt to understand their life-style. The study discovered that most of the beachboys speak fluent French or German and, because of the seasonal nature of tourism, they also find alternative employment in the off season. The majority live off their beachboy savings, with average earnings in the high season ranging from $80 to $240 a month.

Conclusion

The introduction of an easy money, good times, *children for sex* subculture into the fringes of the Sri Lankan tourism economy—juxtaposed with the harsh reality of economic rationalism, increased poverty, and unemployment—has led to a mythification of tourists and their homeland. Reinforced by Western media and a deluge of imported luxury goods, the myth allows beachboys to encroach upon low-income families and entice them to let their young children go with the tourist for a chance of a better life. The knowledge that the child will be sexually exploited is either ignored or misunderstood.

The beachboy behavior, seen as deviancy by mainstream society, is nothing more than conformity to the subculture to which they belong. Their motives are neither more nor less deviant than their role as tourist guide or drug dealer. The beachboys adapted to the earlier hippy culture by providing goods and services for what the market demanded. Further along the continuum, the beachboys have provided their services once again as the market has demanded, this time as "agent" or pimp to foreign pedophiles and child molesters who come in search of younger children for sexual gratification.

Tourism development in Sri Lanka should have been a case study of excellence. From the late 1960s onward, tourism planning was prioritized and supported by national and international authorities. Plans focused on the need to develop infrastructure and provide a conduit for foreign exchange. Sri Lanka was at the forefront of sustainable tourism planning. But planning did not account for the influx of hippy and budget travelers during the 1960s and 1970s or political, economic, and social change brought about by civil war during the 1980s, austerity programs, economic rationalism, or the scourge of child sex tourism over the last decade.

The current legal framework in Sri Lanka has only recently changed to allow for the criminalization of child sex tourism. Although having ratified the United Nations Charter on the Rights of the Child in 1991, Sri Lanka had done little to reform the legal system until the amendment to the Penal Code in August 1995. However, further questions need to be raised about whether this legal reform will be enough to change the patterns that have emerged over the past 10 years. Poverty alleviation, social welfare, and education policies, particularly in regard to those displaced by tourism, also have to be addressed. But policymakers, tourism operators, and tourists will need to take a long, hard look at the impact of host-guest interaction in the informal sector, particularly the effect of liminal *out of time and place* behavior on children and young adults. It is easy for us to classify foreign visitors into categories depending on their motives and behavior, but children do not make these distinctions. Any foreign visitor is simply a tourist, especially when the norms of tourist behavior change over time and are determined by tourists themselves. There is no doubt that if child sex tourism ceases to exist in Sri Lanka tomorrow, the beachboys will still be there, reacting to the whims and demands of the next plane load of tourists.

Chapter 5

Child Prostitution in Southeast Asia: White Slavery Revisited?

Jody Hanson

Are current accounts of child prostitution in Southeast Asia similar to the propaganda used during the turn-of-the-19th-century campaign to end the white slave trade in North America? Goldman (1970), an anarchist writing at the time of the so-called white slave trade, theorized, "It is significant that whenever the public mind is to be diverted from a great social wrong, a crusade is inaugurated against indecency, gambling, saloons, etc." (p. 19). Does the literature in either case call for eliminating the structural causes of prostitution? Are the moralists, indeed, concerned with diverting our attention and is the general public accepting the accounts with which they are presented without question? When reading contemporary accounts of child prostitution in Southeast Asia, I am often left with a feeling of déjà vu, with the distinct impression that this is all so hauntingly familiar. Spender's (1983) book, *There's Always Been a Women's Movement This Century*, serves as an example of this pattern of historical theme and variation.

Rather than offering an interpretation of turn-of-the-century popular press material on the white slave trade, a polite term for prostitution, and reviewing the contemporary reports about child prostitution in Southeast Asia in a conventional academic manner, mainstream writings from the two periods are juxtaposed so readers can judge the tone, style, and content for themselves. In this chapter, I examine the similarities of contemporary child prostitution and the white slave trade. Topics that are juxtaposed fall under the rubric of rural–urban migration in an industrializing context and include employment options, recruitment practices used to entice girls into prostitution, and "escaping" from the sex industry. A discussion calling into question the class origins of the writers, the tones of the texts, and the mission to "save" women from prostitution follows. The policies of protection and the limitation of the proposed solutions are also examined, as are the suggestions to eliminate the "problem." The works of writers who view prostitution from an "It's a job" perspective are then presented. In the last section, the data base is the transcripts of taped interviews and the field notes I compiled while in Thailand and Vietnam in December and January of 1995–96. This field trip was part of my continuing study of the international sex industry. Rather than a conclusion, this chapter ends with questions for further consideration.

Historical and Contemporary Accounts

The primary source for turn-of-the-century literature is the book *War on the White Slave Trade* (Bell, reprinted in 1980). In the preface, he wrote "For the protection of the innocent, for the safeguarding of the weak, for the warning of the tempted and the alarm of the wicked, the truth must be told—the truth that makes us free" (p. 9). Contemporary accounts come from a variety of sources, including publications that consider themselves alternative press, and samples were chosen for their reflection of what is generally regarded as mainstream thought on the issue. I agree with Black (1994) when she writes, "In the phrase 'child prostitution,' both words are questionably accurate—as far as the majority are concerned. And as for 'forced' into sexual work, in many cases the 'force' is metaphorical. There is often a strong element of volition, if not to enter, certainly to stay" (p. 12). This also helps explain why programs to "save" women from prostitution have met, over the years, with very limited success. Given space limitations, readers wanting clarification are advised to consult the original works to better understand the context of the brief quotations (Table 5.1). This juxtaposition of the literature serves to illustrate how the issues today were already of concern some 100 years ago. Hence, although some may view sex tourism and prostitution, especially with women in or from developing countries, as a modern phenomenon brought about by the mass tourism phenomenon, it is indeed something that has occurred for a long time.

Middle-Class Accounts and Proposed Solutions

Both the turn-of-the-century and the contemporary literature reviewed thus far reflect middle-class values and liberalistic concerns. The moralistic tones of the texts, in both instances, often represent second-hand accounts, and are stories that appeal to our sense of injustice. Harry A Parkin, Assistant United States District Attorney, for example, wrote:

> A very few days ago this pitiful case was, in an official way, brought to my attention. A little German girl in Buffalo married a man who deserted her about the time her child was born. Her baby is now about eight or nine months old. Almost immediately after her husband ran away she formed the acquaintance of an engaging young man who claimed to take deep interest in her welfare, and in that of a certain girl friend of hers. He persuaded them both that if they would accompany him to Chicago he would immediately place them in employment which would be far more profitable than anything they could obtain in Buffalo. . . . "Madam, do you know that this is a house of prostitution?" (Bell, 1980, pp. 330–331)

The theme of wanting to "save" women from prostitution is apparent in both eras. The "discourse of decision," which may be an extension of survival in an industrial-

Table 5.1. Juxtaposition of the Literature

Circa 1900	Contemporary
"Employment agents have been convicted for sending girls out as house servants to immoral places for the ultimate reason of making them inmates in the house." Clifford G. Roe, Assistant State's Attorney of Cook County (in Bell, 1980, 171–172)	"The road to prostitution may start in early years with female children working as domestic servants. They become easy prey to the sexual hunger of their masters, their master's friends and relatives." Nayyer Javed (in Sekhar, 1980, p. 23)
The parents gave their consent, thinking that through the girl's life upon the stage their position in life would be raised, and they sent the little girl on to Chicago with this man, bidding her 'God-speed'." Clifford G. Roe, Assistant State's Attorney of Cook County (in Bell, 1980, p. 166)	"They talk to [the parents] about their debts and get them to believe that their children will be better off doing a nice job like selling flowers in the city." (Roberts, 1988, p. 23)
"The white slave trade may be said to be the business of securing white women and of selling them or exploiting them for immoral purposes. It includes those women and girls who, if given a fair chance, would, in all probability, have been good wives and mothers and useful citizens." Edwin W. Sims, United States District Attorney (in Bell, 1980, p. 14)	"Agents of the sex trade take advantage of women's vulnerability to violence. Often, women run into the trap set by these agents to escape violence. . . ." Kripa (in Sekhar, 1995, p. 28)
"The country girl is more open to the enticements of city life, being more truthful, perfectly innocent and unsuspecting of those whose business it is to seek their prey from girls of this class." Miss Florence Mabel Dedrick (in Bell, 1980, p. 105)	"Large numbers of children and young women—mostly from poor families in Burma, southern China, Laos, Cambodia, Vietnam, the Philippines and Taiwan—were sold to pimps and forced to work in sex dens throughout the region." Hildebrand (in Sekhar, 1995, p. 10)
"A girl reared in the country is not taught to suspect everyone she meets, unless a rare occurrence presents itself, and when involuntarily the defence instinct asserts itself." Miss Florence Mabel Dedrick (in Bell, 1980, p. 105)	"Some of the women and children are abducted from outside their house or while they are at work." Nayyer Javed (in Sekhar, 1995, p. 28)
"It is through the lack of education of the fathers and mothers along these lines, particularly in the rural districts that Satan has been aided in his onward evil march. Some one has said, 'No reform will ever be successful till people know the truth'." Miss Florence Mabel Dedrick (in Bell, 1980, pp. 113–114)	"Sometimes, I think, it's innocence on the part of the parents when they sell their children," Dahlin said. "They think really they will work in a factory or in a restaurant or in an office. But some parents know exactly what their children are going into." (Kelly, 1990, p. 2)

"How many hundreds of innocent American and European girls have been led away to heathen and Mohammedan lands, on false promises of good positions as teachers, governesses, or even as missionaries, only the open books of the day of judgment will disclose." (Bell, 1980, p. 28)

"One girl, in telling me how she had been led astray said she had only been getting $3.50 a week. Seeing an advertisement for experienced workers at $5.00, she answered it. For two weeks they kept it from her that she was in a house of shame." Miss Florence Mabel Dedrick (in Bell, 1980, p. 101)

"One victim was found and rescued in Winnipeg. Several others disappeared and have not been found. One daughter of the Parsonage, now fatherless, from across the Line, was rescued and restored to her mother from a resort in British Columbia." Rev. J. G. Shearer, D, D., Secretary, Moral and Social Reform Council of Canada (in Bell, 1980, p. 345)

"If, in spite of all this, a girl should be brave enough or rash enough to try to make her way out of the dive, and escape, almost nude, as she is kept, into the street, perhaps she would be allowed to go." (Bell, 1980, pp. 241–242)

"If the young girls who are seeking a living upon the stage could know of the pitfalls that are in their way, I believe many of them would seek other employment. One of the girls is now married and living very happily." Arthur Burrage Farwell, President Chicago Law and Order League (in Bell, 1980, p. 233)

"Two girls were brought before the registrar general, both of whom pleaded for protection against their owner, stating that she intended to sell them to go to California. One of these had been bought by this woman for eighty dollars; the girls saw the price paid for her." (Bell, 1980, pp. 214–215)

"In other parts of Europe, the Middle East, Africa, and Asia, there are several thousand less fortunate women who are held in captivity as virtual sex slaves working in dingy prostitution dens or classy nightclubs and restaurants operating as fronts." Angeles-Forster (in Sekhar, 1995, p. 1)

"These young women who come from remote local areas or overseas are lured by illegal recruiters into accepting nonexistent decent jobs in the cites and abroad." Angeles-Forster (in Sekhar, 1995, p. 2)

"There are more Tanyas and Martas in other parts of the world, some whisked away to oblivion, others luckier to have been rescued." Angeles-Forster (in Sekhar, 1995, p. 2)

"In the last few years, it has become harder for girls to escape prostitution and the reality is usually very different from what they have been promised." (Mannion & Ridge, 1990, p. 60)

"In many countries throughout the region, the flesh trade is fully integrated with other, quite legitimate businesses. the health cubs found in many hotels are often mere fronts for brothels, offering a range of services to hotel patrons." (Mannion & Ridge, 1996, p. 59)

"She was still in primary school when her mother sold her to a teahouse for $275. For her mother it meant a television and a bottle of whisky. For little Pim, it meant the beginning of life as a sex slave, being forced to take customers for $1.75 each in a room behind the restaurant. She was just 12 years old." (Kelly, 1990, p. 2)

"Others are first seduced, then half willingly go, this seeming to them a less evil than facing the shame at home. Still others are wooed, won and wedded in cold blood by heartless slavers, then inveigled or forced into the segregated colonies in the great American cities." Harry A Parkin, Assistant United States District Attorney (in Bell, 1980, p. 335)

"Other women have been tricked into marrying foreigners, sometimes with the help of illegal marriage brokers, only to end up working in brothels abroad." Angeles-Forster (in Sekhar, 1995, p. 2)

izing country, however, is absent. Subsistence farming holds little appeal for anyone other than romantics. Is it any wonder then that sex work attracts young women when "The average wage for a Government employee [in Cambodia] is $20 a month. A female child can earn three times that much in a week through prostitution" (Thompson, 1994, p. 53)? Thompson dismissed the economic factor as inconsequential, and she failed to discuss the idea that in Cambodia children are expected to contribute to the family income. She did, however, report that Tony, an Australian who works with World Vision "has resorted to photographing and following some of the men to try to stop them taking advantage of the desperate children" (p. 53). Why are the wages of parents, in relation to the goods and services they can purchase, not questioned? After all, poor parents have poor children and poor children have to contribute to the family income if they are all going to survive. Could it be that poverty, not prostitution, is the issue?

Both at the beginning and end of the 20th century, the charitable solutions being proposed by well-meaning liberals are of limited value, by my estimation. Mannion and Ridge (1996), for instance, acknowledged "And if a girl enters domestic service [in Thailand], the expectation is usually that she will provide sexual favours to her male employer who, if he is feeling generous, may extend those same favours to his friends" (p. 59). They then went on to endorse the work of the Daughters' Education Programme where they "snatch girls—some as young as seven—in immediate danger of being sold into prostitution, and provide them with up to three years education or vocational training" (p. 61). Granted, it keeps the young women out of the brothels for 3 years, but does it also mean that they will be better servants, which is about the best job one could hope for with minimal educational skills? As Mannion and Ridge (1996) established, many servant positions also include sexual services, so whose interests are really being served? The need for domestic servants being directly related to middle-class interest in "saving" girls from prostitution has been documented (Henriques, 1963; N. Roberts, 1994).

In Thailand, groups, such as Empower and NET, are working with prostitutes and, given their peer education focus, girls in the sex industry are more likely to have access to condoms and sexual health checks than are their domestic servant counterparts. At a brothel at Soi Cowboy in Bangkok where I was a frequent visitor, for example, there were safe sex posters on the back of the doors in the woman's toilets and above the men's urinals. The girls who worked there said they used condoms and a couple of them pulled some of out their pockets and bags to show me (personal fieldnotes). Samantha, a 59-year-old prostitute who has been in the business for many years, told me she always insists on condoms and that she counsels young women to do the same. It is the clients who do not want to practice safe sex, not the prostitutes.

As well as the moralistic tones being consistent in both eras, the policies of protection are similar in intent and international in scope. In the case of the white slave trade:

> An international project of arrangement for the suppression of the white-slave traffic was, on July 25, 1902, adopted for submission to their respective governments by the delegates of the various powers represented at the Paris conference, which arrangement was confirmed by formal agreement signed at Paris on May 18, 1904, by the Governments of Germany, Belgium, Denmark, Spain, France, Great Britain, Italy, the Netherlands, Portugal, Russia, Sweden, Norway, and the Swiss Federal Council. (Bell, 1980, p. 15)

Given that these laws were already in place, it seems to be an extension, rather than a new statute, that "Germany, Norway and Sweden have passed laws allowing prosecution of child abusing sex tourists in their country of origin. Australia, France and New Zealand are considering similar legislation" (Sekhar, 1995, p. 9). By passing the laws, it seems, the campaigners are relieved of some of their moral responsibility. After all, by prosecuting the offenders in their home countries, they are now "protecting" the young women of Asia from the hordes of sex tourists who are often portrayed as perverted dildo-wielding, video-packing pedophiles. Exactly how this prosecution is going to take place—who is going to lay the complaint, how is evidence to be gathered, how are the women going to testify in a foreign language and in a foreign land—is yet to be established and, except for a few showpiece cases, the legislation is unlikely to do much other than create a "See we're doing something about this problem" sense of relief.

The "It's a Job" Perspective

Child prostitution is about as emotive an issue as one can find these days. Every-one, it seems, has an opinion on the topic. Black (1994) rightly warned, "As with all child labor, it is extremely difficult to challenge the conventional wisdom without being accused of condoning what cannot, and must not, be condoned" (p. 12). Like Black, I do not think prostitution is necessarily the worst occupational choice a woman can make. Again, the economic realities and the discourse of decision also have to be taken into account. Further, like Black, I have trouble with the idea that a girl can be married at the age of 13 and become a mother at the age of 14, but is categorized as a child prostitute until she is 18. "The overwhelming majority of 'children' in prostitution are well past puberty, mostly in their mid-teens, and many are beyond both the legal age of marriage and of sexual consent" (Black, 1994, p. 12).

While in Southeast Asia on two occasions, I spent quite a lot of time in a sweat-shop factory where the women sewed silk clothes for Western women like me. I also visited a number of brothels in Bangkok, Surin, and Ho Chi Minh City. At the end of the day, I had no problem whatsoever understanding why women opt for sex work. Working in an oftentimes poorly lit, poorly ventilated factory for 14 hours a day, 6 days a week for low wages is, by Western standards, unacceptable. Still, many women find it more appealing, more profitable, and more social than subsistence farming (personal fieldnotes). What about sex work? Yes, some of the clients are drunk or obnoxious. Incidentally, the vast majority of customers are local, as international sex tourism is a small, but highly publicized, percentage of the actual market (see Chapter 15). Of course, there are chances of catching sexually transmitted diseases. For some women, these occupational hazards—when weighed up against the odds of violent husbands or sweatshop conditions—make prostitution the preferred occupational choice. Sex work also allows prostitutes to send more money home to their families: "They can earn easy money, and especially when they have a large family which they have to feed. They are so poor. So this job can bring money very quickly so that they can use it for emergencies, immediate expenditures" (Hanson, 1996a).

At the turn of the century, poor and working-class women in America, both native-born and immigrant, had few real options. In short, they could marry a farmer, go to the city in search of work in a factory, seek employment as a servant, or become a prostitute. Goldman (1970) argued:

> "The wife who married for money compared with the prostitute," says Havelock Ellis, "is the true scab." She is paid less, gives much more in return in labor and care, and is absolutely bound to her master. The prostitute never signs away the right over her own person. She retains her freedom and personal rights, nor is she always compelled to submit to man's embrace. (pp. 26–27)

Were the employment opportunities for American women at the turn of the century similar to those available to uneducated rural women in Southeast Asia today (see Chapter 16)? Unlike the reformist writers of both periods, I find that prostitution is often a conscious occupational decision for young women, as mentioned earlier, insofar as it appeals more than working in a factory for low wages or subsistence farming. Further, most prostitutes get into the sex industry because they already know someone, oftentimes a relative, who is already working there. The following account serves as an example and is from the transcript of an interview with Miss Min, the translator at the Sex Worker Outreach Project in Ho Chi Minh City, Vietnam (Hanson, 1996a):

> Many prostitutes have very little education, and they are poor. Maybe they start off, not with sex work, but with something else. But life is harsh, and they see other people very beautifully dressed up and they think "Why don't we try it?" And they do the same and they earn a lot. So they come back to the rural areas and talk to other people and they see that many just follow suit because they see that their life in the rural area is very difficult, and they cannot earn as much money. . . . When [parents] need money they even send

their children to prostitution. Perhaps they have a 16 year old daughter and they need money, so they just take her into the business.

More Questions and Further Considerations

Returning to Goldman's (1970) idea that sensationalist and emotive campaigns are waged to divert us from more serious issues gives me pause. Although I do not claim to have the answers, I do have some questions. Could it be that Goldman (1970) was right when she wrote that "To the moralist prostitution does not consist so much in the fact that the woman sells her body, but rather that she sells it out of wedlock" (p. 25)? Why are the reformist people, in both instances, willing to settle for limited measures, such as providing at-risk girls with minimal education? Could it be that calling for the elimination of the causes of prostitution also means calling for the elimination of the capitalist system that currently supports it? As Southeast Asia becomes industrialized and produces inexpensive goods, an increasingly number of rural people are moving to the urban areas in the hopes of finding work. The market images of Coke, McDonalds, and Reebok, to name just a few, create consumer needs. Along with these needs comes the obligation to have enough money to purchase the desired goods. So if prostitution is a way to make fast and relatively easy money, why should people be surprised when young women exercise this option? Again, it goes back to the ideas of supply and demand.

While people voice their concern about child prostitution in Southeast Asia, child prostitution going on in their own countries, cities, or even neighborhoods is often ignored or, when it does attract the attention of the press, is often passed off as an isolated incident. Once, for instance, I asked a 54-year-old New Zealand prostitute how long she had been in the sex industry. She looked at me and said "I've been cracking it since I was four years old and my step-father would not give me enough to eat unless I came across" (Hanson, no dates). So why, then, it is that many liberals are content to see child prostitution as a problem "over there" while ignoring it at the local level?

Some of the attitudes about child prostitution and sex tourism are, indeed, naive: "I don't see why paedophiles from Australia and New Zealand should be able to go to other countries and do things to children that are totally illegal and punishable in their own countries" (Ansley, 1993, p. 9). Does that mean Australian and New Zealand children are somehow safe because the pedophiles now go overseas? It seems unlikely given that most children are molested by someone they know.

Since it seems that all accounts of child prostitution start with what Black (1994) called a "gut-wrenching" account, I thought I would turn it around and end this chapter on a positive note. Goldman's (1970) optimism comes through when she writes "And educated public opinion, freed from the legal and moral hounding of the prostitute, can alone help to ameliorate present conditions" (p. 32). Yes, child prostitution, along with other forms of child labor, can be eliminated. But in doing so we also have to eliminate the capitalist system that underpins economic, social, and cultural exploitation. Could it be, as Goldman suggested, that a war against child prostitution is being waged to divert our attention from the real problems? The effects of capitalism, on not only young women, but all people who are not in positions of power, are being lived in Southeast Asia on a day-to-day basis. And perhaps the harsh realities of having to cope with what that means is more than we can handle. It is easier, therefore, to concentrate of a small and moralistic crusade to save a few child prostitutes rather than to question the system that leaves them with few other choices.

Chapter 6

Bar Girls in Central Bangkok: Prostitution as Entrepreneurship

Joan Phillip and Graham Dann

Given that prostitution in Thailand is illegal, several studies have attempted to account for its dramatic growth. Table 6.1 shows, for instance, that, with one exception, as the number of tourist arrivals has increased, so has the sex industry correspondingly expanded to meet consumer demand.

Several commentators (e.g., Bond, 1980; Cohen, 1982; Ech & Rosenblum, 1975; O'Grady, 1981; Stol, 1980; Truong, 1983) additionally noted that there is a strong association between prostitution and travel to the Third World. The male bias in such visitor statistics is evident in the Thailand figures for 1993, where 64% of the 5,760,537 tourist arrivals were male; 46% were repeaters.

Several other hypotheses have been offered as explanations for the rapid development of the sex industry in Thailand. Truong (1983, 1990) for example, utilizing a global structural analysis, argued that the sex industry in that country would not have reached such magnitude without the internationalization of capital and the concomitant incorporation of leisure into the international division of labor. She further maintained that the emergence of collective sex tourism through the agency of packaged tours purchased by individuals and groups or by transnational firms as fringe benefits for their workers indicates an ongoing process of direct capital accumulation.

Some theorists have also shown that prostitution in Thailand is grounded in tradition and history (Goughlin, 1950; Phongpaichit, 1982; Truong, 1983). They pointed out that concubinage and brothels have existed since time immemorial, although with distinct class connotations. Other observers have argued that the culture of Thailand has been such that it has promoted the growth of prostitution within the context of the sort of global economy described by Truong (1990). Traditional Thai culture emits contradictory messages, which facilitates conflicting interpretations of the nature of Thai society and the extent of change in Thailand (Cohen, 1993).

Table 6.1. Estimated Number of Prostitutes in Bangkok and Thailand and Tourist Arrivals

| Year | Prostitutes | | Tourists to Thailand |
	Bangkok	Thailand	
1957	10,000	20,000	
1960			81,340
1964		400,000	
1970			628,671
1976		400,000	
1980		500,000	1,858,801
1982	200,000	500,000	
1984		700,000	
1990		150,000–200,000	5,298,860

Source: adapted from Muecke (1992).

Many point to the patriarchal nature of Thai society, which encourages men to gain sexual experience before marriage in a brothel, whereas women are expected to remain chaste. Thus, the prerequisites for an occupation are established where women are required to be submissive (DaGrossa, 1989; Kirsch, 1975). Such segregated sex typing is, however, not exclusive to Thailand. It is familiar enough elsewhere, ranging from the prudery of Victorian England to the machismo of Latin America (Truong, 1983).

A corollary of the culture hypothesis has been the highlighting of the role of Theravada Buddhism in the lives of Thai people. The beliefs in "merit for the next life" (the doctrine of karma) and the exclusion of women from the "merit field" of the monastery have tended to differentiate the moral obligations of sons and daughters with respect to their parents. A son is able to repay his gratitude and exonerate his filial responsibility by becoming a monk. A daughter cannot. She has only one way to demonstrate her thanks—by providing for her parents during their lifetime. Frequently, she is unable to do so because of her poor economic status, hence her engaging in prostitution in an effort to repay the debt owed to her mother and father (Chapter 5 and Chapter 16; DaGrossa, 1989; Tantiwiramanond & Pandey, 1987).

Kirsch (1975) and Khin Thitsa (1980) argued that the inferior way in which women are regarded in Theravada Buddhism conditions them to become prostitutes:

> With the low value attached to the female body and the female spirit by Buddhism, woman has been sufficiently degraded already to enter prostitu-

tion. If historically woman has served man helping him as wife, minor wife or mistress, it is not such a big step to become an actual prostitute. Indeed, the traditional emphasis on polygamy in Buddhist society encourages the widespread practice of prostitution in modern Thailand. (Khin Thitsa, 1980, p. 23)

Khin Thitsa's argument has been severely criticized by Keyes (1984), who maintained that women in Theravada Buddhism in fact hold an elevated position. She also believed that it is the influence of the "Western market" mentality, with its urban secularized image of women, that is to blame for women's entry into prostitution (Cohen, 1993).

Another hypothesis that seeks to account for Oriental prostitution points to the recent empowerment of the Western female. According to this view, Western feminist ideology has reduced the world to a surfeit of unadjusted males, helpless in finding ways to cope with these new developments, and unable to find ways to restore their feelings of masculinity (see Chapter 16). Hence the compensatory alluring trips to the East in search of a "lost paradise" inhabited by traditionally submissive women (del Rosario, 1994; Khin Thitsa, 1980; Lenz, 1978; Odzer, 1990; O'Grady, 1981; Truong, 1983).

The legacy of the United States military bases is also an explanatory factor in the demand for prostitutes. In the late 1960s, for example, 40,000 troops were stationed at air bases in Thailand and Vietnam, thereby creating a conducive climate for entrepreneurs to organize prostitution and to establish "service centers" that now cater to the needs of the tourist (Lubeigt, 1979; Truong, 1983).

Thailand's economic policies since the 1950s have also been offered as an explanation for the entry into prostitution of increasing numbers of women from the Northern provinces. Such policies combine an export-oriented strategy, with the rejection of any program directed towards tight economic planning. The result of this two-pronged approach has been a depression in the agricultural sector and a concomitant mass exodus from the countryside to the city, where a large percentage of these rural migrants have been young women seeking jobs to support their families. However, on arrival in Bangkok, they are faced with severely restricted occupational opportunities. With domestic or factory work, offering earnings that do not reach the 1982 standard daily minimum wage of 64 Baht (approximately US$3), an amount insufficient to support themselves, let alone their dependents, and without the necessary skills to engage in clerical or professional services, the only viable alternative occupation is prostitution (see Chapter 5).

The government, many observers contended, has also played a role in facilitating sex tourism. In Thailand, political leaders have been quite open in their support of tourist-oriented prostitution (del Rosario, 1994; Lee, 1991; Richter, 1989). They readily acknowledge the economic importance of those who encourage tourist spending, thereby contributing to foreign exchange earnings. Whatever the validity of the foregoing hypotheses, there is no denying that a combination of these factors has culminated in the development of a tourist sex industry that is among the largest in the world.

Open-Ended Prostitution in Bangkok

It was Cohen (1982) who coined the expression "open-ended prostitution" in reference to the type of relationship established between a Thai prostitute and a *farang*—a white, foreign, male tourist. He argued that although the relationship might commence as a neutral service, it could be readily extended into a more protracted, diffuse, and personalized liaison, involving both emotional attachment and economic interest. Adopting this same terminology, the present study enlarges his earlier investigation to encompass bar prostitution, and the relationships between go-go dancers and farangs in the tourist bars of the Patpong district of Bangkok.

The current research was carried out over a 15-month period. The techniques utilized were those customarily employed by interactionists—observation, interviews, and analysis of personal documents. The utilization of symbolic interactionism as both a theoretical and methodological approach was justified in order to facilitate an emic appreciation of the phenomenon under investigation.

Methodology.

Thomas and Thomas (1928) argued that situational analysis was the basis of understanding any interactive process. They demonstrated that an individual's behavior in social groups was influenced by his/her subjective definition of objective conditions of the social situation; that is to say, "If men define their situations as real, they are real in their consequences" (p. 41).

In order to define emically the relationship between bar girl and a farang, it was first necessary for the first author to gain entry into the subculture of tourist-oriented prostitution. The objective was to devise a role that would facilitate her successful acceptance into the group, and permit her to gain accurate knowledge of its life, a kind of role that would allow her to share in the sentiments and activities of people in face-to-face relationships (cf. Bruyn's, 1966, axiom on the role of the observer). However, the devising of a suitable role was made problematic by the fact that she was from an ethnic minority and spoke very little Thai; she was also undergoing her own social adjustment to a foreign country.

After a period of what Humphreys (1970) characterized as "getting the feel of the deviant community," (p. 25) while at the same time trying to come up with methods to penetrate its boundaries, she discovered that the only viable means of entering the field was to volunteer as an English teacher with an NGO called EMPOWER, which worked with the bar girls, offering counseling services and educational skills. The role of the teacher was neither forced nor contrived, and fitted well into the normal pattern of bar girl culture, and followed Bruyn's (1966) second axiom of the observer fitting into a normal part of the culture and the life of a people under study. Although EMPOWER stipulated that she could not interview the girls, she was able to utilize the conversational part of the syllabus to explore attitudes and opinions especially relating to their relations with farangs.

In conjunction with observation, informal interviews were conducted with farangs, and letters exchanged between the two parties were analyzed in order to strengthen and reinforce her observational data, as well as to provide a supplementary research tool that could usefully portray how both parties defined their situations. She was able to access these letters, because, in her role as teacher, she was also expected to be a scribe. Although, knowing very little written Thai, she was still able to function effectively as scribe through the help of a Thai coworker, thereby allowing her to compose them in the vernacular.

The Setting

The EMPOWER office is situated in *Soi 1* (Lane 1) of the popular Patpong area on the third floor of a building. Patpong is made up of three sois, each lined with bars, restaurants, supermarkets, bookstores, pharmacies, and VD clinics. During the day, Patpong looks like any ordinary Bangkok city street, but at night it changes its appearance and identity. The latest disco hits blare from the bars, whose neon signs proclaim such names as "Pussy Galore," "The King's Castle," and "Starlight." The bars on the lower levels offer for viewing pleasure satellite television, and a wide variety of go-go dancers, who slither and writhe to the music on a stage. The disco lights make their movements seem even more erotic. They look young, fresh, and very exciting. Drinks are exceedingly cheap and so liquor flows quite freely. The patrons at the bar are all foreign, drunk, and looking to have a good time.

The girls who are not dancing circulate, chatting with customers. They, too, seem to be having a good time. If you scrutinize their "costumes" very carefully, you will see a number discreetly attached to their person, and if you squint and try to focus clearly amidst the disco lights and smoke, you will see maybe a drunk foreigner, with a dancer on his lap, signal to an old woman with a binder note book in her hand. Money is exchanged and the dancer leaves the room, only to return clad in street clothes, whereupon both she and the foreigner will leave the bar hand-in-hand. Or you might see another drunken foreigner climb a few steps to the upper level to the sexual paradise offered by the touts for a cheap price, where he can view sex shows involving a variety of objects and people, or become part of a show himself.

Understanding the Phenomenon: Prostitution as Work

Since the 1970s a new approach has emerged that jettisons the traditional view of prostitution held by mainstream sociologists and radical feminists, the latter considering prostitution as exploitative and the former as a social problem. The "prostitution as work" paradigm, in contrast, is grounded in the liberal feminist perspective, which places prostitution within the context of occupational biology. According to this perspective, women's disadvantaged position in the labor force derives from male-biased norms and values. Because it is this gendered structure that gives women a limited range of occupational avenues, prostitution is thus regarded as an alternative entrepreneurial option for women under the structures of inequality and discrimination in the market place (Heyl, 1977; McLeod, 1982; Phongpaichit, 1982; Rosenblum, 1975), an option that involves risk, innovation, effective decision making, and long-range planning (McClelland, 1961). Liberal feminism further argues that prostitution should be respected like any other "legitimate" occupation (Jenness, 1990), and it is this approach that has been adopted in the present study.

The Bar Girl as Entrepreneur

Using the definition of an entrepreneur as "an individual drawn from a minority group of low socioeconomic status in society, who, in an effort to find alternative avenue of employment consciously decides to undertake an innovative enterprise, assuming risk for the sake of profit," it is easy to see how the bar girl fits the definition. Socioeconomically, she is indeed poor. She has come to Bangkok to find alternative means of employment and has probably worked before in a factory or as a maid. She has decided to take up prostitution in order to survive.

However, in order to examine more thoroughly the idea of the bar girl as an entrepreneur, McClelland's (1961) understanding of the term can be usefully introduced to the analysis. He argued that the first characteristic of an entrepreneur is that of a risk taker. Relatedly, Cohen (1993) indicated that open-ended prostitution is a nonroutine occupation that involves a strong element of risk, both bodily and as regards the precarious opportunity for success and riches. The decision of the bar girl to leave her province and come to Bangkok can also be seen as quite hazardous. In most cases she is preliterate and knows very little of the Capital, in terms of the language, culture, and day-to-day living in a large city.

Once she becomes involved in the trade, Cohen (1993) classified the risks as material, as well as those relating to physical safety and health. For him, material comprises women's exploitation by men, particularly refusal of the latter to remunerate the former.

> From the current research: A case in point was 24 year old Noi, who had an arrangement between the bar owner and a customer. The client wanted Noi for a month, and so told the bar proprietor that he would pay her bar fine for the period (Baht 7,500 or USD 300.) However at the end of the month, the customer refused to pay the bar owner, thereby leaving Noi in debt for the same amount. Noi was not sure what she would do. However one thing was certain. She could not work in the bar until she paid the fine.

The second dimension of risk is the safety factor, which Cohen (1993) and Hail (1980) identified as violence against the bar girl at the hands of the police or dissatisfied customers. The former can take a number of forms ranging from blackmail to rape, whereas the latter includes injuries, some of which result in death (Cohen, 1982).

A third element of risk factor is that relating to physical health, given that venereal disease is widespread among prostitutes (Cohen, 1993; Khin Thitsa, 1980; Suthaporn, 1983). Since the advent of AIDS, there has been an increase in the threat to the health of young women involved in sex work (Anonymous, 1992; Cohen, 1988c; Jensen, 1990). However, whereas a bar girl might understand the ramifications of AIDS and, for the most part, might insist on protected sex, the typical reality of the situation is closer to the following recorded comment: "I tell, that we must (use condoms), but some of them will say I want to feel you, and wait until I turn off the light and take it off."

Risk taking involves bearing responsibility for one's actions. No words are truer spoken than in the case of the bar girl facing material, physical, and health risks. McClelland (1961) argued that a particular feature of being a risk taker is that decision making, although operating under uncertainty, is a function of skill rather than chance (i.e., because the element of chance cannot be totally ignored in life itself and certainly not in any entrepreneurial type of work) (Cohen, 1993; Mosel, 1966). One attempts to reduce the element of chance by making skilled decisions. In this respect, Cohen (1993) saw work in open-ended prostitution as a "skilled game of hazard or 'luck?'" (p. 167). The skill needed to reduce that element of chance is defined as entrepreneurial.

As in any type of work, an aptitude is developed to reduce material, physical, and health risks. Cohen (1993) saw this skill as the challenge faced by women engaged in open-ended prostitution in order to maximize opportunity, while minimizing risks. He argued that such skill consists primarily in the ability to discriminate between dangerous and safe clients. In order to attract the latter and to create an advantageous relationship with them, the bar girl often decides on protracted arrangement. Cohen conceived this skill not so much as "luck," but rather as something that develops over time. The bar girl's work does not totally depend on her physical charms for success. There is also a certain "savvy" or training, which she learns on the job and which has been similarly found in American prostitution (Heyl, 1977) and among male entrepreneurs in other countries (see Chapter 3).

This type of "training" immediately begins on entering the Patpong district, as for example in the transformation of Nuet, a 19 year old.

> Nuet had been in Bangkok for less than a week, when she began her "train-ing." She came to EMPOWER in order to learn English and Arithmetic. She spoke no English, and knew very little Bangkok Thai. She shared a room with a young woman who worked at EMPOWER. Nuet seemed gauche and looked awkward next to the other girls. She wore no make-up. Her hair was not cut into any particular style, and her clothes were quite provincial, when com-pared to the stylish outfits worn by the other girls. As the weeks passed, Nuet's English, as well as her general demeanour and appearance were transformed. She had changed from an unsophisticated country girl from the provinces to a butterfly.

EMPOWER provides the necessary training for bar girls in order to help them in their bar work. In addition to learning the language of customers, the girls are taught how to initiate conversations and are given general information about the countries of potential boyfriends. Girls not only learn how to strike up conversa-tions, but also how to prolong the interaction between a bar girl and a farang. In other words, they are receiving skills training. Such training also extends to appear-ance and dress, and this is achieved via the bar girl's reference group. By looking at fashion magazines, these young women learn to adopt the styles and make-up techniques of the models featured in the glossy pages, and, as Cohen (1993) observed, they come to acquire the style of the tourist-oriented prostitute. Because the ubiquitous jeans and tee-shirt do not really distinguish her from the Thai urban lower-middle class, the bar girl does not stand out in a Bangkok crowd. By day, she fits into any gathering. This ability to merge is also indicative of the skill she has acquired in trying to maintain this type of contrived reality for the farang. Outside of the bar and with the possible exception of her high-heeled shoes, her mode of dress is quite similar to any other young person in Bangkok. For this reason, she does not fit the farang's Western perception of a prostitute (see Chapter 1). As a result, the farang feels quite comfortable in being seen with her outside of the bar setting. He does not feel that she is a prostitute (see Chapter 7).

However, once inside the bar, she becomes transformed by her work clothes of lingerie and skimpy swimsuits. It is in the bar that the natural endowments of the bar girl play a part. The slimmer she is, the more attractive she is to the farang, because, according to the girls, farangs like slim girls, in contrast to their women who are all fat. However, maintaining a trim figure in Bangkok can be quite a challenge, particularly since the advent of fast food chains. It is in the bar that all of the skills, both learned and natural, come into play. The objective then is to find a choice boyfriend, based on the criteria of attractiveness and generosity (Cohen, 1993).

The bar girl has the skill, gained through her own experience and that of her work mates, to identify the ideal boyfriend. This selection is based primarily on considerations of nationality, because, according to them, country of origin is very much linked to generosity. Americans, for example, are thought to be very cheap (*may jeedai*); consequently, an American is selected only in times of dire need. The most generous are considered to be Germans (yellow men) and Saudi Arabians. However, although generous, the latter are also perceived as having a tendency to be violent, thus they too are avoided where possible, unless forced to do so by economic circumstances. The perfect boyfriend is a European in his forties, given that older men generally pay more in an attempt to assuage the guilt of adultery, and to overcompensate for the ego boosting that they receive in being with a young, pretty girl. The higher spending power of older female tourists is also recognized by male entrepreneurs (see Chapter 3).

Another feature of the entrepreneur identified by McClelland (1961) includes energetic and/or novel instrumental performance. This characteristic involves working long hours and undertaking activities in new and better ways. Nothing is more novel than the art to which the bar girl has taken prostitution, in the attempt to veil the eyes of the farang from the true nature of their relationships. She is not only able to successfully hide the "money for sex" character of the relationship, but, in some instances, also to extend the relationship and continue to receive remuneration from it for a considerable period of time (see Chapter 1).

The payment of the bar fine is essentially a pecuniary arrangement between the bar girl and farang, and most of the proceeds go to the bar owner. If both parties decide to prolong the relationship outside of bar hours, the onus then lies with the bar girl to make the relationship profitable for her, while at the same time endeavoring to negate the Western perception of prostitution. The talent that the bar girl uses most in this situation is that culturally ingrained skill of pleasing her sexual partner (Cohen, 1993; de Gallo & Alzate, 1976). The bar girl essentially capitalizes on her renowned charm, naturalness, and innocence. She not only has sex with her customer, but she cooks and cleans for him. She tells him he is sexy, and that she loves him. The client thinks of her as a girlfriend, and she calls him her boyfriend (*feng*). Thus, the relationship is no longer perceived as a Western prostitute-customer liaison, but a normal relationship between two adults (see Chapter 1). The legitimacy of the relationship has been established. The ideal type of scenario has been set in place, the kind of relationship for which Western man has been searching—a compliant partner who is not afraid to please her man inside and outside of the bedroom—something that Western man has lost since the advent of feminism (see Chapter 16). Nothing sums up the attitude so aptly as when a farang writes to his bar girl, ". . . for it is a dream to marry you. . . ."

Remuneration only comes into the picture as compensation for time lost in the bar, as a gift, and as household money for her to carry out her "wifely" duties. Moreover, in order to maintain this utopia, the boyfriend tends to overcompensate her financially, so that she will stay with him. He wishes to save her from a life of hard work, to prevent her from having to work any more in the bar. He is Prince Charming. She is Cinderella.

Because he is so intent on saving her, he takes on all of her financial obligations as well, most of which are familial in nature. "Her mother is sick, the family needs two buffaloes. . . ." This is seen as the "soft sell," rather than hustling the customer to buy a more expensive service, a skill taught to American prostitutes, where the woman learns to extricate money from her customer by appealing to his generosity and his compassion, rather than outright demands for payment, and to attach him to her subserviently while attaching herself to him (Cohen, 1993; Heyl, 1977). She also appeals to his Western perception of himself as a real man who can take care of his woman. Who works longer hours than a bar girl trying to be the Western man's conception of the ideal female?

This skill in telling their personal stories to stress their poverty and financial responsibilities, along with their vulnerability and dependence (Cohen, 1993) appeals to the Western notion of what is manly and princely (see Chapter 1 and Chapter 16), qualities that become united in a fundamental need to prolong the relationship and thereby to extend its profitability. And it is a skill that is taught at EMPOWER by way of letter writing. Nothing can be more novel than the financial responsibilities dreamed up by the bar girl. If one were to go by the bar girl's utterances, most of the families in the North are either sick at home or in hospital awaiting surgery. They are dependent on their daughters, who are languishing in their rooms staring at their boyfriends' photographs, just waiting until they return.

The capacity of the bar girl to manage this tragic portrayal of her life long after the departure of the boyfriend from Bangkok must not be seen only in terms of being innovative. The ability to continue an ideal, contrived relationship from afar is the work of a true entrepreneur, and it is a skill that is largely carried out through the correspondence between the two parties. The bar girl understands the importance of this type of communication so much that she even pays persons to conduct this side of the business in order to reduce such obstacles as time and language. For the bar girl, definite awareness of having done a good job comes with the ability to exist solely off the remittances from her boyfriends. The bar girl who is able to attain this goal is looked upon by her colleagues with respect and envy.

The final feature of the entrepreneurial role is that of long-range planning, along with the allied capacity to organize the activities of others. This too is a role that has been well mastered by the bar girl. She is quite adept at not only prolonging the arrangement between herself and a farang, but also at managing more than one of these protracted relationships at the same time (see Chapter 3). The bar girl schedules the return trips of her boyfriends so that they do not coincide with each other (see Chapter 16), and she herself has become quite the cosmopolitan traveler with a passport showing trips ranging from the United States to Switzerland. It is a quite a skill to be able to play such a large part in the life of a man whom she has known only for a week.

Beguiling the Farang

In analyzing prostitution, most theorists have tended to emphasize its neutral, indiscriminate nature, where a specific act is performed for remuneration (Cohen, 1993). The prostitute is often perceived as a harsh, coarse, painted individual, or in the words of one farang "a two bit whore." The farang typically arrives in Thailand with preconceived notions about the country and its people, which have been passed on from a father, a brother, or a friend. He is told that Bangkok is the "adult Disney land, where you can hook up with a lot of woman easy." These stereotypes become transformed into reality on entering a bar in Patpong. Faced with incredibly youthful and energetic girls gyrating to the latest disco sounds, the farang feels like a child in a candy store facing an array of cheap goodies. For these "sweeties" can be purchased for an amount ranging from Baht 350-500 (US$15-20).

The farang agrees to pay the "bar fine" for one of these girls and takes her back to his hotel. After what many men term as an "incredible time"—because Thai women are so "accommodating, they will do anything"—the girl might additionally clean his shoes, or even do his washing. Thereafter, the farang is "in love" with the Thai girl and the cultural ideal of womanhood that she embodies. Thus begins the point of departure from his preconceptions of prostitution, and the commercial nature of their relationship (see Chapter 1). After all, this is an affair between two consenting adults in paradise. He will give her money, not by way of remuneration for the sexual service rendered, but rather for her to continue her female duties of cooking, cleaning, and laundry, and, most importantly, so that she will not have to work in the bar. Because the bar girl has become his "girlfriend," he will not tolerate her being leered at by his Western counterparts. He therefore assumes a chivalrous attitude in the attempt to save her from them and from her poverty-

stricken situation (Chapter 16; Kruhse-MountBurton, 1995).The farang will speak
of his concerns in his letters to his "girlfriend" about the work that she continues
to do, for instance:

> When I come back to Thailand, I want you out of Patpong—how do you think
> I feel, my girlfriend going with other men?

References are subsequently made to the money he has sent in an effort to sustain
her financially.

The farang has become besotted with the bar girl, for who else will put her hands
around the rolls of fat that surround his waist and tell him, looking deep into his
eyes, that he is sexy and that she loves him? What 18-year-old girl would have sex
with a 60-year-old man, gladly and comfortably? For many farangs, this is what
paradise means, a tropical heaven filled with dusky maidens who are willing to
satisfy every pleasure.As one farang put it, "the bar girl is never seen as a whore.
You can't get a whore in the States for $20, who is good fucking and ego stroking."

The No Face Business

A bar girl who enters prostitution does so in an effort to earn money to support
her family. It is not a moral question for her, but essentially an economic issue.As a
17 year old put it, "I don't like it, but I like money."The burden of her responsibility
is best exemplified by the fact that she remits more than half of her income to her
family, with the average dancer sending about Baht 1500 out of her montly Baht
2,000 earnings. Because Thai culture is such that there is a close association
between love and the gift of money, it therefore follows that the more she gives
her family money the greater is the indication of her love (Chapter 5 and Chapter
16).

The relationship she establishes with a farang typically commences as a mercenary
encounter that subsequently develops along a continuum (Chapter 1; Cohen,
1993).Although feelings can be faked or partially genuine, the reality of the
situation is never lost, as is the case with the farang.The relationship may progress
to what Cohen (1993) calls the "mixed stage," but never to the emotional stage,
where she falls completely in love with the farang. Her familial responsibility is
never forgotten. Open-ended prostitution allows its practitioners to capitalize on
the cultural ideal of womanhood and to sell it to farangs for a profit.Although
Kirsch (1975) speaks of the "loss of face" that is experienced by a Thai woman in
accepting such an inferior status, nevertheless it is through prostitution that she
can afford to fulfill all other cultural roles, while at the same time maintaining a
measure of independence equal to her counterparts in the West. In the words of
one farang, "this is a no face business." Prostitution is simply another form of
entrepreneurship, a way to earn money for survival and/or consumerism, money to
fulfill cultural and social obligations, and given the lack of access to better education and training, possibly the "easiest" way to a better life, at least in a materialistic
perspective.

Chapter 7

Sex Tourism Without Sex Tourists

Armin Günther

In a recently published "survey of German vacationists and sex tourists" Kleiber and Wilke (1995) surveyed 661 German-speaking men in Thailand, the Phillippines, Kenya, Brazil, and the Dominican Republic. To be included, they needed to have had sex with one or more local women. Because of these sexual contacts Kleiber and Wilke judged all these vacationers to be sex tourists. However, their classification did not coincide with the men's self-definition. Asked if they would call themselves sex tourists, the vast majority (78%) answered in the negative (see Chapter 1).

This result points to an interesting question: How is it that tourists having sex with local women in locations of international sex tourism do not perceive themselves as sex tourists? The motivation to defend against a (self-)definition as sex tourist is quite obvious: there is a strong public condemnation of sex tourism and sex tourists. Sex tourism is evaluated as a morally unjustifiable and intolerable degeneration of tourism. The sex tourist is seen as a kind of moral monster. However, the fact that most people would like to avoid being labeled "sex tourist" is not sufficient to explain the marked success of their defensive efforts shown by the high proportion of individuals rejecting this label in the Kleiber and Wilke (1995) study. In addition to this motivation, the involvement in the tourist-oriented sex industry has to be ambiguous enough to allow for alternative self-definitions.

Sexual contacts, mediated in some way by the social institutions of sex tourism, would seem to be clear examples of sex tourism. However, as Cohen (1982) pointed out, intimate relationships between these partners in the context of (Thailand's) sex tourism are "ridden with ambiguities" (p. 411). In a situation of "incomplete commercialization" (p. 420) many settings of tourism-oriented prostitution allow for a personal, noneconomic definition of intimate tourist–prostitute relations. To enforce this noneconomic and self-serving "framing" (Goffman, 1974; Günther, 1992) of the tourist–prostitute relationship, it selectively has to be strengthened, resulting in a reduction of ambiguity. Thus, the denial of one's own role in the sex tourist industry is accomplished through a process of ambiguity reduction, by which the possibility to judge oneself to be a sex tourist is dismissed.

Capitalizing mainly on Cohen's (1982, 1986) field studies of sex tourism in Thailand and Kleiber and Wilke's (1995) survey of German sex tourists, I will analyze the interview of a German tourist to Thailand, which demonstrates this process of ambiguity reduction. In this interview, a self-serving interpretation is constructed, by which the interviewee presents himself in the context of, but not as a part of, the sex tourism industry.

The Case of R.

According to the criteria used by Kleiber and Wilke (1995), the 33-year-old German "R." would be a sex tourist. In an interview, conducted by a student of mine, R. tells about his last vacation, which he spent with a 25-year-old friend in Thailand. The two friends got to know two young Thai women who worked as prostitutes in the tourist center Pattaya. Together, the German men and Thai women spent 5 days until the departure of the tourists. During these days, R. slept with one woman and apparently his friend had sex with the other one. Nevertheless, R. is quite explicit in that he does not consider himself to be a sex tourist. Characteristically, the interview ends with R.'s determined declaration: "Therefore you see, it wasn't sex tourism."

The whole interview may be read as an attempted proof of this finishing sentence, a plea by which R. tries to protest his innocence against the tacit accusation of sex tourism. The interview demonstrates the interpretative work that is needed to transform an originally ambiguous behavior to an unambiguous one. In his attempt to explain to the interviewer what he "really" did in Thailand, R. is confronted with the same question that he had to answer to himself during and after his vacation in Thailand. Having had sex with a local prostitute at an internationally known El Dorado of sex tourism like Pattaya, R. inevitably had to face the question of whether by doing so he had joined the much condemned and despised group of vacationers commonly known as sex tourists. And as he had to convince himself during and after his vacation, R. now has to convince the interviewer that his sexual contacts with a Thai prostitute had nothing in common with "real" sex tourism. At the end, both R. himself and the interviewer seem to be convinced of R'.s innocence: both parties finish with an acquittal. Emphatically, as if swearing an oath, R. declares "with an open heart and conscience" that he "is not a sex tourist and was not a sex tourist." And the interviewer passes his final judgement: "It is without question that R. can't be called sex tourist."

"The Edge of Ambiguity" Revisited

In his interview, R. forwards several arguments against the tacit accusation of sex tourism. The general structure of his argumentation is to demonstrate that he does not feel, think, or behave like a "real" sex tourist. The *argument of lacking intent* says that he is not a sex tourist because he (unlike the "real" sex tourists) did not intend to have sex with a local woman (see Chapter 1; Table 1.3). The *argument of lacking restriction* says that he is not a sex tourist because he (unlike the "real" sex tourists) did not restrict his vacation to having sex with local women. The *argument of lacking promiscuity* says that he is not a sex tourist because he (unlike the "real" sex tourists) did not have sex with several local women (which is only half the truth because R. had sexual contacts with a second woman, only a lack of condoms prevented sexual intercourse). The *argument of lacking amorality* says that he is not a sex tourist because he (unlike the "real" sex tourists) did not allow sexual impulses to control his behavior without restraint by morality.

But the main argument in R.'s defense against the accusation of sex tourism is the *argument of lacking payment*—and this chapter will focus on the analysis of this argument. The argument of lacking payment may be placed in the following syllogism. Sex tourists pay for sexual services (see Chapter 1 and Chapter 6). Neither R. nor his friend paid for sexual services nor have there been any financial claims on part of the Thai women, with whom they had sexual intercourse. Therefore, neither R. nor his friend are sex tourists.

Sex Tourism and Monetary Exchange

R. himself puts it like this:

> It was not sex tourism in that sense, because there has been in no way and at no moment any real financial claim or expectation on part of the girls towards us. It wasn't that way, that the girls would have been financed by us, no, and it has definitely not been in that way, that they were honored by us or that they were payed in one way or another. There were really friendly relations between us four.

That the Thai girls did not claim money for their sexual services from the German tourists obviously is of crucial importance for R.'s interpretation of relationships and his defense against the self-definition as sex tourist. According to him, the absence of payment shows that the two Germans had no commercial relationships with professional sex workers, but rather personal, "friendly relations" with two young Thai women: "We had not prostitutes in this case, we had found two friends."

R. even strengthens the argument of lacking payment: not only did they not pay their Thai friends, but the Thai women once treated the two Germans! In general the tourists—being gentlemen—did pay meals and drinks, but after a visit to a discotheque one of the women insisted on paying the whole check. "These were tourist prices! So it was much more than what a normal worker earns in a month."

At first glance, these are, in fact, strong arguments against the classification of the two German vacationists as sex tourists. In academic research, too, it is often considered a necessary condition for calling someone a sex tourist that he pays for sexual services with money or goods (Beckmann & Elzer, 1995; Pruitt & LaFont, 1995). However, Cohen (1982) drew attention to the fact that sex tourism includes forms to which the concept of prostitution only partially applies. At least, these forms of prostitution differ in a characteristic way from what is common in many First World countries, where the "ideal-type" of prostitution as an exchange of sex for money (or other goods) on an emotionally neutral basis approximates reality much more. In sex tourism, the deviations from this ideal-type of prostitution make the intimate relations between tourists and prostitutes much more ambiguous, allowing alternative, noneconomic interpretations of these relations like "love," "friendship," or "flirtation." Whereas a German, for example, in his native country hardly can avoid an economic interpretation of a typical intercourse with a prostitute, the same individual finds in Thailand and other countries of international sex tourism intimate relationships to native women, to which a noneconomic meaning is much more easily attached (see Chapter 1).

The operational definition of sex tourists as tourists who have sex with natives in exchange for money or goods does not overcome the ambiguity pointed out by Cohen. Even if there is a transfer of money or goods from tourists to natives in connection to intimate relations between both, the meaning of this transfer depends on the interpretation of these relations. In this way the ambiguity of the tourist–native relations also makes the transfer of money or goods hard to classify. It may be seen as payment of a prostitute but also as a gift or aid to a friend. Here we go around in circles. To judge tourist–native relations as prostitution, we have to look for payments, given for sexual services. However, to judge any transfer of money or goods as payments given in exchange for sexual services, we have to look for relations of prostitution.

Just as the transfer of money or goods is not proof of economically based relations (prostitution), so the absence of any such transfer—be it interpreted as payment, gift, aid or whatever—does not prove noneconomic, personal relations. A more lasting or even permanent relationship with Western tourists is an extremely attractive perspective for many women living in the target countries of sex tourism. By way of marriage, they may hope to escape poverty and economic insecurity of their present existence. Therefore, renunciation of (immediate) payment or even the suffering of some loss can be accounted for within an economic frame: as investment costs, which eventually will be more than compensated by future profits (see Chapter 1 and Chapter 3).

The blatant economic imbalance between tourists and natives creates a situation that I would like to call *structural prostitution*: every noneconomic definition of relationship (love, friendship, flirtation, or mutual sexual attraction) tends to be undermined by the native's strong economic interest in a lasting personal commitment of the tourist. The local women (or men), who often do not consider themselves prostitutes (Cohen, 1982; Pruitt & LaFont, 1995), have an economic interest in the transformation of commercial services relations into a personal love affair. This paradoxical structure—an economic interest in the development of noneconomic relations—explains much of the dynamics that characterize long-term relations in the context of sex tourism (Cohen, 1982).

Interestingly, while explicitly defining sex tourists as tourists who exchange sex for money or other goods, Kleiber and Wilke (1995), in their survey of German vacationists and sex tourists, do not use this criterion to separate sex tourists from tourists who have intimate relations with Thai women on a noncommercial, personal basis. It is true that Kleiber and Wilke asked their respondents whether they paid the last native woman with whom they had sexual contacts, but the answers to this question were not used in their classification of the respondents as sex tourists. If payment for sexual services would have been used as a necessary condition for calling someone a sex tourist, the group of (heterosexual male) sex tourists in this survey would have shrunk considerably. After all, 32% of the 661 respondents answered that they did not pay the last native women they had (sexual) contact with (see Table 1.6). There were, however, marked differences between places of vacation. Out of the 112 sex tourists questioned in Brazil, more than half (58%) stated that they did not pay their last native partner and half of the 78 Phillippines vacationists answered likewise. On the other hand, most tourists questioned in Thailand and the Dominican Republic said that they did pay. But even in those locations there was a nonnegligible minority of slightly less than 20% who did not.

Returning to the case of the German tourist R., if we take the missing payment so much emphasized by R. and perhaps additional expenses of the Thai women as investment costs, then just this case demonstrates that such investments could very well be profitable. R. reports that he and his friend "dreamed" about "how those girls possibly can be helped somewhat, though they were not only interested in picking up big amounts." The two Germans hatched plans to settle down in Thailand and to open a business together with the Thai women. At the end of their vacation they even returned to Pattaya once more, staying there for another 5 days in order to check how this project could be carried out; at least this is R.'s explanation for their return. The fact that this project came to nothing does not contradict the economic interest of the Thai women to encourage such opportunities. Within an economic calculation "spontaneous" sexual contacts and renunciation of payment would be rational moves aimed at encouraging a lasting emotional and, as a result, economical commitment by the tourists. But is it actually true that R. and his friend did not pay the two Thai women? To answer this question, let us take a closer look at the setting in which the relations between the German tourists and the Thai women occurred.

Sex Tourism Settings in Thailand: Massage Parlors and Bars

Sex tourism in Thailand takes place in different settings. Two of them are massage parlors and bars. Concerning their degree of ambiguity, these settings are quite different. Whereas massage parlors allow hardly any doubt that the focus is on exchange of sexual services for money, relations between tourists and natives established in bars, nightclubs, or coffee shops can easily be framed in different ways. Therefore, it should not be a surprise that R.—committed to moral standards that would be incompatible with a self-definition as sex tourist—contacted a Thai prostitute not in a massage parlor, but in a bar.

R. and his friend visited massage parlors in Bangkok, where a local guide showed them the city:

> And of course among other things he drove us to a house, where girls are sitting behind a pane. It was—it was bad, it was actually bad. Inside are five, six Thai boys. And then you have two categories of shop-windows. In the one window there are, well, the normal prostitutes, you know. And in the other window you really just have girls from thirteen years down. You stand inside there and look at it and are completely dumbfounded. And then the boys try to chat or in some way lure you into giving a number, by which the women are labeled. I said to my buddy: "Let's get out of here! Quickly!," as that is not our style, and particularly not mine. Sex tourism—you have to see it, you have to see it. You can't get it out of your head and you will not forget it.

This setting of sex tourism could not be more unambiguous, at least as it is described by R. In his report he makes it quite clear that sexual services are offered as commercial goods: the "girls" are presented in shop windows, labeled by numbers like articles of merchandise and the Thai managers peddle their wares like obtrusive clerks. Though these establishments are officially massage parlors, because prostitution is forbidden in Thailand, R. does not take up this superficial ambiguity at all, but qualifies the women unequivocally and somewhat disparaging as prostitutes. In R.'s eyes, the massage parlor setting obviously is the embodiment of sex tourism, and from sex tourism in this sense he (literally) dissociates himself. With a mixture of moral and aesthetic horror, the friends take flight.

Unlike the massage parlor setting, the bar setting allows for different interpretations of intimate tourist–native relations outside the sex tourism frame. It is in this setting that R. and his friend "S." got to know the Thai women with whom they had sexual intercourse later on.

> We were in this bar and there was a pretty nice girl my friend liked. And then it came to an end and I said to my friend: "Okay, let's clear off, let's go!" And then we left, and S. says to me: "Shit! You are to blame I can't get any action." And I said: "Oh fuck you! But wait one moment," I said, "we'll have that fixed." I went in again and said to the girl. "Hey, if you'd like, we could go for a drink." You need not ask twice; for sure they cling on tourists, that's quite normal. And they went along.

This scene could have happened in the native country of the two friends, at a German bar or discotheque. Two men who chat with two women—nothing could be more ordinary. The invitation to go out for a drink seems to be nothing but a conventional first move in relations between the sexes. The only strange point is the eagerness of the two Thai women to join the tourists. The impression is given that they were waiting for such an offer. And of course, this impression creates a problem for R., as it makes the described scene more ambiguous than he would like. Considering that this scene actually does not happen in a German discotheque, but in a bar at Pattaya, the center of international sex tourism, and considering further that the two women actually are not native guests at the bar, but (as R. tells a little later) employees. The eagerness of the women to join the tourists and their willingness to have sex with them shortly after that can easily be interpreted within the frame of sex tourism: two German tourists hire two local prostitutes. R. immediately reacts to this ambiguity by qualifying the readiness of the women to cling on tourists as "quite normal." But of course this normality could be the normality of sex tourism, so R.'s normalization of the women's behavior actually does not reduce ambiguity. That is why R. adds a much stronger argument. Immediately after the just-cited passage, R. continues with the argument that this was not sex tourism because the Thai women did not claim any money from them (i.e., the argument of lacking payment).

But at a closer look it is seen that the companionship was not at all totally free. In Thailand's bars and nightclubs, a system of release is practiced, allowing tourists to hire employees for 1 night or 1 day on payment of a relatively small fee, judged by Western price standards. In addition to paying this bar fee or "bar fine" to the bar manager, the women has usually to be paid for her services directly—if she is paid at all! So the two German tourists had at least to pay the bar fee for the women. However, this form of payment is interpreted by R. in a very specific way:

> We saw them during the whole 5 days. To see them during the day too, you have to go to the bar and pay ten marks [US$6] as a release fee. If you pay the release fee to the owner of the bar, you can release the girl for the whole day. And if you want her for another day, than you have to bring another ten marks to release her once more. That's the way it works. And they do not have to work then, no, they are released. They are released by the ten marks. They have no obligations then. There's no pressure put on them by a pimp or something like that. They are not pressed to deliver something, as they would have.

R. does not interpret the money they had to pay as rent by which he bought the companionship and sexual services of the woman, but as a payment by which he temporary liberated the women from their obligations as prostitutes. In R.'s interpretation, the fact that he and his friend, shortly after contacting the two Thai women at the bar and presumably paying the release fee to the bar owner, slept with them is split apart from the financial transaction. Framing the payment as a means to liberate the "girls" from their work obligation and not as payment for future social, emotional, and sexual services allows R. to believe that he is not a "john" or a sex tourist. In this way, he is able to interpret the sexual intercourse with the "released" woman as a spontaneous, voluntary act, perhaps an act of gratitude, not as a economic obligation. Surely, R.'s interpretation of the payment would have been totally different if the Thai women would have not been "released" by two smart and fashionable young men, but by one of these European tourists, who in R.'s description, appear to be the embodiment of sex tourists because they "already go on crutches and are much older than sixty years, [but] who walk hand by hand or arm in arm with girls of twelve or thirteen and perhaps even younger or who even smooch with them." In these cases R. surely would interpret the "release" fee payed by the tourists not as a means to free the girls from their obligations but on the contrary as a rent, payed for social, emotional, and sexual services. It becomes quite obvious at this point that the criterion *payment for sexual services* depends to a great extent on the framing of the relationship.

Temporal Dimension

R. and his friend use a form of "open-ended-prostitution" (Cohen, 1993) that allows tourists and prostitutes to interpret their relations in noneconomic, personal frames, as "friendship," "flirtation," or even "love" (Walker & Ehrlich, 1992). These settings of sex tourism provide tourists and natives, in spite of their totally different socioeconomic differences and psychological needs, with an opportunity to dream about a joined and better future, or at least with an opportunity to play (Cohen, 1985b) for a few days "being in love," with all parts of it: flirtation, holding hands, having pleasure together, tenderness, caressing, and—of course—sex. In the Kleiber and Wilke (1995) study, about half stated that they fell in love with a local woman: 30% a little bit, 10% strongly, and 9% percent very strongly. Almost 20% of the men said that they certainly would meet again the same local woman on their next vacation and another 35% considered such a reunion to be possible or probable (see Table 1.7). Almost 30% of the men even stated that they would want to marry one of these women. Even the sexual practices seem to be more similar to those performed in personal relations than in typical contacts to prostitutes in Germany (see Table 1.8). Only 40% of the tourists supposed that their native partners regarded them as a "john," compared to a total of almost 60% who supposed themselves to be regarded as a "friend" (21%), as a "husband for a vacation" (10%), or as a "temporary partner" (27%).

The temporal extension of the tourist–native relations surely is of crucial importance for the interpretation of these relations outside the prostitution frame. R. and his friend spent 5 days at the beginning and 5 days at the end of their vacation with the two Thai women. Likewise, in all but one of the countries covered by the previously mentioned survey, more then 50% of the German tourists said that they spent several days with a native woman (see Table 1.6). Only a small minority of these tourists would be able to afford an escort service of comparable extension in their native countries, granting the same social, emotional, and sexual benefits. A survey of 598 clients of female prostitutes in Germany, conducted by Kleiber and Velten (1994) in 1990–91, showed, that in about 80% of the cases the contact to a prostitute did not last more than 1 hour (see Table 1.6). Consequently, these contacts are much more confined to sexual activities. In this way the commercial character of the sexual services becomes relatively unambigous, even if there may be ways to temporarily ignore the economic basis of the relations. The payment, which is much higher than the comparable payment in sex tourism (1994, p. 83), is made in close connection with the sexual activities and as a rule the payment is made to the prostitute herself. In Thailand, it is much less clear who is paid for what, when a tourist "releases" an employee of a bar for a day or night, based on a relatively small fee given to the manager of the bar (see Chapter 1 and Chapter 16).

As the contact of tourists with prostitutes often lasts several days, the number of sex partners remains relatively small (see Table 1.1). This presumably supports the development of personal relations between tourists and native women. The stereotype of the highly promiscuous sex tourist, who uses one woman after another, does not apply to the behavior of the "normal" sex tourist (see Chapter 1). In the most frequent case, representing 37% of all cases, a male heterosexual sex tourist had sexual contacts with only one woman after 3 weeks in the place of vacation. When all cases are combined, the median and mean of number of sex partners were 2 and 3.8, respectively (see Table 1.1). Thus, R.'s *argument of lacking promiscuity*, saying that he is not a sex tourist because he (unlike the "real" sex tourists) did not have sex with several local women, does not work: the "typical" sex tourist tends toward "monogamy."

Conclusions

Is R. a sex tourist? In accordance with Pruitt and LaFont (1995), one probably would have to answer in the negative. In their case study of foreign women who engaged local men in Jamaica in intimate relationships, Pruitt and LaFort (1995) made a distinction between "sex tourism" and "romance tourism." In sex tourism, the actors interpret their relations in an economic frame, as exchange of sex for money (i.e., prostitution), whereas in romance tourism "neither actor considers their interaction to be prostitution, even while others may label it so" (p. 423). These liaisons are constructed through a discourse of romance and long-term relationship, an emotional involvement usually not present in sex tourism. In these terms, R. would seem to be more of the "romance tourist" than of the "sex tourist" type (see Chapter 1).

To understand sex tourism, it is certainly important to pay attention to the meaning tourists and natives attach to their intimate relations. One may even try to classify these relations by the dominant interpretation forwarded by the actors (prostitution versus romance or love affair), though this may be impossible because the interpretations of the actors fall apart or oscillate between the prostitution and the romance frame (Cohen, 1982). However, to seperate sex tourism and romance tourism as two distinctive forms of tourism is highly questionable. When seperated, the ambiguities disappear; actors inevitably have to face who is trying to establish personal relations in the context of sex tourism. In the context of a tourist-oriented sex industry, any noneconomic, personal definition of relationships has to be defended and reestablished by the actors over and over again. Thus, the line between sex tourism (prostitution) and romance tourism (love affair) has to be drawn and redrawn by tourists and natives themselves. Therefore, to study this process of ambuigity reduction by which sex tourism and romance tourism are socially constructed and by which the possibility to judge oneself to be a sex tourist is dismissed, we must not start with this distinction by defining either romance tourism or sex tourism as our objects of research.

Any psychological definitions of sex tourism and sex tourist that refer in some way to the special meaning attached to tourist–native relations by the respective actors has to cope with the ambiguity of these relations. The degree of ambiguity in the tourist-oriented sex industry is an amazing fact. There seems to be hardly anything an average consumer of sex touristic services could do that would commit him to a self-definition as sex tourist. Rather, there are multiple possibilities to interpret one's behavior in ways that distinguish it from behavior of a "real" sex tourist. The defense against self-definition as sex tourist is accomplished by the construction of this difference, by drawing a line between oneself and the "real" sex tourists.

Instead of psychological definitions of sex tourism and sex tourist, I would like to forward a sociological definition of sex tourism and sex tourist that has as its starting point sex tourism as a social institution (Berger & Luckmann, 1966) and sex tourists as tourists who reproduce this institution by using it, regardless of the interpretation of this usage by the individual actor. Varying the title of this chapter, one could say there are "no sex tourists without sex tourism." A tourist who uses a local prostitute is not a sex tourist, unless there is sex tourism as institutionalized tourist-oriented prostitution at the place of his vacation. Thus, sex tourism as a social fact can be defined as the institution of tourist-oriented prostitution using prostitution in the broader sense of exchange of money for intimate relations. The use of an institution is independent of the interpretation of the single actor who uses it but not independent of the interpretations of all actors; the social institution is superior to the individual. Paying for the release of a local prostitute at an internationally known location of sex tourism and having sex with her, R. without doubt uses and strengthens sex tourism as a social institution. Thus, in a sociological sense, R. is a sex tourist.

In this chapter I have reconstructed, questioned, and criticized the way a German tourist frames in an interview his participation in Thailand's sex tourism. By this, it was neither intended to upgrade sex tourists by lifting them into romance tourists, nor to degrade romance tourists by exposing them as sex tourists. However, to understand sex tourism it is certainly important to pay attention to the meaning tourists and prostitutes attach to their intimate relations, and to handle sex tourism politically, one surely has to question and perhaps criticize these interpretations. By idealizing sex tourists as romanticists who travel in pursuit of emotional relationships, one may easily overlook the fact that these romanticists use and reproduce sex tourism as a social institution. Likewise, by demonizing sex tourists as moral monsters who ruthlessly try to satisfy their sexual desires, one may unwittingly encourage tourists who do not see themselves in that way to overlook their real involvement in the tourist-oriented sex industry.

Acknowledgements

I would like to thank R. For his willingness to tell about his experiences, Ralf Koczorowski for conducting the interview, and Russ Dewey for his invaluable help in editing and discussing this chapter. Of course, I am entirely responsible for the views expressed here.

Chapter 8

Massage Parlors: Clandestine Prostitution

Thomas J. Iverson and John C. Dierking

This chapter describes sexual activities that often fall into a gray area in law enforcement: prostitution in massage parlors. The term "quasi-legal" is often used to describe these establishments, because massages are legal, but the sexual activities that take place in the parlors are often illegal. However, as Ryan et al. (Chapter 10) note, in some countries massage parlors are the official and accepted front for prostitution. The situation on the (US) Territory of Guam is used to illustrate some of the problems and potential solutions associated with this clandestine prostitution. A brief history illustrates the common pattern of rapid growth during times of military expansion and a shift to tourist clientele during subsequent military downsizing. We close with some recent events that have brought this form of prostitution into the public eye on Guam and pose some potential policy mechanisms to ameliorate its negative impacts.

Locational Context

Guam is an island territory of the United States, located in the Western Pacific about 13° north of the equator. Discovered by the Spanish explorer Magellan, Guam has been colonized by Spain, Germany, Japan, and the United States. The economy in the post-WWII period was sluggish, with no major commercial success in spite of attempts to develop farming, fishing, and light manufacturing. A tourism industry was jump-started with economic incentives in the form of tax breaks to the hotel industry. With the exception of US military expenditures, tourism is Guam's economy. Guam is relatively close to the expanding Asian economies. Flight times are less than 4 hours from countries such as Japan, Korea, Taiwan, Hong Kong, and the Philippines. In 1995, there were 243 flights per week to Guam, representing 53,718 seats, for a total of about 2.8 million seats per year. In that year visitor arrivals totaled 1,361,830. Japanese visitors are most prominent, accounting for over 75% of all arrivals in a typical year.

According to a noted Guam historian, prostitution was brought to Guam by the Spanish explorers and was institutionalized by the Americans as early as 1915, when there were 16 local prostitutes servicing military personnel. These prostitutes came to be known as Monday Ladies because the U.S. Navy provided medical examinations every Monday to stem the spread of venereal diseases (George, 1996). Shortly after 1945, taxidancers from the Territory of Hawaii arrived on Guam and caused a stir in the island's conservative community because their activities extended well beyond the dance floor. Local law enforcement officials took no action in spite of loud protests by women's organizations. Finally, because of the persistent demands of such organizations, and at the urging of the Bishop of Agaña, the U.S. Navy exercised its security powers and sent the women home.

In the 1950s, a large labor camp was created on U.S. Navy property in Agat village to house hundreds of contract employees from the Philippines who were working for contractors on military projects. Along with commercial seamen, this created the demand for a continued sex industry on Guam. Typically, the sex industry expands and contracts in relation to the scale of military presence (see Chapter 1). Leheny (1995) cited evidence that, in order to maintain its financial standing, the Thai sex market turned to tourists to replace the military personnel withdrawing from the war in Vietnam. Similarly, on Guam (which hosted US bombers during the Vietnam War) prostitution was more widespread during wartime. In 1969, the United States Attorney stepped in to prosecute a prostitution ring, using a federal statute that makes it a felony to transport women over state lines for the purposes of prostitution (Dierking, 1989). In this case, two defendants were found guilty. The prostitutes were not charged, after giving evidence against their employers.

Although the military may have been the genesis of institutionalized prostitution, recent rapid growth in the visitor industry coupled with moderate military downsizing has led to a much greater reliance on tourists as massage parlor customers. The structure of the industry and the pricing of services most likely adjusted as well. Japanese tourists are known for their generous spending habits, and those who come to Guam are often novice travelers and not very worldly in their knowledge of the pricing of these services. The second largest visitor segment, Korean tourists, are also known for relatively high spending while traveling.

The economic impact of this business has not been measured on Guam. There are 14 licensed massage parlors employing approximately 181 women (Cruz, personal communication, 1996). No figures are available regarding the range of services or the ratio of customers to masseuses. One estimate of the average tourist expense, though, is $250 each (Rodriguez, personal communication, 1996). Incidentally, this business is very lucrative for taxi drivers, who might earn a commission of $25 each on a group of four customers delivered to the establishment, in addition to the regular fare (see Chapter 16).

The Legal Framework

Guam, as a Territory of the US, generally mirrors the legal code of the United States. There, relevant regulations and laws are often geared towards sexually oriented businesses. As defined by the United States Court of Appeals, these include: adult arcades, adult bookstores, adult video stores, adult cabarets, adult motels, adult motion picture theaters, escort agencies, nude model studios, and sexual encounter centers (City of Dallas, State of Texas, USA, City Ordinances, Chapter 41A-3).

Most of these are in evidence to some degree on Guam, but the massage parlors are in a rather unique classification because there are legitimate masseuses who are also in business. One humorous anecdote involved a local man who entered a massage parlor and could not find anyone to actually massage his sore back. Guam does not currently license legitimate masseuses. Guam does not regularly report health statistics disaggregated to the level of the massage parlor industry. A study conducted by one of the authors in 1989 found that, in 1987, there were 26 cases of gonorrhea and 18 cases of other sexually transmitted diseases reported to the health department as a result of massage parlor inspections (Dierking, 1989, p. 20).

In 1994, Guam's law was finally changed to make possible arrests and convictions for the crime of prostitution. Prior to that time the Guam police complained that laws against prostitution were so poor that convictions were impossible to obtain, because the actual act of prostitution had to be done in a public place, a highly unlikely event. Guam's Compiler of Laws observed in his 1994 comment on the 1978 Guam Penal Code that, because of defects in that Code which did not permit the prosecution of prostitution per se, very little has been done in that area.

Through the efforts of three well-known female Guam Senators and at the urging of the Archbishop of Agaña, there was enacted in 1994 a comprehensive revision of the antiprostitution laws that closely follows the Model Penal Code (Guam Public Law, 1994). These revisions toughened the definitions, penalties, and the scope of prostitution laws, regarding where prostitution and the solicitation for it will be prohibited according to the Compiler of Laws (Guam Code Annotated: 2-3).

The Police Department Vice Squad was disbanded several years ago and cognizance assumed by the Special Operations Division. The Police admit that prostitution is very low on their list of priorities, and that because of their shortage of staff they are not able to carry out regular enforcement efforts. Prosecution statistics regarding arrests for prostitution-related crime reveal this effort: 1994 two cases, 1995 no cases, and 1996 two cases (Sergeant Toves, personal communication, 1996). Since 1994, in spite of the improvement of the antiprostitution law, little was done to enforce it until February, 1996 when three indictments were returned by the Grand Jury charging the operators of three massage parlor with prostitution activities. The cases were still awaiting trial in August, 1996.

Regulation Through Health Code Enforcement

Under rules established on Guam in 1984, the Department of Public Health & Social Services (DPHSS) is responsible for regulating the sanitary operation of massage parlors. Massage is defined as

> . . . any method of treatment or therapy of the superficial soft parts of the body by rubbing, stroking, tapping, pressing, shaking, or kneading with the

hands, feet, or elbow, and whether or not aided by any mechanical or electrical apparatus, appliances, or supplementary aids such as rubbing alcohol, liniments, antiseptic oils, powders, creams, lotions, ointments, or other similar preparations commonly used in this practice. (DPHSS, 1984, p. 1)

Operators must provide to DPHSS a list of employees, including name, the date of birth, the sex and addresses of said employees, and shall indicate any and all names ever used by the employees so listed. Also required, every 3 months, is a physical examination, including a skin test for tuberculosis, RPR or VDRL blood tests, and a culture test for gonorrhea (DPHSS, 1984).

The Director of DPHSS became suspicious when it appeared that the number of approved health certificates for masseuses was dropping, while there was no apparent reason or evidence of a decline in their business. An internal review lead to the discovery of apparent corruption and bribery within the department (Rodriguez, personal communication, 1996). Bribes were deemed necessary to prevent inspectors from reporting the clandestine prostitution taking place in the parlors. These actions were reported in the local news media. The Director reported to the *Pacific Daily News* that inspectors not only found evidence of prostitution, but caught persons actually engaged in acts of prostitution during the process of the health inspection. Additionally, drug paraphernalia was also found in one of the parlors. Law enforcement authorities were brought in. In an inquiry lasting more than 3 months, investigators uncovered allegations that health officers received bribes and free sexual favors in return for the issuance of health certificates without inspection (see Chapter 16).

Criminal charges brought against the eight health inspectors and one office clerk include conspiracy, official misconduct, unlawful influence, receiving bribes, and tampering with public records. Although this crackdown may appear to be just another skirmish in the war against public corruption, it also may be viewed as a potential policy weapon that might be used by communities to lessen the effects of clandestine prostitution. Admittedly, a middle-ground position regarding the ethics of this sort of sex business, the use of health regulation enforcement might provide a reasonable complement to sometimes ineffective local police forces.

Ethical Considerations

The authors share the opinion that massage parlor prostitution is an ethical concern. This concern is for the employees of the parlors, the clients of the parlors, and the public who are uncomfortable with this fairly open form of prostitution. Others within the community of Guam with a more libertarian view suggest that prostitution will always be around and it is simply a commercial transaction between consenting adults. Another view expressed by officials in both law enforcement and health regulation seeks to manage and control this form of prostitution as a compromise position. This morally neutral position accepts the inevitability of the sex trade and proposes tighter regulation to lower the incidence of infectious disease. Others argue that desperate men, whether sailors or tourists, will look for sex and the massage parlors keep them away from their daughters.

For some, the approach towards this business depends on the demographic composition of the clientele. If the customers are primarily tourists and this behavior is deemed a part of their (acceptable) social mores, then a laissez-faire approach may be presented. A local health official espoused this view when he was quoted as saying, in regard to Asian customers when a visiting businessperson is here and you are responsible for entertainment, part of the offer is women (George, 1996). Haralambopoulos and Pizam (1996), in reviewing several studies connecting tourism and prostitution, note that, in Korea, women are part of package tours. In areas where there is strong divergence between the social mores of tourists and those of the host community, this could lead to friction. Clearly, the ethical position that one establishes has a direct bearing on the policy recommendations that would follow. Without considering the mechanism used to establish a community ethical stance (e.g., referenda, polls, etc.), we turn to a brief discussion of potential policies that might be used to deal with clandestine prostitution.

Policy Recommendations

Public policy towards massage parlor prostitution, in democratic societies, would reflect the prevailing attitudes of the citizenry. One role for educational institutions is to openly discuss these issues so that the citizenry is fully informed. Beyond this, there are specific recommendations that follow from the ethical position established through consensus means. For those who consider massage parlors in opposition to community values, strengthening of the legal code is a viable option. This also implies that additional funds must be provided to investigate and prosecute the resulting crimes. A variety of policy tools are available to more closely regulate massage parlors. Health regulation enforcement may lower the incidence of sexually transmitted disease. The efficiency of this regulation might be enhanced through the use of land use planning to designate commercial zones for sexually oriented businesses.

Specific efforts may be directed toward the related problems of bribery and corruption of health inspectors and police officers. As many of the pay-offs are taken out in trade and where most of the prostitutes are female, the use of female inspectors could lessen the amount of graft. The licensing of legitimate masseuses could lessen the harassment and humiliating propositions that they incur. One interesting ordinance regulating massage parlors was enacted in San Rafael, CA. In addition to requiring a license and certified massage technicians, establishments must be closed between the hours of 10:30 pm and 7:00 am (Dierking, 1989).

A key unanswered question following stricter enforcement would be the extent to which the business would simply move to different venues. Some argue that the level of prostitution on Guam would remain the same but the form of delivery would adapt to less-visible organizations. There is some evidence that the network to facilitate this change, involving taxi drivers and hotel desk clerks, is already in place (Rodriguez, personal communications, 1996).

Conclusion

Massage parlor prostitution sometimes falls into a gray area of enforcement and community concern. Perhaps this would not be so if the establishments carried signs reading "Prostitution Available Here." Viewed by many as a consensual business with no third party consequences, it is often not a high priority for law enforcement. Yet, there are what economists term external diseconomies to this business. The spreading of venereal diseases, the intermingling of the mores of the tourist and host cultures, and the potential for the development of organized crime and increased drug use are all important concerns. Public health regulation provides an alternative to traditional law enforcement methods to more effectively control clandestine prostitution. This method is perhaps a compromise notion that will lessen the negative effects of the business while we learn more of the socioeconomic impacts of massage parlor prostitution.

Chapter 9

The Legal and Political Dimensions of Sex Tourism: The Case of Australia's Child Sex Tourism Legislation

C. Michael Hall

In October, 1996, Raymond John Jones appeared in the Melbourne Magistrates Court charged under child sex tourism laws with encouraging others to have sex with a child outside Australia (ECPAT Australia, 1996a). Jones was not being charged with engaging in sex while a tourist, but, in what was believed to be a world first, a promoter of sex tourism was facing the courts. Whether successfully convicted or not, Jones' case highlights the potential reach of the newly developed laws regarding sex tourism. Furthermore, the media attention devoted to this and other sex tourism and child sex cases in Australia, Germany, and the Philippines at the same time raises numerous issues about legal control of sex tourism, international relations, and the political dimensions of sexuality.

This chapter discusses the politics and legal dimensions of sex tourism with specific reference to the Australian situation. It is divided into three sections. First, a brief discussion of the politics of sex tourism out of which legal frameworks for control of sex tourism are derived. Second, it provides a case study of the development of the Australian sex tourism laws. Finally, it provides some conclusions about the legal and political dimensions of sex tourism and notes the way in which efforts to control sex tourism, and child sex tourism in particular, are related to the wider politics of gender and sexuality.

The Politics of Sex Tourism

The politics of tourism is poorly understood, the politics of sex tourism even less so. It is surprising that for what is often regarded as the world's largest economic sector, so little research on politics and policy of tourism has been conducted

(Hall, 1994a; Hall & Jenkins, 1995). Nevertheless, tourism is a highly political activity. As Peck and Lepie (1989) noted, "the nature of tourism in any given community is the product of complex, interrelated economic and political factors, as well as particular geographic and recreational features that attract 'outsiders'" (p. 216). Decisions affecting tourism policy, the nature of government involvement in tourism, the institutional arrangements surrounding tourism activities, and the involvement of business and lobby groups in influencing policy emerge from a political process. This process involves the values of actors (individuals, interest groups, and public and private organizations) in a struggle for power.

The study of the politics of tourism is therefore the study of power. *Politics is about power, who gets what, where, how, and why* (Lasswell, 1936). Power may be conceptualized as "all forms of successful control by A over B—that is, of A securing B's compliance" (Lukes, 1974, p. 17). The use of the concept of power is inextricably linked to a given set of value assumptions that predetermine the range of its empirical application. For instance, a pluralist conception of the tourism policy-making process, such as that which underlies the notion of community-based tourism planning (P. E. Murphy, 1985), focuses on different aspects of the decision-making process than a structuralist conception of politics (S. Britton, 1991), with each operating within a particular value and political perspective (Hall & Jenkins, 1995). However, given the policy analyst's "need to understand the dominant groups and ideologies operating within a political and administrative system" (Jenkins, 1978, p. 40), it seems reasonable to assume that the use of a wide conception of power—capable of identifying decisions, nondecisions, and community political structure—will provide the most benefit in the analysis of the political dimensions of tourism.

The study of the politics of sex tourism can therefore be analyzed at three different but related levels. At a macro-level, the policy environment, issues of power, values, and institutional arrangements arise. At a meso-level, the policy arena, institutions, interested groups, institutional leadership, and the activities of significant individuals are the subjects for investigation. Finally, at the micro-level—the level of specific policy issues—concerns arise over policy demands, decisions, outputs, and outcomes (Hall & Jenkins, 1995). This following case study will describe the passage of Australia's child sex tourism legislation and highlight the manner in which the issues surrounding sex tourism and the development of the Australian child sex tourism legislation, in particular, reflects the role of certain interests and values.

The Australian *Crimes (Child Sex Tourism) Amendment Act 1994*

Although the introduction by the Attorney-General on March 22, 1994 of the notice to present a bill to the Australian Commonwealth (federal) parliament to deal with child sex tourism represented a milestone in Australian legal and political history with respect to control of sex tourism, it was not the first time that sex tourism issues had been raised at the federal level. During the 1980s, Australian

federal police and a number of parliamentary committees rais(
with the involvement of Australian criminal elements in Filipi
with mail-order brides in Australia (Hall, 1992). However, while sex
ceived a moderate amount of media attention, it was only with the onset or w.
coverage of the impact of AIDS on Australia and Southeast Asia and increased
activities by lobby groups, such as ECPAT (End Child Prostitution in Asian Tourism),
in the late 1980s, that concerted action began to be taken. On December 17, 1990,
following pressure from ECPAT and members of the Australian Council for Overseas Aid (ACFOA) such as World Vision and UNICEF, Australia ratified the United
Nations *Convention on the Rights of the Child* with the Convention coming into
force on January 16, 1991 (House of Representatives Standing Committee on Legal
and Constitutional Affairs [HRSCLCA], 1994). Under Article 34 of the Convention,

> States Parties undertake to protect the child from all forms of sexual exploita-
> tion and sexual abuse. For these purposes, States Parties shall in particular
> take all appropriate national bilateral and multilateral measures to prevent:
>
> (a) The inducement or coercion of a child to engage in any unlawful sexual
> activity;
> (b) The exploitative use of children in prostitution or other unlawful sexual
> practices;
> (c) The exploitative use of children in pornographic performances and
> materials.
>
> The obligations set in place by the Convention and the ongoing campaign by
> ECPAT and ACFOA for the Australian government to be active in the control
> of child prostitution in Asia were lent support by the activities of the Austra-
> lian Human Rights Commissioner and the visit of Vitat Muntabhorn, the
> Special Rapporteur of the United Nations Commission of the Program for the
> Prevention of the Sale of Children, Child Prostitution and Child Pornography
> in 1992. Professor Muntabhorn proposed that the Australian government
> considered the possibility of extending national jurisdiction to cover the
> involvement of Australians overseas in 'transnational sexual exploitation.'
> (Muntarbhorn, 1993, para. 106)

In response, Australian Federal and State Attorneys-General agreed in June 1993 to
frame new laws to enable prosecution of Australians who travel abroad to have sex
with children and of Australians who encourage or arrange for that to happen.
According to the Attorney-General of New South Wales, "If they [Australian tour-
ists] are convicted on these sex tours they could lose their passports and not be
allowed to travel. . . ." All of the states will be moving to introduce mutually
consistent legislation to make sure this field is completely covered and appropriate
criminal sanctions will be introduced ("Sex Tourists Targeted," 1993). The Commonwealth Minister for Justice foreshadowed the introduction of criminal laws to
facilitate the prosecution of extra-territorial offenses against children when, on
November 4, 1993, he announced that the Commonwealth proposed to amend the
Crimes Act 1914 to make it illegal for Australians to engage in sexual activities with
children overseas.

ιe first reading of the *Crimes (Child Sex Tourism) Amendment Bill 1994* took place on March 23, 1994. Following a series of votes and proceedings in the House of Representatives and the Senate, the bill was eventually passed by the Senate on June 30, 1994.

The *Crimes (Child Sex Tourism) Amendment Act 1994* came into effect on July 5, 1994. It inserted a new Part IIIA into the *Crimes Act 1914* to deal with the activities of:

- Australians who travel overseas for the sexual exploitation of child prostitutes;
- those responsible for organizing overseas tours for the purpose of engaging in sexual relations or activities with minors; and
- those who otherwise profit from child sexual exploitation.

The Act makes such activities the subject of criminal offenses punishable in Australia and sets out

- the nature of offenses committed under the new Part IIIA;
- defenses to these offenses;
- the provision of evidence by video link in proceedings under this Part; and
- the provision of rules relating to the conduct of trials under this Part.

The Act makes special arrangements for the protection of children giving evidence. If the attendance of the child witness at the court to give the evidence would cause the child psychological harm or unreasonable distress or subject the child to intimidation or distress, the court can direct that the child's evidence be given by video link. The court may also order payment of expenses incurred in connection with giving evidence in this manner. However, although the Act received general bipartisan support, sections of the Act were not without controversy.

According to the Minister for Justice (Kerr, 1994):

> The principal aim of this legislation is to provide a real, and enforceable deterrent to the sexual abuse of children outside Australia by Australian citizens and residents. . . . The Bill also focuses on the activities of those who promote, organize and profit from child sex tourism. Provided they operate from Australia, or have a relevant link with Australia, they, too, will be able to be prosecuted for their contribution to the abuse of foreign children. . . .
>
> The Bill aims to achieve these ends by creating sexual offences, relating to conduct outside Australia, which will be punishable in Australia, and offences of encouraging or benefiting from child sex tourism, which may be committed in or out of Australia, and will be punishable in Australia provided there is a relevant link with this country. All these offences will have substantial penalties, ranging from 10 to 17 years imprisonment, or correspondingly high pecuniary penalties if a company is involved. (pp. 1, 2)

In recognition of potential criticisms of the Bill, the Minister noted that some people may wonder why Australia would enact extra-territorial laws and why "the foreign country should not protect its own children" (Kerr, 1994, p. 1). He then went on to argue that the Bill was a substantial contribution to the development of international institutional arrangements surrounding children's rights which "should send a clear message to child sex abusers and those who profit from their activities" (Kerr, 1994, p. 2). However, the Minister also emphasized that the legislation must be more than window-dressing and must be enforceable. As the Federal Attorney-General observed, "proof is the difficulty" ("Sex Tourists Targeted," 1993).

The issue of proof was a clear concern in the comments of parliamentarians on the bill. The legislative difficulties in establishing age and consent of minors in countries outside of Australia and presentation of evidence in Australian courts were the most common substantive points raised in debate on the Bill. Indeed, a number of members stated that, while they doubted the effectiveness of the Bill, they would support it because of the ethical and moral issues involved. The comments of one member are typical of this stance:

> Whilst I support this legislation, I am not especially confident that it will be effective on a day-to-day basis. We should not be discouraged by this. We need the law as a backstop. Australians should always know that this law exists and that it will be used. Whilst it may not be perfectly effective, an offending Australian will never be sure whether or not it will suddenly be effective towards him. This fear is a good thing and hopefully will give some benefit to abused children in Asia. (House of Representatives, 1994a, p. 146)

Concern over the legal standing and effectiveness of the Bill was such that the House of Representatives took the unusual mechanism of referring the Bill to the House of Representatives Standing Committee on Legal and Constitutional Affairs [HRSCLCA] for consideration and an advisory report, where usually such referral may occur in the Senate.

The HRSCLCA report on the Bill was completed by May 30, 1994. The Committee held a series of public hearings that were addressed by lawyers, medical staff, politicians, members of government departments, and members of interest groups, such as ECPAT and civil liberties groups. Perhaps significantly, the national Coordinator for ECPAT was the first person to speak at the public hearings. It is also interesting to note that no representative of the tourism industry either spoke at the hearings or presented evidence to the Committee.

Space does not allow for a detailed evaluation of the Bill in this chapter. However, it is important to recognize that whereas the Committee recognized the social significance of the Bill they also highlighted a number of practical difficulties arising from the Bill including:

- costs of prosecuting a case;
- costs of defending a case;
- problems of the video link;
- collecting evidence of the proscribed conduct;
- control of evidence: perjury, blackmail, and perverting the cause of justice;
- age of the child;
- protection of witnesses;

...led consequences of the bill, including other countries legislat-
... carried out in Australia; and
... accused to a fair trial and accepted Australian standards of

Furthermo... he Committee also noted that there was a lack of consultation in preparing the legislation. According to the Vice-President of the Queensland Council for Civil Liberties, "The consultation process up until the time this bill was introduced into the House was restricted to the law enforcement lobby. . . . The consultation has been one way and one way only. That . . . is why there are so many problems with this bill" (Transcript 303, 304 in HRSCLCA, 1994, pp. 20–21). The Committee also commented strongly on the consultative processes associated with the Bill:

> It is clear that consultation involved the Commonwealth Director of Public Prosecutions and (presumably) members of ECPAT and others concerned to address the social problems underlying the Bill. The Committee's concern is that there has been an absence of consultation with experienced practitioners, particularly those experienced in defending criminal cases. (HRSCLCA, 1994, p. 21)

Despite such broad concerns, and a separate statement regarding an expression of concern by a member of the Committee, in the final report (1994, p. 79) the Committee noted that "the arguments for passing the legislation as soon as possible go to social policy considerations" (HRSCLA, 1994, p. 60) and recommended accordingly. Of the 37 recommendations made by the Committee, the Government accepted 25, rejected seven, and held four over for further consideration with one recommendation being deemed irrelevant through acceptance of other recommendations (Attorney General's Department, 1994).

Following the tabling of the Committee's report, the bill was read for the second time, amended and agreed to by the House of Representatives on June 29 and by the Senate on June 30, 1994. The Act was assented to by the Governor General on July 5, 1994 ("Legislation," 1994), thereby becoming law.

The Significance and Success of the Act

From a legal perspective, the Act was significant in terms not only of the subject matter of the law but also in applying Australian law extra-territorially. In March 1996, the first Australian charged under the Act, Anthony Carr, who sexually abused children in the Philippines, was convicted and sentenced (ECPAT Australia, 1996b). However, the evidence for this apparently was discovered when the alleged offender was arrested for child sex offenses allegedly committed in Australia, rather than as a result of any investigation directed at the overseas activity ("Man on First," 1995; Parliamentary Joint Committee on the National Crime Authority [PJCNCA], 1995).

In evidence presented to the PJCNCA's Inquiry into Organised Criminal Paedophile Activity in Australia some witnesses expressed concern that the legislation would not be seen as credible and therefore have a deterrent effect, until a conviction occurs under it (e.g., World Vision Australia, Evidence: 47 in PJCNCA, 1995). Similarly, the Australian Federal Police Association argued that "Unless there are some significant successful prosecutions under the legislation, it runs the risk of eventually being seen only as posturing" (PJCNCA, 1995, para. 4.55). Indeed, the Association argued that there is no evidence on whether the legislation has had a deterrent effect. In contrast, the Minister for Justice and the Australian Federal Police (AFP) both indicated to the Committee that they believed that the legislation was having some deterrent effect ("Ending the Sex Tours," 1995; Evidence, 149-50 in PJCNCA, 1995, para. 4.54), although whether this effect had been more on the casual "sex tourist" than the determined pedophile was less easy to determine. As an AFP Detective Superintendent stated, "I'm inclined to think that the real pedophiles are just being more cautious about their activities and going to ground. . . . I think the act has probably had a real effect on the casual sex tourist" ("Ending the Sex Tours," 1995).

Despite questions as to the efficacy of the Act as a deterrent to sex tourism, the Act and surrounding publicity has had considerable media and political profile in Australia. For example, the PJCNCA (1995) noted the considerable efforts that have been made to publicize the new legislation, particularly to Australian residents departing for overseas through the distribution of leaflets by both ECPAT and the Australian Customs Service. Furthermore, in the diplomatic arena the leader of the Australian government delegation to the World Congress Against the Commercial Sexual Exploitation of Children noted the Australian efforts with respect to the adoption of extra-territorial laws, and trafficking in children and child pornography (Muntarbhorn, 1996).

The issue of pedophile activity and child pornography is now a significant issue in Australian politics. The Australian Department of Foreign Affairs and Trade (DFAT) is conducting an inquiry into pedophilia among Australian diplomats (ECPAT Australia, 1996c). The New South Wales (NSW) Royal Commission into Police Corruption has revealed details of pedophile activity, police corruption, and police lack of action and mismanagement of cases (ECPAT Australia, 1996d). For example, there are allegations that a police informer and self-confessed pederast, Colin Fisk, had been assisted by police in visiting Thailand during a previous Royal Commission ("Inquiry Into Pederast," 1996).

In the case of the NSW Royal Commission, it has become apparent that there was an awareness of pedophile activity but that it was often not regarded as a serious crime, and allegations, particularly involving institutions such as the Catholic Church, were often not acted upon. Similarly, with respect to the passage of the Child Sex Tourism Act, it was stated: "We have all known for years that the child prostitution racket is very widespread in Asia and that it exists in Australia" (House of Representatives, 1994a, p. 146). All this begs the question, why has government taken so long to act given that sex tourism has been an issue for at least 20 years (Hall, 1992)?

The Politics of Reason? Lobbying, International Relations, Health, and External Affairs

Media publicity is only a small part of the answer, as articles on the subject have appeared in the media for many years without sustained action being taken. Crucial to the passing of the Act was the appearance of an interest group, ECPAT, who were able to undertake sustained lobbying of politicians for several years. The success of ECPAT can be indicated when one examines the various parliamentary speeches made with respect to the Act. Over two thirds of the speeches make direct reference to ECPAT or clearly refer to ECPAT material. For example, Ms. Henzell, member for Capricornia, directly quotes from Ron O'Grady of ECPAT in discussing the Bill:

> Tourism is the selling of dreams. It gives ordinary middle class people from Western nations the chance to live like royalty. In their own country the tourist income and savings may appear modest and they may have a some-what boring and servile occupation, but once they enter a poor country they have the instant capacity to live as if they were rulers. (House of Representatives, 1994a, p. 164)

ECPAT have been able to create an awareness among both politicians and the public about child sex tourism in Southeast Asia. Ethical concerns over undesirable social impacts of international travel were at the forefront of debates over the Act. The moral indignation of many members is likely warranted. Unfortunately, perhaps, such "awareness" of the negative impacts of tourism has been restricted to Asia. Little concern has been expressed in Federal Parliament about the sexual activities of international visitors to Australia and the various campaigns of the Australian Tourist Commission, which have sought to display bikini-clad women in order to create a favorable and attractive image to certain market segments.

Ethical issues were not the only major concern expressed in Parliament; almost as important were worries over the damage that Australians engaging in sex with children might do to Australia's image. Five speakers to the Bill emphasized the importance of the Act to help protect Australia's international reputation. The HRSCLCA report (1994) noted that the conduct of Australians overseas impacts on bilateral and multilateral relations. One of the most direct statements regarding the need for the Act came from Ms. Worth, Member for Adelaide, "in terms of self-interest, it is also imperative that such legislation be created. Our material well-being is increasingly a function of our relationship to Asia" (House of Representatives, 1994a, p. 150). The export dollar and diplomatic relations therefore provided a more material basis for the passage of the Bill.

An additional justification for the passage of the Bill, again on more material grounds, was health. Four members spoke in detail of the threat of AIDS and the extent to which the Act may assist in curbing the spread of the HIV virus. Indeed, Hall (1994b) argued that although overt forms of sex tourism do appear to be on the decline, the reasons for this probably relate more to the threat of AIDS to the visitor rather than widespread concern for the sex worker or fundamental changes in gender and economic relations.

Finally, a fourth dimension to the passage of the Bill is to be found in Australia's domestic political arena. The constitutional basis for the Bill lies in Australia's international treaty obligations, common known as the "external affairs" power, and the United Nations Convention on the Rights of the Child in particular. The use of the external affairs power is one of the most controversial areas of Australian politics because is enables the federal government to override the states if a federal law is seen to be giving effect to international treaty obligations. Such a power has, for example, been used by the Commonwealth to create World Heritage areas in the face of state opposition. The positive use of the external affairs power was referred to by a number of speakers in support of the use of such a power, which more conservative members of Parliament argue takes power away from the states and gives more power to the federal government. However, in the case of the Child Sex Tourism Act, the moral and material imperative created in the main through the activities of a pressure group, ECPAT, meant that state rights issues were to be secondary concerns.

Conclusions

One cannot condone sex tourism, especially child sex tourism, if it is exploitative in nature and if the parties involved clearly wield unequal power. However, it is also important that decisions and policies that are formulated with respect to sex tourism are given serious and considered debate. In the case of sex tourism in Australia, this has not happened. The Child Sex Tourism Bill was able to pass because it focused on a small area of sex tourism policy on which moral, and to a lesser extent, ideological consensus could be reached. Such was the success of the ECPAT campaign in creating moral indignation and therefore political action that it almost passed by without notice that the term "sex tourism" is not even defined in the Act. As a member noted, "that the bill should more properly be entitled the Crime (Overseas Exploitation of Children) Bill. . . . I think that name is a more appropriate name for the bill. The bill's title at the moment tends to be emotive, but I suppose that is a matter not of substance" (House of Representatives, 1994b, p. 2345).

Child sex tourism is an important issue, but the numbers of children engaged in prostitution because of tourism are nothing like that of those sex workers who are above the age of consent in the countries in which they work. As the PJCNCA (1995) observed,

> Most sexual offences against children are committed by their relatives and neighbours who are not paedophiles in the strict sense of the term and who do not operate in any organised or networked way. . . . There is no evidence to suggest that organised paedophile groups have ever resembled what are traditionally thought of as "organised crime" groups in size, aims, structures, methods, longevity and so forth. . . . There is no evidence of any current

organised promotion or arrangement of tours by Australian paedophiles to overseas destinations known to be attractive to them. However, informal networking among paedophiles may assist some tourists going overseas to commit paedophile offences. (para. 3.85)

Tourism is clearly an element in the reason for prostitution occurring in certain locations in Southeast Asia and Australasia, but so also is gender, culture, the pattern of economic development, racism, poverty and wealth distribution, highly patriarchal societies, and material interests. In examining media reports and, more particularly, government reports and parliamentary debates on child sex tourism there is often an impression given that "something has been done." Perhaps it has. Nevertheless, broader questions are being left unasked and extremely significant issues, such as gender, economic, and power relations, are typically relegated to academic rather than policy discussions. Governments of countries, such as Australia, while taking action on child sex tourism, fail to recognize that, in their own tourism advertising, they also promote the commodification and objectification of the sexual body. But, of course, the portrayal of available female bodies on Bondi or Bali has absolutely nothing to do with child sex tourism—*does it?*

It is vital that, in attempting to control sex tourism, governments and individuals of conservative political and religious persuasions do not engage in homophobic witchhunts as has started to occur in Australia (Senate, 1994, p. 2495) nor fail to see the wider sociopolitical context within which sex tourism occurs. As Lindblom (1959) stated, "one chooses among values and among policies at one and the same time" (p. 82). Similarly, Simmons, Davis, Chapman, and Sager (1974) noted that "It is value choice, implicit and explicit, which orders the priorities of government and determines the commitment of resources within the public jurisdiction" (p. 457). In examining policy developments on sex tourism and the associated sets of values that they portray, it is therefore just as important to examine what is left out as what is left in.

Chapter 10

Tourist Demand and the New Zealand Sex Industry

Chris Ryan, Helen Murphy, and Rachel Kinder

The purpose of this chapter is to describe some of the features of tourism and the sex industry that currently exist in New Zealand. In doing so, the authors are building upon past research published elsewhere (Ryan & Kinder, 1994, 1996a, 1996b), and research continues into this subject. Consequently, this chapter will present a short factual outline of the present position in New Zealand concentrating on the relationship with tourism, but generally ignoring wider social implications.

New Zealand is not often considered as a destination for sex tourism. Yet it possesses a system of licensed massage parlors and escort agencies that operate not only in the main centers of population but also in the smaller towns. Massage parlors are legal under the 1978 Massage Parlours Act, which negatively defines the area of application by explicitly excluding application of the Act to massage undertaken for sports purposes or by those "pursuing massage under a licence or registration in pursuit of a profession." Licences for a Massage Parlour are obtained from the local Magistrates Court and will be granted if the person making the application is judged to be suitable and if the police do not object. Any person can operate as a masseur or masseuse if he or she has not been convicted of crimes relating to prostitution under the 1961 Crimes Act, or under legislation pertaining to the misuse of drugs. However, sections 147 to 149 of the 1961 Crimes Act deal specifically with "brothel keeping" (section 147), "living on the earnings of prostitution" (section 148) and "procuring sexual intercourse" (section 149), and under section 147 of the Crimes Act, 1961, "everyone is liable to imprisonment for a term not exceeding 5 years who keeps or manages, or acts or assists in the management of any brothel. . . . (for an assessment of the Act see Ryan & Kinder, 1996a, 1996b, and Jordan, 1991). Currently there are signs that the Ministry of Health will seek to introduce new legislation with the effect of clarifying the situation, but it is thought that this will seek to legalize rather than decriminalize prostitution with possibly the legislative situation of the ACT, Australia being used as a model.

Agencies and Parlors

The number of massage parlors and escort agencies can be estimated from a survey of the Yellow Pages section of the telephone directory. Table 1 is derived from those pages and lists the number of businesses and a "population ratio"' for the towns or regions where they are located. In 1994, Auckland had about 40% of the escort agencies and massage parlors in New Zealand while accounting for just under 29% of the population. This imbalance between population and size of the sex industry is caught in the final column, which indicates the mean population per number of escort agencies and massage parlors in a given area. Can it be concluded that those locations with the lowest ratios have important tourist industries, as is the case with Auckland?

Closer examination of Table 10.1 reveals a mixed pattern. The locations can be divided between those with a low average population per sex industry outlet of

Table 10.1. Distribution of Escort Agencies and Massage Parlors in New Zealand

	Agencies		Parlors		Total		Average Population per Sex Industry Outlet
Directory Area	1994	1996	1994	1996	1994	1996	1996
Auckland	48	52	52	48	100	100	8,856
Blenheim/Marlborough	2	2	2	2	4	4	15,184
Christchurch	13	23	21	22	34	45	6,418
Dunedin	5	5	5	5	10	10	10,950
Gisborne	0	4	0	0	0	4	31,484
Hawke's Bay	6	7	2	1	8	8	13,777
Invercargill	5	1	4	2	9	3	5,776
Manawatu	5	10	4	5	9	15	7,813
Nelson	2	4	3	1	5	5	9,478
Northland	0	0	1	1	1	1	31,620
Queenstown	0	0	1	1	1	1	15,123
Rotorua	1	4	2	3	3	7	7,671
Taranaki	3	5	4	4	7	9	15,317
Tauranga	4	1	2	2	6	3	11,800
Taupo	3	2	2	2	5	4	30,721
Timaru	0	0	1	0	1	0	42,400
Wairarapa	0	0	1	1	1	1	29,129
Waikato	14	13	4	7	18	20	8,256
Wanganui	3	2	2	2	5	4	8,242
Wellington	13	17	12	18	25	35	9,027
Westcoast/Buller	1	0	0	0	1	0	20,191
Total	128	152	125	127	253	279	

Sources: Yellow Pages (1994, 1996); New Zealand Year Book (1993, 1996).

below 10,000, those with a medium population range, and finally those with over over 20,000 per sex industry outlet. A low ratio implies that the sex industry is able to sustain itself comparatively easily, and by implication must be attracting clients from outside the town, city, or region. Those areas with a high ratio of population to sex outlets imply that the sex industry is less able to sustain itself, and requires a higher population to trade, indicating perhaps that tourism is less important. Two caveats to this analysis exist. First, the number of workers at any parlor is assumed to be within a constant range. Second, it needs to be recognized that massage parlors are licensed, and hence local police and council policies are important in that some authorities may be more opposed to granting licences. Nonetheless, even where magistrates are more readily granting licences, there must still be a demand in order for the parlors and agencies to trade successfully. Areas with low population to sex outlet ratios include Auckland, Wellington, Invercargill, Manawatu, Wanganui, and Waikato. Auckland and Wellington are two of the major conurbation areas in New Zealand, and the two major centers of trade, commerce, and government. Additionally, Auckland is the major disembarkation point for visitors to New Zealand, while being a major trading port. It contains the main red light district in New Zealand around Fort Street, and this can be counted as a tourist area in the same way as places like the Walletjes, Amsterdam's red light district, albeit on a much smaller and more circumscribed way. For example, there are no women sitting in "shop windows" as is the case in the Dutch city. Wellington is of interest in that its share of sex outlets appeared, in 1994, to be approximate to its share of the New Zealand population, but there is a growing tendency for prostitutes to work privately or in small cooperatives. The data in Table 10.1 thus underestimate the relationship between population and sex industry for Wellington, even allowing for the growth in numbers of sex industry outlets between 1994 and 1996. The cases of the other low ratio centers are of interest for a number of reasons. Palmerston North in the Manawatu is a major conference and sporting venue, whereas Hamilton in the Waikato is approximately 1-2 hour's drive from Auckland. Both Hamilton and Palmerston North are also university towns, as are Wellington, Auckland, Christchurch, and Dunedin. Some respondents saw this as a significant factor, if only because it helps create extra conference and visitor business. Invercargill is the major (and only) city in Southland, and acts as a regional center. Of these cities only Auckland, Dunedin, and Christchurch can be said to have a major recreational tourism business, but all the others attract a significant amount of business tourism, and in the case of Palmerston North, sports and conference tourism. Informal discussions with sex workers and representatives from the New Zealand Prostitutes Collective indicate that businessmen traveling away from home are an important component of the business of the parlors and agencies. In the case of Auckland, Ryan and Kinder (1996a) conservatively estimated that the sex industry offered employment to about 1500 women whereas tourists, both domestic and international, accounted for at least 10% of the total business. They estimated the earnings of the sex workers in Auckland alone as being approximately $40 million.

Economics and Demand

These estimates are supported from the figures made available at the time of the closure of the Wellington escort agency, Corporate Associates, in June 1996. The police estimated that the agency had a turnover of $1.4 million during its 7-month existence. The prosecution presented evidence that business records showed that 30 women worked for the company for different periods of time, and the women handled about 1100 appointments a month ("Brothel Took $1.4 m a Year," 1996). The figures imply that, on average, women had about 6–10 appointments per week, which is consistent with the assumptions made by two of the authors in their earlier work. An analysis of the figures produced in the courts would imply that the women working for Corporate Associates earned, in total, approximately $800,000–900,000 during the period the agency was open. The escort agency itself, after payments to the women and taxi drivers, retained about $650,000, out of which payments had to be made for the accommodation used, including bedrooms in various hotels, and other business expenses. The figures were not disputed by the defendants, either in court or in a subsequent radio interview on National Radio.

It is of interest to note that the major tourism centers of Rotorua and Christchurch feature as "low" ratio centers, respectively. Christchurch has a significant tourism industry and also has an international airport with direct flights from Australian airports and some Asian cities such as Singapore. The increase in the number of outlets in Christchurch between 1994 and 1996 is shown in Table 10.1, and this might at first thought to be linked to developments in other aspects of tourism. Not only has there been an increase in international flights using the airport, and an increase in tourist numbers, but also, in 1995, a new casino opened. Condom distribution figures by the New Zealand Prostitutes Collective reveals a growing number of condoms being distributed in Christchurch. In the period April to June 1996, 7778 condoms were distributed by workers with daily visits being made to the parlors. Yet, in spite of a seeming growth in the industry, the picture is confused. Workers in the industry are reporting that the casino is actually taking money away from the prostitutes; as one said, "there is now a new addiction." Although there appears, at first sight, to be a linkage between tourism growth and the sex industry, in fact the relationship is far from simple. What might be happening is that there is an increase in the supply of sex services, and that supply to some—undefined—extent is based on a premise of their being more custom, perhaps because of tourism growth. However, demand is not expanding as fast as supply, with the result that prices have been falling. It would seem that most of the clients are *Pakeha* (European) New Zealanders and it was stated to the researchers that Asians are not a prominent group of customers. To some extent this is explained by the type of Asian-based tourism New Zealand is attracting. A significant proportion of this is packaged family tours and, as one informant commented, the coach schedules permit little time for visits to massage parlors.

Registration and Legality

Unfortunately, there are limitations to the use of the Yellow Pages as a source of information. Although the law might be clear as to the distinction between a licensed massage parlor and an escort agency, which is not so licensed, the practical distinction is less clear. First, some escort agencies seem to operate in a manner very similar to that of a massage parlor in that they have permanent premises where "ladies and gentlemen" might meet. These are generally known to the police, and may in fact be massage parlors in all but name and are operations awaiting licensing from the magistrates, having made an application for a licence. Second, a perceived although unsubstantiated "legality" might exist. In Wellington and Christchurch, and some other towns and cities in New Zealand, the police require those working as prostitutes and escorts to register with the police. Indeed, for example in Wellington, it is not possible to advertise in the press unless a woman has so registered. The police authorities argue that it is a measure designed to protect the women, but the women have different views. It has been put to the authors that, as in Christchurch, the need to be photographed holding a name card is akin to be treated as a "criminal." In Wellington, when the need to register was introduced, at least two sets of reaction were noted. First, there was scepticism and concern expressed by women about police motives and the privacy of the database. Many women have not informed parents or partners of their occupation. Also, although in the great majority of cases the women involved in sex work are driven into it by a need for finance, not all women are in such a situation—some hold what are deemed to be socially respectable positions, and hence, like all sex workers, feel vulnerable to "blackmail" (see Chapter 11 and Chapter 12). Another category is students who use prostitution as a short-term means to help finance their tertiary education, and who are fearful of a loss of long-term job prospects if their current occupation was known. The second reaction was that the very act of registering was interpreted by many workers as meaning that they were, in fact, "legal"—a situation that is not correct.

Another reason limiting the usefulness of Yellow Pages as a source of research information is that some places offer both parlor and agency services, but may be advertised in only one section of the telephone directory. Although Yellow Pages cannot be regarded as an infallible research source for the level of activity, they are nonetheless important for clients. For a client's viewpoint, it can be noted that a contributor to the "alt.sex" bulletin board service on the internet stated that:

> Since street walkers are generally those who are unable to get a job in a parlour or escort agency they also tend to be the bottom of the heap and therefore the best place to go is to a massage parlour.

> These are in all the major cities and those with a large tourist industry. Mainly Wellington, Auckland, Rotorua, Tauranga, Palmerston North, Queenstown, Dunedin and Christchurch. They are always easy to locate through the classified section of the local newspaper or *alternatively the yellow pages* (authors' emphasis).

Changing Times

The Yellow Pages also provide evidence of the rate of change within the industry. For example, the Manawatu Yellow Pages, within which Palmerston North is located, show that in 1992 there were four escort agencies and one massage parlor. By 1994, there were seven escort agencies and two massage parlors. In 1995, the respective figures were 12 and three. A year later, there were nine agencies and four parlors, while the city's first strip club had also opened. However, parlors might be compared to restaurants, in that names and decor might be changed to indicate novelty even while the management remains the same. Of the 1992 escort agencies, only one trades today under the same name. The only massage parlor trading in 1992 was subsequently purchased by the owner of another, which commenced trading in 1993. The city's one strip club, which opened in 1996, is owned by the same people who closed a massage parlor in Levin and added to the numbers they owned in Palmerston North. The Yellow Pages, however, are not the sole source of information, for newspapers also carry advertisements for "Adult Entertainment." Indeed, such advertisements were a prime source of information for a later section of this chapter. As is indicated, such advertisements may be misleading. Much depends upon the organization of the industry in a locality. In some cases, the advertisements that appear to be placed by independent women are in fact placed by male-run escort agencies or parlors that are simply increasing apparent choice by advertising under the names of specific women. However, in the case of Wellington, recent years have seen a growth of women's "cooperatives" in the sense that small groups of three or four women will rent a flat and operate from it. Such arrangements extend the same safety provided by working in a massage parlor, while offering a potentially higher return because no commissions are paid to the parlor operator. A "better deal" might also be provided for the client because no "door payment" is made, and possibly clients might feel that greater anonymity is being offered because they cannot be seen entering the doors of a massage parlor. It is estimated by Catherine Healy, national coordinator of the New Zealand Prostitutes Collective, that up to 10% of the women previously working in massage parlors or for escort agencies within the last 3 years have "gone private." However, such women tend to be the older women, or women with at least a couple of years of experience or, if younger, who know such women to work with.

The trend to cooperative working is, it is thought, related to economic factors. These are important in explaining the increase in supply of sex workers and outlets, the current slower growth in demand for sex services, and the falling prices. In spite of New Zealand's economic recovery since 1992, single females with families continue to be particularly vulnerable to low incomes and financial difficulties. Both the literature (e.g., Jordan, 1991; Silver, 1993) and individual interviews for this study reveal the common story of women turning to prostitution for money to support young children after being left by their partners. The 1993 report *Child Poverty in Aotearoa/New Zealand* noted the "increasing numbers of New Zealand children belong to families that are poor by New Zealand Standards" (Jackman, 1993, p. 3), and cites a respondent who commented about the "frustration and powerlessness which saps the strength I need for my children" as a reaction to benefit cuts (1993, p. 34). Easton (1980) noted that in New Zealand "At the termination of the marriage the housewife loses her job. There is a case for redundancy payments, particularly to enable her to re-establish herself" (p. 151). Certainly it can be contended that, for many women, divorce can indirectly cause a loss of full-time employment because of commitments to young children. Prostitution offers potentially well-paid employment with schedules that can be convenient for solo female parents. However, as Ryan and Kinder (1996b) argue, in New Zealand in particular, other motivations besides the simply financial can also apply and there is little doubt that, for many women, the income that prostitution provides apparently permits them to have greater control over their lives than might otherwise be the case. The word "apparently" is deliberately chosen, for the constructs and constraints of that control need to be carefully assessed, although such an assessment is beyond the scope of this chapter (see Chapter 16).

However, as a source of finance, prostitution in 1996 is less rewarding than in 1994. For example, in 1994 the normal price for an hour in a Wellington massage parlor was about $100 to $120 in addition to the entry fee of approximately $50 to $60. By June 1996, the prices had fallen to such an extent that in the local newspaper one parlor was offering a $50 "all inclusive" for 30 minutes. The same trend can be observed in Auckland.

The phenomenon of changing supply in the Auckland region is evidenced by an analysis of advertisements that appeared in a New Zealand Sunday newspaper over a period of 6 months from January to June 1996. This analysis only covered heterosexual sex with male clients. It excludes those changes associated with the growing gay and lesbian scene, some of which details, incidentally, can now be accessed on the Internet. A total of 1299 advertisements was categorized from six issues, revealing 333 female names and 51 massage parlors and escort agencies. The descriptions of individual workers allowed a tracing exercise to be carried out: of the total number of female names, 88 appeared only once on the database. On the other hand, 107 of the names appeared four or more times from the six issues, indicating continuous advertising and full-time employment in the industry.

What emerges from this analysis and other information is an industry of movement and yet also stability. There are many women who work but infrequently when a financial need becomes pressing. Others work only the ships that come to port—the "ship girls" who entertain sailors. Certainly, there is anecdotal evidence of female students working to meet the costs of their education, but no substantive evidence exists of any faster increase in the numbers of such students as a result of New Zealand's recent educational policies on tertiary fees, which has led to students having to pay increased percentages of steadily increasing university fees since 1994 in particular. Stability exists, however, in the fact that many managers and owners of the parlors have long been in the business; indeed, until quite recently, most of the Auckland business was in the hands of three men.

Street Workers

Finally, before turning to the relationship between tourism and prostitution, mention needs to be made of "street workers." Street workers form a category of sex workers different from those working in the escort agencies or parlors and are a group of workers who, for a number of reasons, do not work in more organized settings. Although it might be thought the reasons include those of finance, it would seem that in practice they earn much the same per client as other workers. Given the conditions of "working the streets," and the greater potential physical harm they face, reasons for such work must lie in other directions. For some, it is a clear preference, giving them a freedom of work in terms of use of time denied to massage parlor workers. Also, if they do not like the look of a client, they feel they have more freedom to send the client away. But there are also other reasons. Although pimping in the worst sense of the term is not the norm in New Zealand, it does exist for some workers; and it was put to the researchers that in one area perhaps 10–20% of the women were having to finance a drug habit with even more having to finance the drug habits of their partners. This "scene" is more akin to the street prostitution of the UK or US (e.g., Caplan, 1984; Gibson-Ainyette, Templer, Brown, & Veaco, 1988), and if prostitution is the last resort of those suffering from social or psychological dysfunctional environments, then, in a New Zealand context, this is the area where it is most likely to be found. Although it may be thought that the present law forces women with convictions for prostitution to the streets because the Massage Parlor Act makes it illegal for such women to work in a parlor, the position is more complex, with some police authorities apparently taking a more pragmatic view. However, factors of individual preference by the women, the influence of male partners, boyfriends, pimps, drug habits, the attitudes of massage parlor managers—all of these have to be assessed before any conclusions can be reached about this part of the New Zealand sex industry—and at present little research has been published about these factors.

Conclusion

What conclusions can be drawn from this review? It must be first stressed that the text refers to prostitution in New Zealand, a country of small population and, in world terms, comparatively little international and domestic tourism as measured by the numbers of tourists. Yet, tourism is very important to New Zealand's economy and it is the largest single source of foreign exchange earnings, amounting to approximately $4.8 billion in 1996. But in an international context it accounts for less than 0.2% of international air movements. There are no large-scale organized sex tours to New Zealand, and its only red light district of note is small. So conclusions must be understood as emerging from this context.

First, it is to be noted that, like tourism, the sex industry in New Zealand has a substantial national economic and social impact. A proportion of the income generated by the sex industry is derived from tourism. Although very difficult to estimate, it appears from discussions with those involved in the sex industry that those traveling away from home for business, conferences, and sporting events, and some recreational travel with, albeit small, overseas demand, might, together, account for about 10% of the total business. Most business is local, although intercity travel patterns are thought to exist in some cases; for example, Hamilton meets some demand from Auckland. Additionally, some intracity flows might be detected within major conurbations (e.g., from the west of Wellington to Lower Hutt).

Second, although not explored in great detail in this chapter, both tourism and prostitution share the commonality of being a subset of leisure for both industries meet needs of relaxation, social interaction, fantasy and role play, escape, and indulgence. As a leisure activity for males, the sex industry competes with other demands for expenditure made possible by the level of discretionary income, and there are signs that, within the last 2 years in New Zealand, that income is being squeezed.

A third possible relationship is between the growth in tourism in New Zealand and the price of services provided. Two possible hypotheses exist. The first is that tourism growth has created a demand that has helped to cushion price levels against the fall that has been recorded between 1994 and 1996. This would be true of major tourism centers and it may be no accident that it is in Rotorua and Christchurch that the fastest increase in the number of outlets has been recorded. However, as noted, this may simply be to due to the second hypothesis: that an anticipated growth in demand was identified, and supply increased to meet the expected demand, but this demand has not in fact materialized. It is thought that the truth must lie somewhere between these two positions; that in fact demand has increased, but not as rapidly as supply, thereby leading to a reduction in price even while supply and demand have increased. However, it is difficult to provide any statistics to support this contention.

Tourism in New Zealand has a marginal influence on the sex industry beyond the bright neon lights of the strip joints in Fort Street. It is true that Japanese business-men can be seen paying dollar bills to "be rubbed" by naked dancers—a habit imported from the US as generally New Zealand strippers do not collect "bills"; but so too can be seen male students, farm and office workers. Yet the influence of tourism is important because, like much marginal business in economic terms, it is the extra 10% of revenue that generates much of the profits when a local market is just large enough to cover the costs.

Additionally, from a wider social perspective Ryan and Kinder (1996b) have argued that tourism and the sex industry share commonalities in meeting needs of relax-ation and fantasy. Both are subsets of leisure. It is also to be noted that, in New Zealand, although overseas demand is generally unimportant, domestic demand associated with travel for business, conferences, and sports is high. Hence, the question has to be asked, if New Zealand males develop such habits in New Zealand, do they continue such habits when traveling overseas? The authors have no direct evidence about this. However, it was reported by one Sexually Transmit-ted Diseases clinic that there was a consistent demand for their services from males who had recently traveled overseas. Also, the authors adhere to a view previously expressed (Ryan & Kinder, 1995, 1996a, 1996b) that both tourism and the sex industry reveal much about mainstream society and its working. Krippendorf (1996) commented that tourism is the hospital of society whereas Posner (1992) attributes the economics of commercial sex to the nature of companionate and noncompanionate marriage.

Hence, the current authors argue that sex tourism and the sex industry in New Zealand currently exists because prostitution is attractive to women as an alternative to financial hardship and agree with Posner (1992) that demand is fostered by the state of conventional male–female relationships and other factors like the degree of urbanization. To that extent, the New Zealand situation reinforces work undertaken elsewhere.

Acknowledgements

The authors would want to thank Catherine Healy, National Coordinator of NZPC, and Anna Reed, Michelle McGill, and Helen Frame also of the NZPC, and volunteers with the Cooperative. In addition, due acknowledgement is made to various other sex workers, and those working in Sexually Transmitted Diseases Clinics, particularly that of Palmerston North. The abstract from the alt.sex bulletin board is from August 30, 1995 and with this note, "Permission is granted to freely copy, modify, and distribute this document in whole or in part, provided that it is not done for profit and that this notice remains attached."

Chapter 11

Topless Dancing: A Case for Recreational Identity

Asuncion Suren and Robert Stiefvater

A man wearing a baseball cap swallows a mouthful of beer, then cups his hands around his lips and bawls his approval. The man's buddy gives a comradely slap on the back that is clearly meant to indicate they share enthusiasm for the recreational activity in which they are both engaged. Isolating these two men's reactions from the event they are observing, we might assume they are responding to a baseball player's bat connecting decisively with a perfect pitch, to a prize fighter delivering a debilitating blow, to a power forward slamming down a monster jam. But in fact, the men are watching a woman remove the few clothes she was wearing when she mounted the stage on which she now performs, pleasing her admirers with seductive movements timed to the rhythms of the music they all hear.

Whether you refer to the businesses that host these events as strip clubs or titty bars, the customers of topless dancing establishments are experiencing leisure and are engaged in a recreational activity (see Chapter 1 and Chapter 12). Many people would persuasively argue not only the morality of such an act, but also the legitimacy of topless dancing as recreation or leisure. As leisure scholars, we submit the following interpretation of recreation: it is an activity from which a participant receives pleasure or a sense of restoration. A participant experiencing leisure receives a sense of intrinsic or extrinsic satisfaction from the recreation activity. Consequently, how one defines leisure directly affects the criteria by which one evaluates recreational behavior. If individuals define leisure subjectively then, likewise, they must define what activity (recreation) helps them reach that leisure state. Leisure, as a subjective state of the individual, is characterized by a sense of perceived freedom, intrinsic satisfaction, involvement, and arousal (Unger & Kernan, 1983). Perceived freedom is the psychological sense of having freedom of choice in deciding on a behavior or set of behaviors. Within the context of leisure, intrinsic satisfaction refers to engaging in recreational activities because of the pleasure or enjoyment that one derives from that engagement. Involvement relates to a total or near-total absorption in an activity characterized by intense enjoyment. Arousal entails increased intensity of emotion and feelings and a positive or desired reaction to stimuli (Tinsley & Tinsley, 1982).

Recreation is defined as the "active engagement" whereby one attempts to reach a leisure state (Stiefvater, 1996). One can reach this desired state by choosing a recreational activity as passive as watching the sunset on a beach or as vigorous as mountain biking. Viewing recreation from this perspective is consistent with the "leisure-as-a-subjective-state" perspective, which confirms that recreation as an activity is self-determined (Kando, 1975).

Leisure Services Industry

Leisure experiences offered by businesses and industry seek to capitalize on recreation interests that draw the masses and that create a climate of desirability (Kraus, 1990). The leisure services industry or commercial recreation is "the provision of recreation-related products or services by private enterprise for a fee, with the long-term intent of being profitable" (Crossley & Jamieson, 1993, p. 6). In their definition of commercial recreation, they interpreted "recreation-related" to include any product or service that supports a leisure pursuit.

In an affluent society, people are willing to pay top dollar for their recreation; they are in pursuit of leisure experiences that are exciting, energizing, and entertaining. Russell (1996) noted that commercial recreation businesses "are more likely to be associated with entertainment, popular culture, spectator sports, theme parks, tourism, food and drink, and shopping facilities and programs" (p. 369). Maclean, Peterson, and Martin (1985) identified passive forms of entertainment, such as stage shows, nightclubs, and massage parlors as legitimate commercial recreation businesses. Because they provide customers recreation and ultimately a sense of leisure, and are in the business of making a profit, sex-oriented businesses clearly fall under the commercial recreation domain.

Globally, sex-oriented businesses, of which topless dancing is a part, constitute a flourishing industry. For instance, Thailand's sex tourism industry attracts 1.2 million tourists yearly, a total that represents 60% of all Thailand's tourists (O'Malley, 1988). In Shenzhen China, there are approximately 42 "song and dance halls" (sex shows), which attract 50,000 customers a night (Abramson & Pinkerton, 1995, p. 311). In the US, gross revenues from commercialized sex exceed $10 billion a year (Kraus, 1990, p. 273).

Topless Dancing as a Spectator Sport

Because of the degree of interaction between the dancer and the audience, topless dancing can be construed as a spectator event. Murphy and Williams (1973) identified two recreational behaviors that suggest motivations for engaging in spectator events. One is the desire for a vicarious experience. Ross (1977) noted that the spectator experiences an "element of vicarious pleasure" (p. 111) in watching a performance. People find pleasure in observation (spectation) because of an appreciation for the skill or performance of that which is being observed (Mull, Bayless, & Ross, 1987). The second recreational behavior relates to sensory stimulation, which primarily involves pleasure and the stimulation of the senses including drinking, sexual desire, music, and visual experiences, such as light and laser shows. Commercial recreation businesses take advantage of these motivations for spectation and, as such, they attempt to provide experiences that will attract paying customers—be they spectators interested in basketball games, rock concerts, theme park attractions, or topless dancing.

Manipulating Leisure Environments

No commercial recreation business can "give" a participant leisure—leisure is a subjective state. However, what a business can do is to manipulate an environment in such a way that creates the greatest probability that an individual will experience leisure. Rossman (1995) refered to this manipulation of the environment as *the six elements of place.* These six elements are the generic set of variables that structure leisure experiences through recreational activity: interacting people, physical setting, leisure objects, rules, relationships, and animation. Interviews with a topless dancer and the proprietor of a strip club illustrate how these elements are used to create a leisure experience for the spectator.

The Interview: A Case Study

Tara (all names are fictional) is a junior majoring in tourism management at a Big Ten institution in the Midwest. Tara is an attractive—5 feet 5 inchs, 115 pounds, brown hair, brown eyes—Caucasian woman who secured a position as a dancer in a local topless club. Tara worked as a dancer for approximately 1 year while attending school full-time. Her initial attraction to dancing topless was financial. However, she later discovered an additional benefit of the job. She became a provider of a popular recreation event that cultivated a sense of extrinsic satisfaction for herself and a sense of intrinsic satisfaction for many of the spectators. Our initial interview with Tara revealed a dilemma between three conflicting emotions (i.e., moral, financial, and physical) and her role as a recreation provider.

In an additional interview, the owner of the unpretentious club where Tara worked offered a perspective of topless dancing as a vicarious experience for the men who frequent the club. Sam, the proprietor of Night Life, considers himself a recreation provider. He is in his early fifties and has owned and managed topless dance clubs for approximately 15 years. Sam is committed to operating a "clean" business; no acts of prostitution or drug use are allowed on the premises. Sam is a well-respected businessman in the community. In addition to Night Life, he owns a family restaurant, and a tuxedo rental and sales store.

Six Elements of Place

Interacting People

Having an understanding of the needs, wants, and desires of people who interact in any recreational environment is a key element in establishing a successful leisure experience. An effective commercial recreation agency is able to anticipate the expectations of a specific type of clientele and determine how to design satisfying leisure experiences to meet the expectations of that clientele.

As strip clubs go, Night Life is a middle-of-the-road establishment. It appeals to a wide variety of men, ranging from college professors and business professionals to blue collar types and rowdy college fraternity boys. Unlike some clubs that cater to an up-scale crowd, with their $20 cover charges and $10 drinks, Night Life is a very accessible establishment. It is located in the main business district close to a number of restaurants, hotels, and apartment complexes. The outside appearance of the club is well maintained. The parking lot accommodates a significant number of vehicles and is well lit.

Night Life has its share of regulars and locals, but draws heavily on the transient population of a college town. Students, tourists attending various functions (e.g., sporting events, conferences, shows), and visiting college alumni have all made their way to Night Life. The makeup of the spectators is primarily men who are alone or in groups. According to Sam, however, "we see couples come in here and when a woman comes in alone she is more than likely a lesbian." Each group of interacting people has its own unique and dynamic reason for attending the club. Sam Jones indicated that "lesbian women were perhaps the most aggressive while men, who may attempt a subtle touch, will back down at the first sight of resistance from dancers." Sam points out that men in groups are typically more rowdy then those who are alone. This can be attributed to the consumption of alcohol and the nature of social interaction of men in a "boys' night out" environment.

Tara, on the other hand, described a recreation experience where she entertained at a bachelor party at the club. She indicated that she felt as though she were in on the hazing of this soon-to-be-groom. The bachelor party sought an convivial environment in which to celebrate a right of passage. Tara and Night Life were able to satisfy that desire. Sam expressed that "most men who come to the club alone are either in need of personalized attention, or they need time, after work, to relaxation before going home to their wives."

Tara also related an experience in which she entertained a hearing impaired gentleman. He was simply seeking the attention of a woman. She did not dance for him, but rather they communicated through written notes highlighting her costumes, beauty, and discussing the people with whom she was socializing. Tara stated that, "I think that (it) was truly a different form of recreation . . . it wasn't all fun and games, it was just kind of a form of relaxation or the need to release for that time." It was these experiences that gave Tara a sense of being a recreation provider.

Physical Setting

Rossman (1995) noted that in order to orchestrate a leisure experience that closely satisfies clientele expectations, a recreational event requires unique settings to be successful; settings can be manipulated with decorations, lighting, and other physical alterations to create the best possible experience. Strip clubs require a certain ambiance to be effective. Dim lights, a disco ball, loud/aggressive music, and scantily clad dancers all help in creating the proper atmosphere. Add black walls with colorful splashes of florescent paint, neon lights, and the smell of alcohol and perfumes permeating the air, and Night Life has created a setting in which multifarious and vicarious leisure experiences may occur. According to Sam, the proper atmosphere sets the mood for both the dancer and the spectator: "It offers a sense of fantasy for the men who come to watch the girls, and helps the girls to be more entertaining."

Leisure Objects

Rossman (1995) identified three types of leisure objects: physical, social, and abstract. These objects are critical to enhancing the desired experience of the spectator. Examples of physical objects include mirrors, dance poles, and the stage. Social objects relate to individuals who are essential to providing a successful leisure experience: the dancers, bouncers, and bartenders. Abstract objects could include such expressions as ideas, philosophies, or fantasies.

Physical Objects

A variety of physical leisure objects are present in Night Life and other such clubs. The most prominent and probably the most important one is the stage. The stage is typically the central focus of the club. It is one of the most important elements for the dancer. It separates her from the spectators; it elevates her in their eyes both literally and figuratively. The stage is where she establishes her role as the entertainer, creates the event, and becomes the recreation provider.

A second critical object is the dancer's costume. Costumes must be provocative yet functional. Strippers usually wear "alluring" costumes that are easily removed. According to Sam, for the dancers to keep the attention of the regulars and to continuously make hundreds of dollars, they must dress in sexy clothes yet leave the men wondering. "Men pay their money to see the girls strip down to nothing, they fantasize about what her body really looks like," contends Sam. Tara stated that she often felt sexy wearing 5-inch heels and beautiful sensuous costumes. She indicated this feeling helped her to dance more seductively, which got her big tips.

Two other physical leisure objects that are unique to strip clubs are mirrors and the dance pole. Sam indicated that the mirrors serve a number of purposes. They help create a sense of space in the club. And they help the dancers to perform more seductively. Dancing solo is difficult, particularly in front of a group of people. Sam would instruct the new dancers to look at themselves in the mirrors, which would assist them in providing a better performance. Dance poles date back to burlesque shows when an experienced dancer was separated from a novice by how well she manipulated the pole. Dancers swing, climb, and dance around the pole, providing a more erotic performance. An experienced dancer can use the pole in much the same way a good gymnast uses an uneven parallel bar.

Social Objects

Social objects encompass the key providers in offering a desired leisure experience by the clientele. There are a number of people involved in the strip club. Foremost, of course, are the dancers themselves. Although they may still be performing, dancers are expected to interact with the customers between their sets: conversing with them, playing table games, or listening attentively to their problems and deftly brushing off their advances while maintaining an aura of flirtation.

The disc jockey (DJ) is another key player in the strip club. He or she can control the mood by musical selections. The DJ must attempt to play to the crowd, while keeping in mind the persona and tastes of the performer. The bartender must be a competent "mixologist" yet able to lend an ear to patrons and dancers alike. The bouncer must present an image of authority, and be quick to handle any disturbances.

Abstract Objects

Abstract leisure objects relate to less tangible notions such as customers receiving feelings of self-confidence from interacting with the dancers. Patrons may also experience lust or fantasy while observing the performance. Foote (1954) describes the concept of the counterfeiting of intimacy. This refers to the intimacy between customer and dancer, which actually conceals a mutual exploitation. The dancer's interest in the participant is monetary and the customer's interest in the dancer lies in the objectification of the dancer's sexuality. The customer's interest may also be stimulated by the idea that strip clubs have a reputation of being deviant and that the experience of going to them can be one of mystique and intrigue.

Rules

Rules guide interactions in an activity. According to Rossman (1995), "rules guide how interactions may or may not unfold, and in this sense they make certain interactions possible and constrict others" (p. 44). Some rules are typical of most strip clubs, including Night Life. For example, when dancers thank customers, no hugs or kisses are permitted. In fact, at no time is touching the dancers permitted. Dancers can never date customers for money—prostitution in any form is strictly prohibited. Nipples must be covered by an opaque material and G-strings are not allowed; T-bars must be worn that are at least 4 inches wide in the front.

"No drugs" is one of the most important rules. If dancers are caught using, selling, or buying drugs while on the premises they will be permanently barred and prosecuted without hesitation. When Sam suspected one of the dancers of bringing drugs into Night Life, he had the police and police dogs inspect the dressing room and the dancer's locker. According to Sam, the dog went wild, but when it was opened the locker did not contain any drugs. Sam stated that he likes to make a big episode of suspected drug use; he believes it keeps the dancers honest and his club clean.

Relationships

Recreation providers are encouraged to fully comprehend the impact that relationships have in the interactions of a leisure experience and forecast how these relationships may contribute to or detract from customer satisfaction. Rossman (1995) exerted that it is important for the recreation provider to not structure events in a way that could destroy relational histories. Because people frequently participate in leisure with family and friends, properly designed leisure experiences should first encompass an assessment of the nature of the relationship and, then, their potential impact on the expectations of family, friends, and others alike.

As a college student dancing in a small Midwest town, Tara continuously struggled with three conflicting emotions. First, she loved making a $1,000 or more a week. She was able to use the money to pay off credit card debts, purchase a new car, and finance her college education. Second, she enjoyed the feeling of looking and being perceived as sexy. She looked forward to opportunities to perform at special events. Tara related that "when picked to perform solo at a special function, I truly felt like I was providing recreation for the guys who were involved. These opportunities made me feel special . . . they (event) made me feel sexy." Third, Tara's most emphatic and lasting emotion was an overpowering sense of shame. After nearly a year of performing, Tara absolutely could not overcome her fear of a friend, family member, or classmate appearing as a spectator at Night Life. Tara shares her feelings: "I was nervous that if a classmate saw me perform he might think that I was easy. I am an intelligent woman, I don't want my friends or classmates to think I'm a typical topless dancer." Tara believed that this feeling of shame affected her ability to perform seductively:

> My attitude started to change after several months dancing. . . . I thought moving from my parents house would help me overcome this feeling of fear and shame, but I kept thinking what if my parents saw me up on stage. My attitude really affected my dancing, I couldn't stand the way the guys came on to me . . . I would ask the bouncer to throw people out . . . I started to notice that I wasn't making as much money as the other girls.

Although Tara truly believed that she was "simply entertaining" and "providing recreation," she could not dismiss the negative stigma associated with dancing topless (see Chapter 16):

> In the beginning it (topless dancing and having family and friends find out) was nerve racking. Because it was new and the money was good my attitude was a lot different. As far as dealing with this feeling of shame, I tried to keep it in my head that morally I wasn't doing anything wrong. But as the months went by, I noticed the disrespect from some of the customers . . . they act like you are a slut or something.

Because Tara could not rid herself of this feeling, she decided to spend less time dancing and more time socially interacting with the regulars and the bartender: "I felt drinking with some of the guys who come in all the time would make me feel better. Sometimes when the customers really got on my nerves, I would just spend time with the bartender until it was my turn to perform." Upon Tara's first-year anniversary at Night Life, she could no longer dance. In fact, although she knew that this job would qualify her for field experience hours through the University— a graduation requirement for all recreation and tourism students—she decided that topless dancing would not look good on a resume.

Animation

"Animation deals with how a program is set into motion and how the action is sustained throughout the program" (Rossman, 1995, p. 49). In theater, animation is referred to as "blocking"; in sport it is known as developing a "play." Typical animation in a strip club has the dancer performing to a three-song set. It is not usually until the third song that she removes her costume to reveal bare breasts and a T-bar. The dancer attempts to build the suspense, delivering the obvious in a deliberate and seductive pace, and thus heightening the recreational experience for the customer.

After her three-song set, she will "work" the crowd, collecting tips from customers that were not stage-side. This is usually done during the first song of the next dancer's set. And so on throughout the evening. Dancers can earn upwards to $500 a night, more in the up-scale clubs in larger cities. Dancers at Night Life typically earn between $200 and $300 for a 6-hour shift. Depending on how many dancers an establishment employs (Night Life has 36 dancers), and the number of shifts one takes, stripping can be an extremely lucrative occupation. As previously stated, Tara was able to earn enough money in 1 year to pay off substantial credit card debts, buy a new car, and finance her college education.

Conclusion

Despite the negative connotations associated with sex-oriented businesses, topless dancers offer spectators an opportunity to recreate and ultimately receive a satisfying leisure experience. Tara and Sam revealed many instances at Night Life that clearly illustrate the conceptual relationship between recreation and leisure. Recreation does not occur during leisure so much as it creates leisure. One recreates, engages in passive or active events, with the intent of achieving a leisure state (Maclean et al., 1985).

Night Life, as a commercial recreation establishment, caters to a host of men who choose to engage in passive recreation. Their reasons for spectating perhaps are similar. However, the leisure states derived during the experience differ. For some, the dancers and ambiance offer a sense of relaxation, socialization, or excitement, whereas others are temporarily lost in fantasy, or are recharged from personalized attention, or are hyped by the escape from work and family obligations.

Topless dancing offers its spectators hours of satisfying leisure experiences that occasionally induce a high sense of self-esteem; consequently, sex-oriented businesses are highly controversial where it concernes morals and values—people are strongly opposed to women, and now men, stripping for money. The belief is that this type of behavior leads to corruption and other deviant acts by both the dancer and the spectator. In addition, people often believe that strip clubs are within the seedy parts of town, where the community suffers because of the seedy clientele who frequent the club. Furthermore, there is a belief that dancers are usually from broken homes and are not well-educated and, therefore, are unable to secure a well-respected job.

In some cases this perception may have merit. In fact, Tara resigned from Night Life because of the stigma associated with working in this type of industry. Tara could not handle the disrespect from some spectators, and the constant fear of being found out by friends, classmates, and family. Although she made a substantial amount of money, which helped to finance her college education, Tara eventually felt that the stigma of dancing topless would affect her ability to secure a reputable position within the tourism industry. Even though Tara left Sam's club, she felt just as special as she did ashamed. Tara truly believed that she was providing a meaningful recreational event for her spectators.

Regardless of the type of recreation on which people choose to spend their dollars, leisure experiences are usually sought to heighten one's level of expectation. Although commercial recreation businesses cannot give one leisure, they can design experiences that meet and exceed clientele expectations. Rossman's (1995) six key elements of place clearly illustrates a process that any commercial recreation business can follow to successfully design leisure experiences. Understanding the needs, wants, and desires of people who interact in any recreational environment will satisfy the client expectations and the business financially.

Chapter 12

A Travel Model in the Runway Setting: Strip-Tease as Exotic Destination

Jon Griffin Donlon

Jafari (1987) developed a model that helps to explain the unique circumstances involved in some touristic experiences. Essentially, his model claims that neither the location nor the participants are in "normal" modes for the time period involving the tourist. Paris for the tourist is not, in this view, the Paris of a resident's experience and/or reality, nor is the person traveling in Paris the same self that exists in the work-a-day world back home. This chapter discusses observations of behavior at so-called "runway clubs" or strip-tease joints in order to compare the fit between those participants and the participants of touristic episodes according to the Jafari model.

Briefly, Jafari (1987) offers this model of the tourist. "To begin," he explains, "for a visual metaphor, one may imagine a springboard of resilient material which enables the tourist to leap temporarily into the tourism world and then fall back into ordinary life" (p. 151). In this metaphor, the participant is fairly aggressive, demanding control and acting as the agent of change to actively create or recreate a temporary reality. By extension, failing to "fall back" implies the phenomena of "going native."

Jafari describes the transit as having five general components: ordinary life, the process of emancipation, actually doing tourism, the process of repatriation (the homeward touristic flow), and the ordinary life that has continued apace while the participant was off a'touristing. Obviously, this constructed or play space for the tourist is often likely to be superimposed upon, or imbricated into, real or quotidian space.

Many of us have experienced the feeling of strangeness associated with conclusion of a touristic period. For example, when Hooper (1990) returned from 6 months in

Southern Africa he wrote, "coming back was like I'd never been away. Everything was the same: the people, the places, the mind-sets" (p. 251). Although Hooper's comments, as commercial text, are shaped by publishing convention, he does convey the sense of dissonance between recollection of an exoticized experience and return to one's normal life.

For Jafari (1987), it is existence in ordinary life that ". . . . breeds the need or desire to leave the springboard" (p. 151). Tourism, then, in this interpretation, is not a recent manifestation of a primordial social phenomenon; there is not pressure to create ritual change. The theorists do claim that there is a sort of "recreation" taking place, that the participant is refurbished in some spiritual way beyond the more tangible aspects of having a touristic experience.

In the Jafari model, as the participant proceeds through the phases noted, the originating culture becomes a species of back-drop while the tourist culture swells in importance. According to this model,

> While ordinary needs may be met, it is the ludic forces and leisure desires which are especially awakened when the foreground and backdrop cultures assume their respective positions. . . . The tourist can now play any role of his choice any way he wishes, ranging from the childish games and practical jokes played by the middle-aged conventioneers in hotels, to the loud Hawaiian shirt worn by the conservative bank president. (Jafari, 1987, p. 153)

Jafari's sixth part is "omission." Here he deals with the fact that time, and all its associated events and dynamics, continues to roll on along back home. So, on returning, the tourist has to integrate not only new experiences, but also any changes that have taken place in the interim:

> In duration, the omission is the same as the nonordinary flow; it is the span between the emission and the emulsion points of departure and arrival. As the omitted body lengthens, the re-entry culture shock is more probable and thus more real for the returning expatriate . . . the difference between the re-entry "shock" of the tourist and the expatriate is a matter of degree, not kind. (Jafari, 1987, p. 156)

For Jafari, it is the experience of travel and tourism, much more than the change of locale, that creates or supports the sensation of being a tourist. The sense of being a tourist is brought about by an awareness of exiting the normal orbit of one's activities and life. Based on the model described above, might it be shown that runway clubs or strip joints function to support a temporary visit to a nonordinary site? Do traditional flesh pots function as touristic settings?

One perspective posits that these clubs are normal or ordinary spaces in which performers create a bogus or counterfeit sense of intimacy (Sijuwade, 1995). Because the folkloric truism that women display sexually and men display with resources has been powerfully tested and supported, there is much to say for the theory that strippers offer a performative version of a biological reality. This chapter, however, maintains that such spaces are playful, or ludic, and are designed to allow role malleability.

As might be predicted, market variability, local politics, regional regulatory apparatus, and a lushly varied intuitive sense of probity have interacted to create a tremendous range of expressions of the basic strip club format. In some cases, apparently, the settings include actual sexual acts (Hubner, 1992; McCumber, 1992). Most often there is merely display or ritual sexuality (see Chapter 11). Performance elements may be placed along two axes: amount of undress involved, and complexity of individual events. One club may feature several women in bikinis gyrating on raised daisis. Another club might barrage customers with the spectacle of women table, lap, and couch dancing, friction dancing, booths involving customers showering with performers, a pit with pudding, oil, or mud wrestling, several nude women moving along a raised runway, and an absurdly large chested novelty "ringer" wrapping her breasts around a patron's head. A basic motif does exist, however.

Elements of Typicality

These bars are typically composed of two discreet populations: the visitors/clients and the residents/professionals/workers. The professionals include a variety of operatives such as doormen, bouncers, bartenders, short-order cooks or caterers, and lighting and/or sound specialists. The focus of this chapter is on the performer or dancer as a professional. In particular, strip clubs engage both employees and private contractors. That is, the exotic dancer or performer often contracts for a time slot or shift (some of which are significantly more lucrative than others) and are, functionally, free-lancing or acting as independent contractors. This is rarely or never the case with other categories of club professional.

According to accounts in the popular press, presumably the source of information for most customers, performers very much like the high incomes associated with this line of work (Chapter 11; J. Gould, 1992; Hastings, 1993; Huggs, 1992; Mano, 1993; Silverman, 1993). In a Marxist sense, the exotic dancer not only retains the means of production, if it is assumed that the performance is the product, but they are aware that this particular occupation is situated in a range of less attractive options. In spite of this, as Fine (1991) notes, "We do not instruct our daughters in exotic dance in high school. We honor Martha Graham but not Sally Rand" (p. 89). Why? One obvious but inadequate answer is that exotic dance is sexual. Yet as Hanna (1988) argues compellingly, "all dance is sexual." Is exotic dance self expression or a job? Is it the chore of these professionals to create the touristic setting described by Jafari?

A recurrent theme of these spaces is a perceived, and described, tawdry aroma connected with exotic dance-related performative events. From the perspective of the visitor, presumably at least a part of this "wild side" tone is an attraction of such places. In light of the Jafari model, the ambience contributes to a sense of being outside the normal flow. Runway clubs vary from most other commercial hospitality settings both in this actively risqué reputation and in actual services offered. Although most restaurants and bars or lounges maintain a domestic sense of what MacCannell (1976) called "front" and "back" region relationships, strip clubs aim to blur or reduce the appearance of this barrier. Moreover, whereas many runway clubs offer up-scale decor and serve high-quality food and drink, it is safe to assume that it is the display atmosphere that serves to differentiate stripper and nonstripper milieus.

These clubs commonly cater to male, presumably heterosexual, taste although homoerotic settings do exist as do what might be called "novelty" performances at otherwise mainstream businesses. Male strippers serving heterosexual female audiences may be standard fare at some locations—often, for example, within an exotic tourist domain—or they may perform as occasional acts booked at clubs usually devoted to male entertainment. In the sense that audience members viewing exotic dancers are allowed, or even encouraged, to behave in ways usually considered outside the social "norm" of the home location, during these "ladies nights" the effect is even more clearly defined. To the observer, it seems that it is the desire of the client (acting as a species of traveler in this case) to exit the normal flow for at least part of the time in the club. Professionals, especially the performers, indulge and nurture this desire by acting parts or roles consonant with an exotic setting.

The assumption of familiarity, the intimacy of language between strangers (recall that some theorists believe that it is the creation of a false intimacy, not creation of an ersatz exoticized setting, which is the main function of these spaces), and the willing acceptance of a prolonged, typically male gaze common to consumers in these audiences seems to be expressed even more profoundly when female club goers participate in a male stripper event. That is, the female audience goes further "in country," further from their "normal" flow of daily life. It must be acknowledged that the pro forma behavior variance between the exotic site and the domestic one is presumably broader in the female audience than in a male one.

In commercial social settings, female clients are largely forced to deny that their own overt sexual display is about mate attraction, whereas female performers, whose sexual display is so elaborated and outside the normal flow, are forced to deny—in order to maximize income and profit from their performance—that the activity is about work or maintaining a false "front." This microtravel event mirrors the frisson associated with single women traveling on the macro- or geophysical plane.

As interesting as these considerations may be, the occurrences of male-oriented strip or runway clubs are so much more common that it seems appropriate to focus on the presumed norm, and not on the relative outliers. In addition, of course, this decision allows one to exclude the more difficult and much more trying features of the world of exotic dancers that accumulate at the margins: the lesbian clubs, the cross dressers, the multiple-gender settings, and others.

Regulating Adult Play

Until fairly recently, congregations of strip clubs were frequently relegated to relatively suspect real estate, or were consolidated in well-known adult entertainment areas such as Boston's Combat Zone or New Orleans' Bourbon Street. In these traditional groupings the fit between the Jafari model and club goers seems quite tight, especially when communities actively isolated the clubs as sources of pollution (Douglas, 1966). The need to travel even the short distance to the seedy neighborhoods or special districts reinforces the sense of travel and of becoming a tourist in that other culture region. It may be said that the specificity of the journey to the club constitutes a sort of microtouristic episode on its own. However, more recently, as these clubs become what has been called "up-scale" and more expensive, the money and the glitz have provided entrée into theretofore restricted areas.

On the other hand, what might be described as "rowdy behavior" seems to be, or at least is perceived to be by some employees, reduced in such up-scale settings. In a pattern that exactly reflects the complaints by geographical travelers that a physical location can become "Westernized" and lose much of its exoticism, so, too, do these strip clubs become "normalized" as the behavior is more formally regulated. Jafari's travel model demands that one be able to exit the normal flow, even if the actual world continues on normally—as in the case of the banker in the Hawaiian shirt. The reduction in rowdiness should be conceived—and indeed is conceived—as a threat to the desired reality operant in traditional runway clubs and strip bars.

The reduction of the possibility of transitioning across Mary Douglas' smooth to shaggy, "purity and danger" domains seems to reduce the sensation of exiting a normal realm. Presumably because of this, a number of staff or longtime strip club goers have complained about the change in tone in the same way that travelers, as has been mentioned, complain about a particular destination: it has been ruined by development, made too American (or Europeanized), it is not like it used to be.

Performance Styles and Types

General dancing, such as that which takes place in the club, often consists of each dancer working through three popular songs (similar events may be taking place simultaneously at several locations in large clubs). Although performers place great emphasis on their selection of music, the development of costumes, and establishing particular erotic themes, the literature dealing with strip-tease has been loath to acknowledge any of this as creative activity.

Usually the first song in the "set" involves very little stripping, but a good deal of movement along the raised "runway," which often backs or juts from the wet bar— thus the name runway club. In the more traditional, more rowdy, clubs, the dancer uses this time to assess which viewer is likely to be good for a nice tip, usually by his loud comments, vocal compliments, active body language, calls, whistles, or waving of cash, and other learned cues. The procedure may be likened to a skillful predator casting about for prey. Up-scale clubs usually have a much more restrained give-and-take between performer and client because of more-or-less regularized fees associated with services. Almost certainly, the introduction of the credit card, in conjunction with business lunch deductions, has had a large effect here.

The middle or middle and last song of a successful set devolve toward one client (or client cluster) being "danced to." Frequently, although not invariably, so-called "floor work" is done near the end of a performer's set. Floor work allows an individual exhibition of prowess as well as a generic display of suggested sexuality. Eventually, the stage set should lead to receipt of a good "tip" as well as, perhaps, a request for further performance.

Commercial activity off-stage or off-runway include table, couch, and friction dancing, or mud, oil, or jello wrestler, and related variants. The runway performance constitutes a sort of advertising for the more lucrative specialty work that rounds off the activities of the performers and provides them with most of their incomes. Because the performer is actually employed by the patron for a short time, this procedure results in a much closer fit between effort and payment than is available through incidental tips. Assignment of time slot can have a vast effect on the income opportunities open to the performers.

To the observer, the special atmosphere created in many runway clubs exhibits a package or envelope of interpersonal behavior either entirely outside the usual social norm or, in any event, available in other circumstances only in individualized intimate moments—authentic "back" scenarios among acquaintances, friends, or lovers. For the duration of the club visit, entertainers are certainly freely ogled, with little or no feigned concern for this gaze, and yet are largely in power. Clients are, conversely, forced to operate in a direct quid-pro-quo relationship, entirely based on commercial exchange.

The cat-calls, wolf whistles, and shouts of enthusiastic praise of body parts or corporal shape that are entirely verboten in the normalized flow of most American communities are subverted within the runway clubs. There, dancers utilize these markers to "zero in on" desperate or willing men, ready to exchange cash for a brief visual offering—again, what is called "false intimacy" by some researchers. And because the exchange is, in its essential nature, an honest one, bad tippers are individually and institutionally ostracized; participants are free to act out an array of roles typically forbidden while existing in the normal flow of day-to-day life.

Does the Jafari Model Explain Part of the Club Experience?

Curiously, as the runway or strip club setting becomes more mainstream, sanitized, formalized, and up-scale, it also more fully reflects the normal flow—calls, whistles, and shouts, for example, become less and less common, and grabs and gropes virtually nonexistent. The social barrier between verbal and visual communication and tactile is a sensitive membrane in the strip-tease world. Touching is very commonly regulated, frequently formally forbidden, and virtually invariably moderated by the decisions of the performer, never the client. Touching is a topic of control for both the club owner/manager and the civil authority. Dancers, aware of the power of pressure, may try to circumvent the intent of this regulatory apparatus by striking clients with pieces of their costume or with their hair (which is notorious for being traditionally long). Curiously, a frequently successful dodge is simply to photograph or video tape a patron/client with his favorite dancer sitting on his lap. This obviously crashes through all intents of the barrier and allows a great deal of full-body contact. Presumably the domestic place of the snapshot and the videoed family record as "safe" has been imbricated into the quasi-sexuality of the rendering.

The salient feature here is that authenticity—or the implications of authenticity, of acting at the margins of a "back" area, temporarily exiting the front or norm-related zone—is reduced. Meanwhile, the persona of the exotic dancer becomes more professional and more thoroughly distanced from her former specialty as negotiator and facilitator of role-playing events.

Although Jafari's model usefully describes the structural dynamics of many runway or strip clubs, it only poorly embraces the entire domain, especially becoming weak with the most modern of the settings. If the opportunity to role play, to exist for a more or less short time outside the normal flow, is an important element in the genre, one might expect the evolving form of such clubs to recapture the old patterns of behavior. That is, one might predict a reexoticization of exotic dance and at least the appearance of the diminution of slick professionalism.

Chapter 13

The Virtual Tourist and Sex in Cyberspace

Steven Kohm and John Selwood

The Internet is opening up a whole new "virtual" world of sex tourism. Sex and travel on the Internet are rapidly coming closer to mimicking the experiences available on conventional sex tourism holidays. Indeed, casual sex on the Internet may even offer a more intimate, "real" encounter than one might be able to find in a Nevada brothel, or Amsterdam's Red Light District. Not all of the senses can be stimulated, but enough of them can be sufficiently activiated to allow the imagination to complete the experience. Sex sites on the Internet offer virtual geographies of erotica that can be just as exciting and possibly just as expensive as can be found on a regular sex holiday. From the comfort, convenience, and privacy of the home (or even the office) one can surf the net worldwide for sexual titillation, enjoyment, and satisfaction in almost any imaginable form. Communications technology has overcome the friction of distance to the point where "one's location is of little or no significance for an increasing variety of interactions" (P. C. Adams, 1995). That is, one can now become a "virtual sex tourist" without nearly the hassle, inconvenience, potential violence, or threat of disease connected with conventional tourism travel, and given the relatively anonymous nature of the experience, one might also conclude that cyberspace is the perfect crimogenic environment for the pursuit of illicit sex (Kohm & Selwood, 1997). The question arises: is virtual tourism in cyberspace an "authentic" experience?

Authenticity

The concept of authenticity is widely documented and debated in the tourism literature (e.g., Boorstin, 1985; Cohen, 1988a, 1988b; Crang, 1996; MacCannell, 1976; Squire, 1993; Urry, 1990). Boorstin (1985) has noted that any marketable tourist experience cannot be a "real" event. In fact, "to be repeatable at will they must be factitious" (p. 103). Moreover, in the last century we have seen the rise of completely fabricated tourist destinations that have absolutely no relation to the geography or people at their respective locations (Boorstin, 1985). The principal example of such a tourist attraction is the mother of all inauthentic tourist experiences: Disneyworld. However, others have challenged Boorstin's work. Cohen (1988b) feels that the level of authenticity demanded by "intellectuals and experts" is considerably more than what the average tourist is seeking. Therefore, authenticity must be viewed as a subjective phenomenon, the meaning of which will depend upon the tourists, their expectations, and willingness to "make-believe." Certainly, inherent in cybertravel is the willingness to make-believe. Although people who surf the Internet are keenly aware that the graphics viewed on their monitors are not "real" in the strictest sense of the word, the feeling of having traveled "somewhere" and having done something with some virtual entity on the other side of the globe can be very real. Whether or not these virtual interactions can be classified as "authentic" will vary according to the criteria applied to them.

The question of authenticity has been the subject of a number of studies involving literary and historical tourism (e.g., Crang, 1996; Pocock, 1980, 1982; Squire, 1988, 1994; Zaring, 1977). In the case of literary tourism, Pocock (1982) has pointed out that "we see what we are expecting to see, and overlook that which does not conform to our pattern" (p. 43). Often, literature has shaped and distorted the tourist's experience of place. Squire (1988) has noted that most visitors to Hill Top, the country home of Beatrix Potter "were oblivious to the setting's inherent artificiality" (p. 114). Tourists who visit such places often have formed strong preconceived images of the place through their reading, then look to the actual site for confirmation (Zaring, 1977). Although academics are quick to point out that these tourists are not in fact having an authentic experience, it seems of little consequence to the tourists themselves, or the tour operators.

There is a further manifestation of inauthenticity in tourist destinations: the tourist attraction. "Landscapes of Simulation" (Hopkins, 1990, p. 2) in the form of theme parks and mega-malls are the pinnacle of artificiality. In the case of West Edmonton Mall, shoppers can visit mock-ups of destinations around the world, from Bourbon Street, in New Orleans, to Columbus' ship, the Santa Maria. The tourist visiting the mega-mall encounters the quintessential postmodern experience. The juxtapositioning of a 15th century Spanish ship a stone's throw from a recreation of a 20th century street in the United States, complete with statues of prostitutes (since removed), is as inauthentic an experience as can be had anywhere. Such "imagineering" (Relph, 1987, p. 129) is evident in a number of amusement or theme parks, which have been labeled as "absurd, synthetic places made up of a surrealistic combination of history, myth, reality and fantasy that have little relationship with particular geographical setting" (Relph, 1976, p. 95). An entirely inauthentic form of tourism has grown up around theme parks. Just as with the mega-mall, the theme park offers a contrived touristic experience, often featuring unrelated elements, and always promising to "provide *guaranteed* excitement, amusement, or interest, while eliminating the effort and chance of travel or imagination" (p. 97). The outstanding example of this sort of "disneyfication" (p. 93) is, of course, Walt Disney World, in Florida. This postmodern mecca of inauthenticity was conceived of, and built, as one man's vision of utopia. The built reality, however, is a far cry from that vision. As with most postmodern phenomena, the theme parks built by Disney provide the tourist with an experience akin to channel-surfing with one's television (Sorkin, 1995). The traveler to Disney theme parks is confronted with the question of authenticity like no other tourist. The consumer of heritage tourism might be presented with a somewhat inaccurate portayal of history, or a selection of "snippets and interesting little vignettes" (Crang, 1996, p. 416) that gloss over the mundane. However, in the world of Disney, one has traveled great distances, yet "one has gone nowhere" (Sorkin, 1995, p. 216). Disney theme parks provide the tourist with the most typical of clichés from a variety of destinations around the world. But authenticity is not a static phenomenon. Rather, "'authenticity' is a dynamic, emergent phenomenon . . . and, hence, today's 'staged' attractions may turn into 'authentic' ones tomorrow" (Cohen, 1988a, p. 36). One only has to look at Disney theme parks for confirmation of this statement. What has been harshly criticized by academics as a phoney, staged world of nonsense has, over time, found a secure place within Americana. "For millions of visitors, Disneyland is just like the world, only better" (Sorkin, 1995, p. 216). One might say that Disneyland is "as American as apple pie." Moreover, mega-malls, such as West Edmonton Mall, are becoming legitimate, or "authentic" tourist destinations as well (Butler, 1991).

The Internet is very much like the theme park, and much like television. It is movement, without the necessity of travel. It is a mixture of fact, fiction, and fantasy. As an experience, the Internet does not seem altogether less authentic than a trip through Disneyland. The cybertraveler is able to experience a wide variety of cultures and destinations. One might argue that experiences in cyberspace can be more genuine than those one might have as a tourist on a packaged tour. The Internet permits communication with others around the world in a way that might be impossible or even discouraged on a prepackaged holiday. However, at the same time, those individuals with access to, and interest in, the Internet are certainly not representative of an entire country's population. Nevertheless, cyberspace can be experienced in the same fluid, channel-zapping fashion as Disneyland. Cybertravel is the quintessential postmodern experience: everything is connected, yet nothing truely fits together.

Surfing the Internet can be interpreted as a form of leisure and tourism. Whereas the Internet was once exclusively the realm of a small number of academics, military and government employees, and computer hackers, today it is widely available to the general public. More and more, people are using the Internet as a leisure time activity—even when they are supposed to be at work (Abate, 1996). Just as conventional travel and tourism are popular leisure time activities, the Internet opens up a world of experiences and the opportunity for recreation. Just as the theme park or mega-mall has become "real" and "authentic" with the mass public, so too has the Internet rapidly gained widespread acceptance. Experiences on the Internet have become real and authentic for many.

Virtual Reality

Virtual reality (VR) is a force that promises to have dramatic impact upon the tourism industry in the decades to come. Although still in the early stages of its development, VR promises to alter the way the business of conventional tourism is carried out and, more importantly, it has the potential to rival conventional travel and tourism by enhancing manifestations of "substitute" tourism or by creating a form of "surrogate" tourism (Williams & Hobson, 1994).

Williams and Hobson (1995) have identified several broad areas wherein they believe VR technology will effect change. First, they point to the development of "Virtual" theme parks. At the moment, theme parks offering a sort of VR experience, such as Disney's Star Tours, provide only a partial or pseudo-VR experience. The Star Tours ride does have some of the elements of VR, yet at present has "limited interactive capabilities" (Hobson & Williams, 1995, p. 130). Nevertheless, theme park operators are keen to make use of VR technology because of the potential for profit. Part of the attraction of such "virtual" theme parks is that they are "smaller, cheaper to build and therefore they can be built in densely populated areas, immediately opening up new markets" (Williams & Hobson, 1995, p. 425). Ironically, Disney, in their planned but later abandoned Historical America Park outside of Washington, DC, hope that VR technology will help to make their recreated, and likely sanitized, version of American history feel more "authentic" (Hobson & Williams, 1995, p. 131). Williams and Hobson (1995) suggested that VR has the potential to compete directly "with what the travel agents are offering" (p. 425). Most pertinent to this chapter on the virtual tourist is the the notion that, one day, VR technology may offer a completely artificial form of tourism (Hobson & Williams, 1995; Williams & Hobson, 1994, 1995). Virtual sex tourism has already become an alternative to conventional sex tourism.

In seeking sex on the computer network, the cyberspace traveler already faces a bewildering array of choices. Adult, XXX, or sex-related sites are extremely popular despite desultory efforts to curb them. In addition, with the growing appreciation of the commercial potential of the World Wide Web (WWW), the use of sex to attract customers is becoming widespread, just as it is in the more traditional advertising media (Chapter 2; Kohm & Selwood, 1997; Miller, 1991; Sack, 1988). Sex is used to sell everything from soup to nuts—including sex. Sex is a major commodity, if not the paramount item, for sale on the web.

Virtual Sex Markets

There's something for all tastes in cyberspace, whether it be simply voyeuristic viewing of "naughty" pictures or the satisfaction of the most aberrant needs. Most destinations on the WWW appear to provide services for the more common range of demands. XXX-rated pictures, videos, and CDs, hot chat and phone sex, bondage and discipline (B&D), and "sexual aids" are widely available, whereas the more exotic practices tend to be catered to on the lower profile and longer established Bulletin Board Systems (BBS), File Transfer Protocol (FTP), Internet Relay Chat

(IRC) sites and newsgroups. The latter facilities cater to niche markets for every imaginable form of deviant sexual behavior (Durkin & Bryant, 1995; Rimm, 1995; Rose & Thomas, 1995; Tamosaitis, 1995). Many of these locations carry material judged to be obscene, pornographic, or otherwise unacceptable and are censored by some Internet service providers (ISPs). Such material is therefore marginally less readily available than more conventional sex products and services.

Virtual Sex Tourism Destinations

The virtual sex tourist has many options available, whether they be "authentic" destinations, pure fantasy places, or websites where the location is totally irrelevant to the experience:

a) Authentic destinations conform to the sexually oriented locations of conventional tourism, particularly those that have a national or international reputation. For example, Bangkok, Amsterdam, Tokyo, Sweden, Nevada, and other legendary places receive and supply a great deal of attention. Sweden's *Dreamsex Fantasy World* (www.dreamsex.com) and *Swedish Erotica* (http:pussy.bahnhof.se/Swedish_Erotica) offer a full range of services, as does Amsterdam's *Erotic City* (http://www.euro.net/5thworld/erotic/erotic.htm). Nevada's brothels are featured in *Southern Nevada's Legal Cathouses* (http://www.wizard.com), whereas *Tokyo Topless* features pictures of Asian nudes (http://www.bekkoame.or.jp/~adolf). The pages of the *Single Traveller* (http://www.singletravel.com) provide information on the brothels of Patpong and other Asian centres, as well as various locations in Central America. Many of these sites are essentially travel guides for the person who may wish to visit as a conventional sex tourist, although others merely use the ploy of place to market their wares.

b) Fantasy locations are those that have names which are suggestive of real places, but that only exist in the imagination. Examples of these are: *Eros Island* (http://www.erosisland.com), *Sex Mall* (http://www.sexmall.com), *Intersex City* (http://www.intersex.com), and the like. These sites generally offer a wide range of services, including everything from pictures to various forms of interactive video chat and phone sex lines.

c) The locationally irrelevant sites make no pretense of being geographic places to visit. They focus more on the type of offerings to be expected and/or tend to identify themselves by known personalities or institutions in the sex industry. Names like *Video Vixens* (http://www.videovixens.com), *Amateur Hardcore* (http://www.webpower.com/amateurs), *Hot and Heavy* (http://www.hh.com), *Jordon Lee* (http://www.jordonlee.com) and *Danni Ashe* (http://www.danni.com) the sex queens, *Playboy* (http://www.playboy.com), and *Penthouse* (http://www.penthousemag.com) need little further introduction to seekers after sex. It is also apparent from such names that the "establishment" has invested substantial amounts of capital into the virtual sex trade.

These developments bring into focus the concept of the product life cycle (Kotler & Turner, 1993) and Butler's (1980) model of the tourism area cycle of growth. The sex sites of cyberspace, despite their recent creation, already exhibit similar characteristics to conventional resorts. Sites in the initial or "exploratory" phase of development can be extremely short-lived, or become established and evolve to further stages. Frequently started by an individual as an amusement or diversion, the site may begin to consume too much of that person's time or money to make it feasible to continue. Another complication can be the disapproval of the service provider whose lines become clogged with the increased traffic or who might disapprove of the unseemly use of the site (http://chelsea.ios.com:80/~shyman). In other words, the environment cannot sustain the development, or the host community banishes the developer. If the host is more accommodating, the site moves through the "involvement" stage to the "development" stage wherein the site operator successfully makes the transition from amateur to commercial levels of operation and the site enters into an accelerated growth trajectory. Outside capital flows into the site and the breadth of product offerings increases. Alternatively, heavily capitalized sites may be established along the lines of those created by *Playboy*, that is, they become the sex-oriented cyberspace equivalents of the theme park. The incredibly rapid growth of the Internet makes it unlikely that major sites have reached the "stagnation" stage as yet. User numbers are still skyrocketing and are forecast to continue doing so for some time into the future (Carrol, Broadhead, & Cassel, 1996). New sites are proliferating and existing sites are continually expanding their services as new products, clients, and technologies become available.

The popularity of XXX-rated sites is enormous, although the available statistics are open to challenge. Web counters (e.g., http://www.netcount.com) record the number of "hits" made on a site, but they do not necessarily measure the true nature of its use. For example, *Adult Erotica* claims some 15,000 users daily, but with over 1,000,000 hits a day on its adult sites (http://207.30.50.110/archive.htm). However, usage levels can vary quite dramatically according to time of day, season, weather, demographics, and a number of other variables (O. Friedrich, MBNet Systems Operator, personal communication, 1996). Casual browsers will touch on a site, but not stay there to do more than sample the wares. Visits in transit are particularly high on sites containing large numbers of links to other sites, performing much as major transport hubs where travelers converge before moving on to other destinations. However, unlike the conventional traveler, the virtual tourist can rapidly backtrack and select a new destination. Another problem arises out of the practice of some site operators hitting their own site, thereby artificially raising its ranking on web counters. Nevertheless, there is no arguing with the fact that there are literally thousands of sites that offer XXX-rated material and that their popularity far outstrips that of other sites providing other material. Table 13.1 provides some data, albeit obsolete, that give an indication of the relative rankings of the top XXX-rated sites relative to the overall rankings.

Persian Kitty's Adult Links, the top-ranked site, featuring numerous links, registered an average of some 169,500 hits a day during the last half of June 1996 (http://counter.digits.com/wc/—info=yes/—name=pkadult1996). The level of activity keeps growing as more people join the web and the web offers more to its users.

Table 13.1. Top Twenty Ranked Sites, January 1996

All Sites (Including XXX Adult Sites)		All Sites (Excluding XXX Adult Sites)	
Average Hits per Day	Name	Average Hits per Day	Name
158,477	Persian Kitty's	11,862	This site has EVERYTHING
74,815	Persian Kitty's	6,478	The webWaYs
53,273	The Cream of the Adult Crop	6,081	CyberCite
27,312	Adultery	6,071	Cy-Development
24,809	Netbabes	5,338	A absolutly free page
22,653	XXX-Archive-Free-Girls	5,223	Validate-#1 Age Verification
22,401	Geronimo's Random XXX	5,217	Home Away From Home
19,173	Nikkita's Outrageous Fantasies	4,360	Homepage of Kenneth Lam
16,372	Persian Kitty's	4,355	Wanker Nanny
15,041	The Web's Youngest Women	4,016	Ian's Page of Wonder
14,377	Cybex goes Ballistic	3,977	Roland Rabien's Home Page
13,747	The Beaver Palace	3,874	Alpine World's Web Guide
13,668	The Best Adult Links	3,417	Hanthorn on the Internet
12,346	Deb of the Web	3,162	HomeNet
12,250	For Your Eyes Only	3,114	Internet Services Add Page
11,915	Athena's Nasty Habits	3,070	The Goddess Page
11,858	This site has EVERYTHING	3,048	All Pictures—The Web's
11,690	New Bourbon Index	2,888	Internet Service
11,598	Free Porn Pics	2,842	Cool Page of the Day
11,588	Naughty Lynx	2,825	Wanker Automated Mail

Source: Web counter http://www.digits.com

There is no denying the Internet's capacity to provide authentic experiences. Numerous stories attest to the system's ability to create the full gamut of genuine romantic and sexual encounters, whether these result in casual one-time sex or eventually lead to marriage (Rose & Thomas, 1995:Toufexis, 1996) Even the internationally syndicated columnist, Ann Landers (1996a, 1996b), is now dealing with testaments to the Internet's having brought romance, happiness, and marriage to some, while bringing heartbreak and abuse to others.

On the other hand, virtual reality offers opportunites to dissemble and the anonymity provided by the net carries with it elements of deception. People may not be as they appear. "Gender Bending," mainly by males pretending to be women, is fairly common and can become sinister and traumatic (Durkin & Bryant, 1995, p. 190). Indeed, the net allows its users to disguise their true identity and to indulge in fantasies far more readily than possible in "real" relationships. This is in part because of the volume of users and because elaborate measures have been developed for maintaining user anonymity (Rose & Thomas, 1995). Participants can thereby be persuaded that illicit behavior is rendered safe, with cyberspace a perfect crimogenic place. However, the user is still open to discovery and the contents of so-called private meetings and exchanges can be disclosed.

The Drive for Reality

To become real, virtual sex requires high levels of interactivity. Past trends in sexual activity on the Internet have seen rudimentary email exchanges develop into newsgroups, then "chat lines" involving "Tiny Sex" (sex-based exchanges). These then incorporated MUD (multiuser dungeons), but were still "text only" (Rose & Thomas, 1996, pp. 122–129) and, for the most part, noncommercial in nature. However, with creation of the WWW, commercial chat lines have proliferated, first relying on 1-900 phone connections, but now incorporating both "live" video and real audio at the receiver's end (Carroll et al., 1996). Computer Telephone Integration (CTI) will now permit live chat to move to fully merged and synchronized voice/action, whereas Microsoft and the French company, Thomson SA, now have prototype hybrids that integrate the Internet with big-screen television. Three-dimensional images are becoming available with Virtual Reality Modeling Language (VRML), whereas "hands on" interaction and reaction are available through avatars and TFUI (Touch-and Feel-User-Interface). Each of these technologies is enhancing and heightening the virtual sex experience, leaving less to the imagination and drawing participants into a more comprehensively authentic, yet virtual, experience—at least it does for those who are able to afford the necessary equipment and access charges.

The average virtual traveler still has to submit to the "travails" associated with conventional tourism. As yet, the exchange of experiences is highly likely to be dulled by the sometimes deadly slow transfers across telecommunications channels. The big bottleneck is the lack of bandwidth, largely because of the system's dependence on the almost ubiquitous copper coaxial cables. Replacement with fiber optic cables is regarded as essential, but this will take years to complete. Meanwhile, other developments hold promise, although efficient two-way communications presents problems yet to be overcome. In the more immediate term, seasonality and highly variable traffic over periods of the day should encourage web tourists to travel at off-peak times or be prepared to suffer sometimes interminable delays due to traffic congestion, being bumped (timed out) from their connections, or left hanging because of some system breakdown. Privileged users can avoid much of the inconvenience and discomfort, but the costs can be high. Although sign-on costs can be minimal, subscriptions, passwords, and other tickets to preferred destinations can be extremely expensive, running into several dollars a minute for connection time.

Virtual Sex and the Law

Another impediment to sex on the Internet is government regulation. People have been indicted for distributing and receiving pornography (particularly that involving children) on the net in a number of jurisdictions. The United States, with its heavy traffic, probably boasts the highest number of offenders (Durkin & Bryant, 1995), but other countries, including Canada, China, and Japan, have also been cracking down on such activity.

The United States' Communications Decency Act, designed to prevent children from viewing XXX-rated material on the Internet, made law by President Clinton in February 1996, had a signal impact on the presentation of sexually related material over the net. Major providers such as Compuserve and America On Line (AOL) took steps to curb such content, and despite screams of outrage over the limitation of freedoms, many websites tempered their offerings, no longer making available more extreme forms of sexual activity. However, the myriad USENET and other groups appear to have been largely unaffected by the law. Ironically, the threat of regulation has probably raised prices and increased the costs of access to consumers of sexual material on the net.

The recent Philadelphia Federal Court Panel's injunction blocking the Decency Law and the very rapidity of technological change affecting the Internet suggest that cybersex is here to stay. Although the Federal government is appealing the decision at the United States Supreme Court, it appears doubtful that much more stringent measures can be applied, or that the network will itself develop the capacity to do more than inhibit the exchange of money for sexual services that continues to proliferate. Net providers are beginning to team up with government in seeking self-regulatory solutions to the various emergent problems of the network (Pihichyn, 1996) and this will probably lead to the drafting of a code of ethics to which members will be asked to subscribe. However, the already immense and dramatically rising volume of traffic on the Internet renders effective policing virtually impossible.

Meanwhile, websites are taking steps to protect themselves. Visitors are required to acknowledge their willingnes to view offensive material before gaining access to depictions of explicit sex. Home regulation by parents using software packages such as *Surfwatch*, *Net Nanny*, and *Cybersitter* is also being widely touted by XXX-rated websites. Adult verification systems are also becoming popular. These operations, such as *Adult Pass*, *Adult Check*, and *Validate* charge a fee, with a percentage going to the website generating the business, for obtaining proof of age from the visitor. However, skeptics doubt they will be very effective. Ultimately, it seems that the principal apparatus for regulating the sex trade in cyberspace will be the price. It will certainly ration use of the system.

Conclusion

Judging from the statistics on usage, there will always be the sex tourist searching cyberspace for satiation. Sexual satisfaction from cyberspace will only be limited by users' ability to pay, their personal needs, and their imagination. Sexual encounters are already authentic, although, technically, virtual reality is still in its infancy. Links and transfers are currently slow, but the computer and communications industries are driven irrevocably to provide ever faster exchanges. The experts are also constantly producing new hardware and software that will bring "virtual reality" closer to being REAL. The "feelies" of Aldous Huxley's (1932) *Brave New World* come to mind. And the sex industry will be there to cash in.

Chapter 14

Business Travel and the Emergence of the Modern Chinese Concubine

J. S. Perry Hobson and Vincent Heung

> Having a concubine is another form of prostitution. The only difference is you
> pay monthly and its much safer. (Mr. Wong, *Next*, 1994)

Sex tourism is usually viewed by tourism researchers from the perspective that it
is leisure travel, where the major motivation is be involved in short-term commercial sexual encounters. In this chapter, a different form of sex tourism is discussed.
Here, the type of travel is not for leisure but for business purposes, and the sexual
encounters form part of an established relationship. However, what are regarded as
the main components of sex tourism—travel, sex, and financial exchange—are still
present.

Marriage, the Family, and Concubines

In traditional Chinese society, marriage was seen as a long-term commitment.
Baitou daolao—meaning "to be together forever"—was seen as the goal for Chinese couples. Historically, a number of feudal practices surrounded marriage in
China. Among these were various forms of arranged marriage such as child betrothal and "blind" weddings, as well as the selling of brides. One of the duties of
the wife was to provide a son for her husband. The significance of having a male
descendent was that he could carry on the family name, provide for their parents
in their old age (part of the filial duties), and inherit land or take over the family
business.

Inequality between the sexes was institutionalized within Chinese society. For
women, fornication, adultery, and premarital sex were unacceptable and considered a "sin." Although divorce was theoretically available, in practice it was only
possible under extreme conditions, and was normally only available to the husband. Any problems with a marriage was automatically seen as being the fault of
the woman. In comparison with Western society, one feature of Chinese norms

surrounding marriage was that men could take a number of secondary wives as concubines. This was a right that the "primary" wife had no legal right to prevent. The man would have to be able to support the concubines, and traditionally they would live in the same household as the "primary" wife. Concubines provided not only additional sexual services for the male but could be used to reproduce. If the primary wife could not have children, or did not provide a son, a concubine could be used to provide an heir. Given that China has essentially been a feudal society throughout most of its history, only wealthy men could afford to keep both a wife and concubines (Parish & Whyte, 1978).

After the 1949 Communist revolution, the Communist Party set out to change the ancient feudal practices, particularly those relating to the family and marriage. Traditional values such as filial duty and ancestor worship had no place in a Communist belief system. The 1950 Marital Law outlawed concubinage, child betrothal, and the sale of sons and daughters into marriage or prostitution. Other sexual relationships outside marriage were considered unlawful and women were permitted to sue for divorce (Davis & Harrell, 1993). In the intervening years, the Communist Party has tried to prevent the traditional practices it banned from reemerging. But social engineering has not been easy. Given China's rapidly growing population, it was in 1979 that Communist Party decided to become even more intrusive on the family, when it instituted its national "one-child" policy. In the following year, the new 1980 Marriage Law was passed, which laid down minimum ages for marriage: 20 years of age for women and 22 for men.

Hong Kong—Its Changing Social Norms

Hong Kong is located in the southeast part of China at the mouth of the Pearl River Delta. Since 1841 it has been governed as a British territory, but it was returned to Chinese sovereignty as a Special Administrative Region (SAR) in July, 1997. It is a small and crowded place, with limited natural resources and a population of some 6 million. Hong Kong is an economic success story and, over the past two decades, its economy has more than quadrupled in value. It has established itself as a major international trade and financial center and in 1995 was ranked the eighth largest trading entity in the world.

It should be remembered that the vast majority of the residents of Hong Kong left China in the last 40 years. They are migrants, who have often left behind not only their extended family, but also the traditions of a rural society in exchange for a highly urbanized one. Given the strictly limited numbers of mainland Chinese permitted to emigrate legally into Hong Kong, families have often been split and dislocated for years. The recent historical experience of China has included a Communist revolution, a socialist economic system, and limited influence from the West. On the other hand, Hong Kong has experienced not only sustained economic growth in a capitalist system, but also a stable and semidemocratic government structure. The residents of Hong Kong have been exposed to Western thought and ideas through the influence of the British school system, the media, and the ability to travel freely and study abroad.

Consequently, many traditional Chinese values concerning the family are no longer held as absolutes in Hong Kong. As with other overseas newly industrialized Chinese-based societies, such as Singapore and Taiwan, couples are marrying later and having fewer children. In Hong Kong the average age for marriage is 28.2 years for women, and 30.5 years for men (Hong Kong Census and Statistics Department [HKCSD], 1991). Married couples are also opting to have fewer children, and the fertility rate in Hong Kong has declined from an average of 3.46 children per female in 1971 to 1.23 children by 1991 (HKCSD, 1991). Furthermore, much less emphasis is now placed on having a son. The status of women in society has also changed. Women have a high labor participation rate in Hong Kong's workforce, they are often financially independent, and many have leading roles in society. In addition, they are increasingly unlikely to put up with the traditional customs and roles that they were supposed to subscribe to. The role and rights of the Chinese male have been challenged as women have been able to assert their position in society.

One unique social factor that has affected many marriages and families in Hong Kong also deserves mention at this point. It relates to the preemptive actions taken in the lead-up to the resumption of Chinese sovereignty in 1997. Following the Tiananmen Square incident in 1989, many Hong Kong families have been looking to acquire foreign citizenship. They have hoped that such an "insurance policy" will safeguard the future for themselves and their children. This has often meant that the families have had to establish residency in a foreign country (usually a period of 2–5 years) before they can acquire citizenship and a passport. It is believed that at the moment there are already up to 600,000 Hong Kong Chinese holding some type of foreign passports or residency agreement. One result has been that it is not uncommon to find family members separated for an extended period of time. A typical pattern of the relocation is for the wife and children to live in the adopted country (such as Canada, Australia, New Zealand, or the US) where a second home is established. Meanwhile, the husband commutes to and from Hong Kong for much of the time. In Hong Kong these commuting husbands are commonly refereed to as "astronauts"—because they spend so much time above the planet.

Table 14.1. Hong Kong Divorce Statistics, 1985–1994

	1985	1988	1991	1994
Petitions filed[a]	5,047	5,893	7,287	9,272
Divorce decrees	4,313	5,098	6,295	7,735

[a]Figures include defended cases.
Source: HKCSD, 1995

Hong Kong is acknowledged to be one of the world's most stressful cities in which to live. In such a highly pressured environment, which has experienced such rapid social change, it is perhaps not surprising to see that the institution of marriage and family has suffered. In the last 10 years, Hong Kong has experienced a steadily increasing divorce rate (see Table 14.1) with approximately one in three marriages ending in divorce. Although such figures do not reveal all the facts, they are perhaps an indication of such social change.

Hong Kong and China: The New Economic Relationship

After WWII, Hong Kong developed itself into a low-cost manufacturing center as well as a trans-shipment point for China. Following the end of the "Cultural revolution" in 1978, Deng Xiaoping launched his "Open Door" policy and a range of economic reforms. His official call to China's citizens was that "to get rich is glorious." In order to encourage rapid economic growth he urged China's population to "cross a new threshold every few years." In 1980, a number of Special Economic Zones (SEZs) were established in southern China (Table 14.2), and by this time Hong Kong was no longer such a cheap manufacturing base. Its standard of living had dramatically improved, and land and labor costs were rising. Consequently, many of Hong Kong's factories were relocated to China to take advantage of lower land and labor costs. In the intervening 15 years, Hong Kong has shifted the focus of its economic base from being a manufacturing center to that of a service sector economy. By the mid-1990s, the importance of the service sector was clearly reflected in its contribution to over 80% of Hong Kong's GDP and employment of some 78% of the entire labor force (Hang Seng Bank, 1996). By contrast, Hong Kong companies now employ about 3 million people in the Pearl River Delta of China, more than they actually employ in Hong Kong itself (Linn, 1995).

Business Travel to China From Hong Kong

Since 1980, the economic relations between Hong Kong and China have become much closer, necessitating a considerable volume of business-related travel. The migration of Hong Kong manufacturing base to southern China has also meant that an increasingly large number of Hong Kong owners, managers, supervisors, techni-

Table 14.2. China's Special Economic Zones (SEZs)

SEZ	Location	Area (sq. km)	Time of Establishment
Shenzhen	Guangdong	328	August 1980
Zhuhai	Guangdong	121	August 1980
Shantou	Guangdong	53	August 1980
Xiamen	Fujian	131	August 1980
Hainan	Hainan	34,000	April 1988

Source: Huang (1989).

cal consultants, and truck drivers have had to make business trips to the new plants. Consequently, the number of visits by Hong Kong Chinese across the border into China has been steadily increasing (see Table 14.3) and, in 1994, 25 million trips to China were made by Hong Kong residents.

Internal Migration Patterns in China

The implementation of Deng's economic policies has seen the SEZs and the surrounding parts of southern China develop rapidly. The last 18 years of economic growth have, however, increased the economic disparity between the coastal region and the hinterland provinces. As a result of this growing income inequality between the regions, substantial numbers of workers from inland provinces have migrated to the more developed and prosperous areas of Southern China (Anonymous, 1996). Despite attempts by the Chinese authorities to limit who can live in the SEZs, the prospect of making two-to-three times the average rural wage has kept the waves of migrated workers coming. In Guangdong province, with its need for labor, the total number of migrants has grown from 5 million in 1989 to 11 million by 1995 (B. Gilley, 1996). The SEZs have developed rapidly. To put the growth in perspective, it should be pointed out that in 1979, the year before Shenzhen was declared a SEZ, it was a small border town with a population of less than 40,000. Some 15 years later, Shenzhen has been transformed into a city with a population of some 3.7 million.

China has pushed a "one-child" family policy. In many rural areas, the economic prospects for women have not been good. Whereas it is more likely that the men were able to stay on the land and farm, young women have had to look elsewhere to earn a living that could help support their family. In looking for cheap, compliant, and diligent factory labor, Shenzhen has attracted millions of young women from across China. In Shenzhen alone, the *da gong mei* (working sisters) account for over 50% of the migrant labor force and heavily outnumber the local population (B. Gilley, 1996). Such an influx of women has massively distorted the normal population statistics. In the early 1990s the gender ratio of females to males in Shenzhen was officially put as 5:1 (Chan & Tsui, 1993), though some informal

Table 14.3. Trips to China Through Hong Kong 1990–1994

Year	Hong Kong Visitors (Millions)	Growth (%)	Foreign Visitors (Millions)	Growth (%)
1990	17	10	1.2	20
1991	19	14	1.4	12
1992	21	13	1.7	28
1993	23	8	1.9	10
1994	25	7	2.0	5

Source: HKCSD (1995).

studies have indicated that it has reached as high as 7:1, if all the women who are living illegally in Shenzhen are included.

Increasing Availability of Sexual Services in Southern China

There is a Chinese saying that "people ridicule poverty but not prostitutes." The sheer numbers of single women brought to work in the SEZs have been significant, but the conditions in which they are expected to work and live are notoriously poor. Lax health and safety regulations have seen periodic industrial accidents, killing workers in the factories or while they sleep in the dormitories. In addition, many of the women that come to the SEZs do not have permission from the Chinese authorities to be there. This has sometimes made getting official employment difficult. Furthermore, there is considerable pressure to remit money to their families in the rural areas they came from.

With the demand for sexual services from the increasing number of Hong Kong and international visitors, prostitution has become a flourishing industry in Shenzhen (Anonymous, 1995). Whether it is in the "barbershops" or karaoke bars, sexual services are widely available. As Elliott (1996) noted, "Prostitution is more blatant in Shenzhen than just about any other Chinese city. Dolled-up girls try to wrestle pedestrians into the barbershops that front for brothels" (p. 11). But a number of new twists on prostitution have been developed in Shenzhen. Hong Kong's *East Magazine* (Yik, 1995), reported that five or six "porn stables" have been set up in the lounges of Shenzhen hotels. The prostitutes, known as female "horses," have to pay a HK$50 (US$7) entrance fee. The men then pay HK$200 (US$25) to take a horse to their table, additional services at the horse's table cost upwards of HK$750 (US$100). Another derivative reported by *Next* magazine (Cheuk & Chon, 1995) includes luxurious yellow "sex tour" coaches with female tour guides who are available to provide sexual services to the guests while they are on the bus. Reportedly most of the men came from Hong Kong, Taiwan, and Japan. Although Shenzhen does not have a defined red light district (though it should be noted that the Chinese associated the color yellow with the sex industry—and not red or blue as in the West), the city thrives on a get-rich-quick-anyhow mentality.

It is clear that the availability of sexual services has recently grown in southern China. What is interesting to note, however, is that in addition to increases in prostitution, the SEZs have also witnessed another social phenomenon. This has been the reemergence of one of China's ancient traditions—that of men taking a concubine.

The Emergence of the Modern Chinese Concubine

The economic prosperity of Hong Kong means that many of the men traveling into China have significant amounts of disposable income. Many Hong Kong men are either making frequent business-related trips into China or are there for extended periods of time on their own. Such Hong Kong travelers could use a series of prostitutes during their visits. However, keeping a woman on a financial retainer as a concubine has now presented itself as a viable option. It appears that there are a number of advantages. It is safer than having multiple sexual partners and cheaper than paying for individual prostitutes, and it offers the conveniences of being "at home." In addition, the border between Hong Kong and China provided an additional amount of security in keeping the relationship hidden from the wife and family in Hong Kong.

To many young mainland Chinese women, finding a Hong Kong man to pay the bills is much more lucrative and stable and less dangerous than prostitution or working in a factory. A young peasant woman from a poor province in northern China could make more as much as 20 times the average wage. She might even have a child, possibly one day gaining the right to live in Hong Kong. Because of these factors, most women really do not care if the man has a wife across the border (Elliott, 1996a). If a Hong Kong man wants to establish a woman as a concubine, he normally rents her a flat. The rent for a flat with two bedrooms and a living room costs HK$900–1,500 (US$120–200) per month. He will then pay HK$2,000–4,000 (US$250–550) to cover food, clothing, and traveling expenses ("Crackdown on Concubine Keepers," 1995).

Needless to say, there has been considerable speculation in Hong Kong about the number of men involved and the extent of this phenomenon. When looking into a subject such as this, it must be accepted that it is notoriously difficult to get meaningful data. However, a survey in *Next* magazine (Yiu, 1994) of 200 Hong Kong male and female residents (see Table 14.4) revealed that 29% knew someone that had a concubine in China. The survey found that the majority of men (54%) seemed quite happy with the notion of taking a concubine. Interestingly, a similar percentage of women (56%) were concerned that their husbands might actually do so if they went to work in China. The main attraction (38%) seen by men for having a concubine over the border in China was that it would be much cheaper than having one in Hong Kong. On finding out that their husband had a concubine, the main response anticipated by Hong Kong women was ending the marriage by divorce (41%). Although it should be acknowledged that this survey is not representative of the wider Hong Kong population, it does lead someway towards an understanding of some current social attitudes surrounding this issue in Hong Kong.

The different social values of Hong Kong men and women are also reflected in the comments of those who were surveyed. Many men seemed to take a financial view of the situation. Typical comments included, "It's no big deal to have a concubine if you have extra money." A salesman who worked in Hong Kong felt that, "It's nothing to do with right or wrong when one party is willing to pay for the services provided by the other party. Although it is immoral to have a concubine, it actually is helping in developing the Chinese economy." Such views were not shared by the women surveyed. Some women clearly recognized that men may be too tempted if they travel into China for business. A secretary for a legal firm, pointed out, "If my

Table 14.4. Survey on Attitudes of Hong Kong Residents to Concubines

General question to both male and female respondents:
(1) Do you know of any person that has a concubine in China?
      Yes: 29%
      No: 71%

Questions to male respondents:
(2) If the opportunity arose would you take a concubine?
      Yes: 54%
      No: 28%
      Don't know: 18%
(3) What is the main reason for having a concubine in China?
      Its cheap: 38%
      The women are not so demanding: 18%
      Easier to get rid of one woman and get another one: 15%
      No need to get married: 14%
      All of the above: 15%

Questions to female respondents:
(4) Would you worry if your husband had to work in China?
      Yes: 56%
      No: 15%
      Don't know: 29%
(5) What would you do if you discover your husband has a concubine?
      Divorce him: 41%
      Ask him to leave the woman: 28%
      Tolerate it: 6%
      Use violence: 2%
      Don't know: 23%

Source: Yiu (1994).

boyfriend has to work in China, I will definitely ask him to quit his job. It's too dangerous!" Some women seemed to recognize the inevitability of the "concubine phenomenon." A nurse observed that, "Men need women mentally and physically. When a man works in China alone, it's normal to get a concubine. The wife shouldn't tolerate this though" (Yiu, 1994).

At first, it might be assumed that having a concubine would be the sole prerogative of middle- or upper-class males from Hong Kong. However, the anecdotal evidence suggests that initially most of the concubines were kept by working-class males from Hong Kong, particularly by truck drivers. On investigating this, *Next* magazine (Pat & Chan, 1994) reported that they believed that a significant percentage (80%) of truck drivers that deliver goods from China to Hong Kong had a concubine on the Chinese side of the border. Most of the women are kept at a place called Huangbeiling, which is near to the main Shenzhen's border crossing points for trucks. Locally, the area is know as "Concubine Village" ("Case Studies from the Concubine Village," 1995). Hong Kong truck drivers have to make frequent trips into China, and it is not unusual for them to have to stay overnight in China. Whereas they may have low socioeconomic status in Hong Kong, the value of their Hong Kong dollars gives them considerably higher standing in China. As Pamela Pak, a Hong Kong radio talk-show points out, "In Hong Kong they might be a truck driver or even a street sweeper, with no status. . . . But, when they go across the border to their concubines they get treated like gods" (Elliott, 1996b).

To more fully comprehend the phenomenon of the modern concubine, it is perhaps useful to review some case examples in order to get a better understanding of the situation.

> **Case 1:** Tao, a 19-year-old girl, became a concubine after working in a "karaoke" bar for three months. She earned HK$3,000 (US$390) per month before she met a driver from Hong Kong. After spending the first night together, the man, Chan, asked Tao to be his concubine. Initially, Tao did not take the idea seriously because she thought Chan did not mean it. After a few days, Chan came back and this time they discussed the proposal in detail. Chan asked Tao to live with two other women, who were the concubines of his friends, in a three-bedroom flat. Chan paid the rent for Tao and gave her a further HK$4,000 (US$520) for living expenses. The condition was that Tao had to give up her job in the karaoke bar. Her view was "Yes, my boyfriend has a wife and two children in Hong Kong. But it doesn't matter, provided that he can take care of me and let me save some money for my family, that's good enough. There is no commitment between us. He can leave me anytime, and I can leave him whenever I want." (Pat & Chan, 1994)

It would appear that an increasing number of middle-class males are now taking concubines. The *Hong Kong Economic Journal* (Leung, 1995) reported that, "Having a concubine is not only restricted to the lower levels of society anymore, many middle level and professional people are also becoming involved" (p. 3). When reporting on the new concubine phenomenon, Chen and Choi (1993) found that for Chinese migrant women Hong Kong managers were the most desirable. In an informal survey conducted in Shenzhen, the rating scale of the most popular type of man was (1) the Hong Kong factory manager, (2) a Hong Kong supervisor, (3) a local Shenzhen-based business owner, (4) a local Shenzhen-based supervisor.

> **Case 2:** Heung is a 20-year-old Chinese woman. Her "husband" is a Hong Kong businessman who has a factory in Guangzhou. Heung used to be an trainer in the factory, but after a while she became the concubine of the owner. She is given a total allowance of HK$6,000 (US$780) a month, and lives in a well equipped 800 sq. ft flat with three bedrooms and two living rooms. Heung knew that the man had a wife right from the beginning. She pointed out that, "All men are like this. I don't mind being a concubine as long as he's nice to me." Heung said she wanted to marry the man one day, but she knew that it would be very difficult for the man to get divorced after so many years of marriage. ("Case Studies from the Concubine Village," 1995)

Effects on the Family in Hong Kong

Considerable concern has been expressed in Hong Kong in the last 10 years about the ever-growing social problem of extra-marital affairs. In 1994 ("Extra-marital Affairs," 1995), the Caritas Family Services and the Department of Social Work and Social Administration at the University of Hong Kong looked into some case histories. They examined 421 couples who had sought marriage counseling from Caritas Family Services. It was found that the most likely person to be involved in extra-marital affairs was male (93%), over 40 years of age (53%), was in a job requiring overtime or frequent business trips (68%), and earned HK$10,000–20,000 (US$1,300–2,600) per month. In terms of the types of extra-marital affairs, it was found that the majority of these affairs (70%) were stable long-term relationships. However, a significant percentage (20%) were found to involve the partner paying for a concubine in China or using prostitutes. The minority (10%) were occasional affairs.

> **Case 3:** Mary Chan, 42, is a Hong Kong housewife and mother of two teenagers. Her husband works as a trader in China, and began having casual affairs in Hong Kong. Then he began going to China on lengthy business trips. Slowly it became clear to her that he had taken a concubine over the border. She pointed out that, "He says I have no right to question his other relationships. . . . I can't interfere." In this situation, history was repeating itself, as Mary's mother was the first of two wives. As has been noted, Chinese women are not supposed to questions what their husbands do. If the men seek out other affairs, then its automatically the wife's fault because she is obviously neglecting her husband's needs. She concluded by pointing out that when she discovered what was going on she was "devastated, but I just have to keep quiet." (Harris, 1996)

It would appear that fewer women in Hong Kong are prepared to "keep quiet" and put up with their husband's infidelities. As indicated, Hong Kong women are prepared to take action by initiating divorce proceedings. However, there is considerable concern that the breakdown of the family in Hong Kong is leading to a number of other social problems in the territory. Issues such as the increase in youth crime and looking after the elderly are seen as problems flowing from the breakdown of the traditional Chinese family structure (Leung, 1995).

Action Taken by the Authorities and Wives

Although the Hong Kong authorities can do little about the concubines, the Chinese Public Security Bureau (PSB) in the SEZs has periodic crackdowns. The Chinese authorities have found that most of the concubines are living in the SEZs illegally, and a number of them have also been found to engage in part-time prostitution in the karaoke bars while their "husbands" are back in Hong Kong. If the women are caught and their "home-away-from-home" status is discovered, their "husbands" can be detained and face questioning by the PSB for aiding and abetting residents from other provinces to live illegally in the SEZs ("Crackdown on

Concubine Keepers," 1995). The concubine would be arrested and sent back to her home village.

However, the seriousness of some of concubine-"husband" relationships has meant that a number of Hong Kong men have taken the relationship a step further—by actually marrying their concubine. Needless to say this has caused a variety of complications for both the Hong Kong and Chinese authorities. Polygamy is illegal, but getting the evidence and proof can be difficult. But as Case 4 shows, legal actions have been initiated by some Hong Kong wives.

> **Case 4:** In a case reported in 1996, Mr. Lu, who had a wife in Hong Kong, took a concubine in China. Meanwhile, his wife was moved to Canada to establish residency. In the meantime, he married his concubine in China. His wife found out, and gave her husband three months to make up his mind what he wanted to do. But as he refused to make a decision, his wife took both her husband and the "second wife" (concubine) to a local ZhongShang court in China for polygamy. In the ensuing trial, the "second wife" claimed that she did not know that her husband was married. Both of them were sent to jail—the man for one year and the "second wife" for three months. (Yan, Chen, & Lee, 1996)

Conclusion

> The concubine problem will be solved automatically once the economy of China improves, because it will be too costly. (Mr. Leung, *Next*, 1994)

Unlike other forms of sex tourism, it is unlikely that this new concubine phenomenon has resulted in a significant increase in the flow of travel between Hong Kong and southern China. In this case it would appear that the majority of trips were initiated by, or are associated with, some form of necessary business travel. But it should be acknowledged that Hong Kong residents with concubines may be making more trips than they would otherwise need to, and may also be staying longer. Unfortunately, it is virtually impossible to assess the impact of the "modern concubine phenomenon" on increased travel. Rather, this phenomenon is of interest to tourism researchers as it has brought to light a range of other social impacts that have occurred as a result of business travel.

Clearly a number of other factors have contributed to the reemergence of the concubine phenomenon. The social and economic situations in Hong Kong and China have been in a state of flux. This will continue into the foreseeable future. As the power of the Communist Party wanes in China, a number of the traditional "feudal" practices are reemerging and becoming acceptable practices again. Davis and Harrell (1993) have noted that, "The retreat of the state during the 1980s may have permitted a revival of cultural preferences and economic forces that the Maoist state held in check, but did not eliminate. During the 1980s, teenage marriages and even child betrothal began to reappear in rural areas. There was also an explosive increase in marriage expenditures and the return to lavish dowries and high bride price" (p. 6). Along with reemergence of these practices, concubinage is another recognized Chinese tradition. The "Open Door" policy and its economic reforms brought not only Hong Kong capital to southern China, but also capitalist ideas about being able to make money and getting rich. The massive inflow of single women into the SEZs, connected with the increasing number of Hong Kong business men to China, meant that there was a plentiful supply of women who were looking to change their economic circumstances. The realignment of social values in China, and the economic and labor situation in the SEZs, has meant that a significant number of mainland Chinese women have been willing to accept financial payment to become the concubine of a Hong Kong-based business traveler. It has ended up as a modern twist to an ancient tradition.

After 1997, Hong Kong will be further integrated into China (Hobson & Ko, 1994). As communications and freedom to travel improve, the border may become less of a barrier and it may be harder for men to keep their concubines a secret from their Hong Kong wives and the authorities. Furthermore, as the economic disparity between the Hong Kong Special Administration Region (SAR) and the SEZs lessens, it may become too costly to keep a concubine in southern China. But given the sheer size of China, it is unlikely that the problem will be totally solved. There are numerous poorer regions in the hinterland areas of China, where the emergence of the "modern concubine phenomenon" will again offer single women an economic and social alternative. Consequently, China's modern-day concubines are likely to be with us for some time yet.

Chapter 15

Where There Are No Tourists . . . Yet: A Visit to the Slum Brothels in Ho Chi Minh City, Vietnam

Malcolm Cooper and Jody Hanson

The 11th General Assembly of the World Tourism Organization (WTO), held in Cairo in October 1995, condemned organized sex tourism. The resulting declaration rejected all such activity as exploitative and subversive to the fundamental objectives of tourism. The declaration requested governments of both tourism destination and origin countries to issue guidelines to their tourism industries insisting that they refrain from organizing any form of sex tourism and from exploiting prostitution as a tourist attraction. We argue in this chapter that this type of approach to regulating the sex industry creates a "them/us" approach, which ignores the economic realities of its position in most societies.

The declaration overlooks the local supply and demand components of the sex industry in modern society. It also ignores the simple fact that people are survivors: if there is a societal demand for sex, then there are people who will supply it at an economic price. Rosa Luxemburg, writing at the beginning of the 20th century, noted that

> Prostitution is as little specifically Russian as tuberculosis; it is rather the most international institution of social life. But although it plays an almost controlling part in our modern life, officially, in the sense of the conventional life, it is not approved of as a normal constituent of present-day society. Rather it is treated as the scum of humanity, as something allegedly beyond the pale. (Luxemburg, 1927, p. 348)

For many people, in the developing world especially, it is one of the few realistic options for earning a decent income, particularly for young uneducated women from rural areas. Given that the wages of factory and domestic servant jobs—the other two options open to women in this group—are so low, it is little wonder that they opt for prostitution. There is no real alternative economic choice for this group. For others associated with the sex industry, such as bar owners or pimps, it may be their only way of trying to increase their financial base and establish personal power and control.

This chapter looks at the sex industry and tourism within the reality of Vietnam as a developing country where rural overpopulation and the demands of an emerging and diversifying urban economy are rapidly transforming economic and social relationships. And one where the outside world, in the guise of tourism, is also beginning to impinge on national and local life-styles. The sex industry has always been a significant part of socioeconomic relationships in the personal service industry within any human community; therefore, the sex industry in Vietnam must be analyzed within this context to be properly understood. As a consequence, any analysis of the Vietnamese sex industry in relation to emerging patterns of tourism must also acknowledge that tourists merely constitute a particularized and specific market for that industry. This is not to say, however, that the patterns of power and control inherent in the operation of the sex industry in many countries do not have significant implications for the safety, health, and welfare of the people involved in it, particularly the women who work as prostitutes. In many countries, the sex industry is an important part of the system of political and financial control in the economy (see Chapter 16), exercising a role similar to drugs, arms, and other forms of illegal trade. Often too, it is controlled or heavily influenced by foreign interests as well as by indigenous criminal elements.

It is the intention of the authors to examine briefly the characteristics of the sex industry in relation to tourism as revealed in neighboring countries and, thus, to highlight the similarities and differences observed during field trips to Vietnam. The suggestion is made that as a developing industry in postwar Vietnam, the sex trade need not experience the same oppressive forms of power and control as evidenced in other countries. Nor does it have to be influenced by foreigners who become involved in the sex industries in other countries, if it is kept in local hands and does not become, as the WTO characterizes it, part of a organized pattern of sex tourism originating from and for the benefit of nationals of other countries.

Economy, Tourism, and the Development Debate

World interest in tourism as a development option stems from its foreign exchange employment, income, government revenue, and regional development potential (Walton, 1993). From the point of view of the WTO and many governments, the benefits to be gained from the development of tourism can—if properly har-nessed—be used to overcome resource problems, increase economic well-being, and further facilitate development (World Tourism Organization [WTO], 1994). This perspective on tourism is widely supported in the literature, although its draw-backs are now beginning to be outlined (Sinclair & Vokes, 1993).

Tourism as an Economic Growth Generator in Asia

In the 1980s, especially in the latter part of that decade, many Asian governments strongly committed themselves to the development of an international tourist industry in the firm belief that to do so would bring substantial economic benefits. Foreign exchange earnings and the creation of employment opportunities were identified as the major reasons for tourism development, with other factors such as an ability to promote regional development also being taken into consideration. Moreover, it was believed that tourism, as one of the world's fastest growing economic sectors, could bring relatively rapid returns to investment. Vietnam is just the latest Asian country to declare the importance of tourism to national development (Vietnamese National Administration of Tourism [VNAT], 1995).

Although there has been some variation in strategies, Asian governments have generally accorded high priority to tourism development through special investment and tax concessions. They have also substantially increased financial backing to revitalized or recently established tourist promotion boards and programs (Din, 1989; Oppermann, 1992; Shen, 1993; Tisdall & Wen, 1991). However, the desirability of these measures has not been accepted by all members of their societies and the growth of tourism has been questioned from both moderate and extreme points of view (Richter, 1993). The latter view argues that tourism should be banned altogether whereas the former suggests that the economic benefits from tourism should be weighed carefully against the environmental and social, as well as economic, costs of tourism development (Hall, 1992).

Employment and the Sex Industry

Even if favorable economic impacts should occur in Vietnam, it is important to realize that the pattern of overwhelming concentration of low-paid employment opportunities within the tourism sector in most countries will also occur. The rapid rural–urban migration found in developing nations has changed the circumstances in which many young people now have to live, the towns in which they live, and how they have to earn a living. Often the only jobs they can get are as waitresses, receptionists, bar girls, dancers, tour guides, and street merchants. The extent to which they engage in sex-for-cash is often in direct relationship to their ability to earn money in other low-skill occupations in the rapidly growing cities.

In northeast Thailand, for example, the girls from poverty-stricken rural areas seek to perform the expected filial duty of providing support for their families when they are recruited into Bangkok's massage parlors. Initially, it is not their aim to enter the sex trade as a preferred life-style. Where the new cities beckon as a way out of rural poverty, urban employment is often viewed as an economic safety net for the families who remain on the farm, rather than as a "new horizon" for all. The young leave to find work and money to send back to the village. In the sex trade they can earn, relatively, a lot of money (Black, 1994).

Nevertheless, as Cohen (1993) noted, although prostitution for local customers is far more prevalent, the foreign customer-oriented sex trade remains extremely important to Thailand's accumulation of foreign capital and also to political influence in that country. In Thailand, the sex trade is centralized and oligopolistic (Fish, 1984), with active involvement of the military and the police. As a result, brothel owners are a strong political and economic force (Leheny, 1995).

The supply and demand factors related to employment in any country, together with different cultural views of prostitution in different settings, are the most important influences at work. The role played by international tourism—especially pedophile tourism in promoting prostitution—has been much overrated (Cohen, 1993; Leheny, 1995). The world's oldest profession has always been plied around men away from home: soldiers, sailors, traders, pilgrims (see Chapter 1). The international businessman and the tourist are just today's most numerous and usually most free-spending customers. They contribute to an expansion in the sex industry generally and, to that extent, they play an important role, but the majority of customers for prostitutes are neither foreigners nor tourists. Except in a few special resort locations, tourists are not the demons of commercialized sexual abuse, as they have been portrayed by the media (Hanson, 1996a).

As Black (1994) suggested, the onus of guilt carried by tourists is partly explained by their visibility. There is the fact that very few societies want to admit that they, in part, rely on the sex trade for significant economic benefit or that they condone prostitution. And where the evidence is undeniable, it is often easier to blame the "unclean other"—decadent foreigners with their incomprehensible tastes and misbehaviors. However, there is in fact no need to look further than the rigid control of girls and women, which used to and often still does operate in most societies, to recognize that the notion of innocence perverted by the evil outsider is far-fetched. Most societies were by no means so simple that they did not per-ceive the risk to girls of lascivious male intent, but the circumstances in which they can continue these protections—customs such as early marriage and purdah (which women activists deplore)—are vanishing and nothing has been put in their place. Girls venture out into the world and are obliged, for one reason or another, to enter the workplace. They are young, sexually mature, undereducated, and ill-prepared for adult life. Their options are limited and the outcome is often a fore-gone conclusion (Richter, 1993).

Despite near universal literacy in Vietnam, for example, the majority of the sur-veyed labor force in the tourism industry remains virtually untrained (Table 15.1).

Table 15.1. Estimated Number and Qualifications of Tourism Employees, 1995

Employment Category	Number	Level of Training	Number
Tourism service	6,000	technical training	25,000
Hotel service	60,000	on-job training	20,000
Related to hotel service	15,000	university degree	2,000
Management	7,500		
Total employees	88,500	total trained employees	47,000

Source: VNAT (1995).

The general conclusion that international tourism can be of significant economic benefit to people in developing countries should not obscure the fact that this so-called gain is often brought about by significant rural–urban migration, low-paid part-time employment, and employment in industries such as the sex trade. The task confronting policymakers in Vietnam is to foster the development of tourism while lessening the impact of development on their people. The role of the brokers of tourism—agents, guides, and the hotel and brothel owners, the police and the politicians—will be crucial in this transition.

Vietnamese Tourism: An Alternative Sex Tourism Plan

Vietnam has significant potential for tourism development. It has attractive natural resources such as beaches, lakes, forests, mountain ranges, and many rare species of fauna and flora, as well as a rich and diverse cultural heritage. Some of the recent war sites, such as the Cu Chi tunnels, have also become tourist attractions. The 1995 Master Plan for Tourism Development outlines the expected main features of the Vietnamese tourism sector to the year 2010. This plan, developed by the Viet Nam National Administration of Tourism (VNAT, 1995) on the basis of work carried out by the World Tourism and Travel Organization, is a comprehensive document covering the development of the Vietnamese tourism sector since 1989 and shows that Vietnam has significant potential for tourism development over the next 15 years. In the longer term, the wider Indochinese region has similar potential and Vietnam hopes to act as a gateway for the rest of the region, particularly Cambodia and Laos.

The Tourism Master Plan identifies the tourism sector as a significant potential earner of foreign exchange for Vietnam. Turnover from tourism (not including transportation) is predicted to reach US$1.06 billion by 2000 and around US$8 billion in 2010 (1989 US$). In 1993, the "tourism branch" of the economy made up 2.8% of Vietnam's GDP. When transport and other tourism-related "branches" are included, the sector contributes 5.8%. This is expected to rise to around 10% by 2000 and to 20% by 2010.

Vietnam experienced the highest rate of growth of all the East Asia/Pacific tourism destinations during 1994–1995 (22.8%) with the Philippines (20.4%) and Indonesia (14.7%) second and third, respectively. Statistics from the Tourism Master Plan (TMP) indicate that the single largest group of tourist visitors to Vietnam (21%) are "overseas Vietnamese"—emigres returning to visit. The next largest groups are Taiwanese (20%), French (10%), Japanese (7%), Americans (4.5%), and British (4%). A further 27% are described as "others."

These figures suggest that, with organized Japanese sex tourism declining in recent years due to changes in the composition of Japanese outbound tourism (Leheny, 1995), and the other major groups not to date being noted for promoting this aspect of tourism in host communities, it may be that the Vietnamese need not see the development of this aspect of the sex trade, or, at least, it might see its development as something outside of normal sex trade parameters.

The Sex Industry in Vietnam: A Case Study of the Brothels and on the Streets of Ho Chi Minh City

Is it possible to set aside moral issues and regard sex work as part of the personal service industry? Or a way that young women (and some men) in developing countries can earn a living? The evidence of Black (1994), Cohen (1993), and Leheny (1995) has underpinned our argument that sex work is in fact employment in the personal services sector and, by regarding prostitution as a fee-for-service occupation without the moral stigma, it becomes rather ordinary work at that.

In some countries (e.g., parts of Australia, Germany, Turkey) prostitution is legal, but is heavily regulated by governments and, as a result, part of the industry is driven underground. Decriminalizing prostitution in Vietnam, in a similar way to the measures being proposed by the New Zealand Prostitutes Collective (NZPC), is essential because "It will be difficult to educate prostitutes in those parts of the sex industry which are underground. If AIDS is to be kept out of the sex industry , the sex industry must be brought out of hiding" (New Zealand Prostitute's Collective [NZPC], 1989, p. 7). Further, decriminalizing the sex industry will give prostitutes more power over their working conditions and will help break the cycle of financial dependency on brothel owners and pimps.

Although it is important to examine official government policies, projections, and documents regarding tourism flows to understand the development opportunities in that industry in Vietnam, we argue that in order to understand the sex industry's role in that development it is also crucial to make contact with people who are actually working in the sex trade. To that end, the remainder of this discussion is based on interviews with prostitutes, madams, and Save the Children Fund (SCF) outreach workers and translators in Ho Chi Minh City.

Using "life history methodology," as developed by Middleton (1993), these interviews start from the premise that: "I assumed that the women were telling the truth about their lives insofar as they understood and remembered the events. There was no reason for them to lie. The techniques of revisiting and reinterpreting the material in subsequent interviews . . . ensured that the stories were consistent" (Middleton 1993, p. 68). All interviews were conducted with the help of an SCF translator.

A report prepared by SCF estimates that there are 149 brothels in Ho Chi Minh City (Save the Children Fund [SCF], 1995). Many of these establishments are, officially, bars selling beer to Vietnamese clients. Through Catherine Healy at the New Zealand Prostitutes Collective, who did peer-training workshops in Vietnam, the names and addresses of contact people were secured prior to going to Vietnam (Catherine Healy, Wellington, New Zealand, 1995, personal communication). Once in Ho Chi Minh City, the Commercial Sex Worker Project people were contacted. Following an initial meeting, two former sex workers and Miss Min, a translator, arranged a tour of some of the brothels found in the slum area of the city. In addition, some of the street kids (a number of whom are sex workers) and some of the homeless women who live in a park in the downtown area of the city (again, a number of them are prostitutes) were also interviewed.

The first visit was to a slum area near the edge of Ho Chi Minh City where there is a series of brothels that use selling beer as a front for their activities. In front of each beer-drinking establishment there is often a cluster of young girls. At least they get to sit out in the sun, unlike their clothing factory counterparts. Some of the girls looked to be 13 or 14, but we were told they were 16 and 17. How they came to work in the sex industry is a fairly consistent story: these young women had moved to the city from the provinces in hope of gaining decent paying employment, but it was not forthcoming. One girl had had a fight with her family and had left. Another girl, for instance, had worked in a factory for a while and she had ended up drifting towards prostitution simply because it paid more money and required fewer hours and less work.

Over a 3-day period, 60 of the young women sex workers were surveyed. When asked what they would be doing if they were still in the provinces, their answers were: "Nothing," "Looking after the house," "Watching children." The question as to whether they perceived that they were better off socially and economically being in the city or staying on the farm was always met with startled looks. Everyone said she was much better off here, thank-you very much.

The prostitutes were open about relaying information and discussing issues, undoubtedly because of the SCF women translators whom they already knew. The researcher was introduced as "a foreigner who was looking at the spread of AIDS and STDs and that kind of thing." Following our first stop, we went down the road a little farther to another brothel, where there were three young girls sitting in front of the pub. Again, they were from the provinces and again they thought they were not doing too badly financially, even though they did not really see all that many clients a day. An older women, whom we later learned was in fact 50 years old, came across the street. She sat down and said she was sort of the "madam" of the establishment, although she insisted that they were only selling beer these days because the police raided the area three or four times a day rounding up prostitutes.

When sex workers are arrested in Ho Chi Minh City, they are taken to a detention center at the Local Committee level. Some of them may be sponsored for their release by the brothel owners. The brothel owners raise money and pay under the table for their release, but once the sex workers are out, they have to work and pay back the money. Because the interest charged is very high and especially because the amount of money paid under the table is large, the sex workers have to be loyal to the brothel owner. For those who do not have anybody to sponsor them, they must just let their life take its course in these circumstances (Hanson, 1996a).

After our visit to this particularly poor area, we went to another section of the suburb that was slightly more prosperous, judging from the buildings and the way people were dressed. In the second area, the brothel was run by a very attractive and articulate woman. Miss Min later advised that this woman had been a working girl herself, then she had married, and her husband had left her for another sex worker. She had a child (who would be about 2 or 3 years old) to support, so she had set up a beer parlor business. Although she lived elsewhere, the brothel was built beside the bar and carried on an obvious business. Besides the madam, there were three girls of about 17 or 18 years of age sitting in front of the bar. More kept joining us.

The girls seemed to be quite congenial group and, for the most part, the place was quite clean and rather well kept—much better than some of the South East Asian hotels where the researchers have stayed. The working girls here, like working girls in so many other places, seemed to wear a lot of make-up and put more effort into their hair and clothes than do factory workers. The observation that consistently came through (common, in fact, to prostitution elsewhere) is that girls often get into the industry because they know someone else who is already working. They are from rural areas and are making a transition to urban living. They often start by doing some other kind of work, be it in factories or restaurants or whatever, find that they cannot make enough money doing that, and then drift into prostitution to make enough money to support themselves and to send sufficient funds back to their families.

Working girls in Ho Chi Minh City see mostly local clients. The prostitutes confirmed that absolutely no foreigners go to the first area we visited, except possibly the occasional Taiwanese business man who is looking for an out of the way place, or for very cheap sex. The women on the street told the same story: their clients are locals. Even in the more wealthy areas, the major prostitution market in Vietnam is local. An analogy might serve better to illustrate this point: sex trade workers are on a par with the pedicabs. Yes, tourists use them, and when they do they are very noticeable, but most of the pedicab clients, most of the time, are still locals.

Working safely in the sex industry requires that prostitutes be taught safe sex practices and that they be aware of the health and safety issues surrounding their work. One of the ways this is currently being done in Ho Chi Minh City is through the SCF, which, in its official literature, reports that "Peer educators and peer counselors serve as credible and impactful disseminators of preventive/protective knowledge and behavior skills, and as positively reinforcing role models and change agents in the referent target populations (including sex workers)" (SCF, 1995, p. 4). Consistent with the SCF literature and the high degree of literacy in Vietnam, the awareness of sex workers is very high; as a result, many refuse sex without condoms.

Educating prostitutes through peer education is an effective strategy (Hanson, 1996b, in process). On the street, an Outreach worker reported that "At first it might be difficult to bring in some girls for a STD checkup, but as we develop a relationship with them, and develop some trust, they see that we come to them with respect. We come to them with empathy, so they readily participate actively" (Hanson, 1996a).

If their work is regarded as contributing to society, rather than as a crime, it stands to reason that more sex workers will become conscious of the health and safety issues in the sex industry. As the tourism sector in Vietnam grows, it also stands to reason that so will the area of the sex industry that services foreign tourists. By preparing for that development, rather than adopting a knee-jerk, anti-sex industry, anti-foreigner reaction, Vietnam can support the prostitutes who will work in that part of its tourism sector.

Considerations and Recommendations

Vietnam has an opportunity to set a precedent for tourism in other countries in the Indochinese area, specifically for Laos and Cambodia, by decriminalizing prostitution and supporting the sex industry as an important part of its developing economic structure. Unlike, for example, Thailand or the Philippines, where foreign interests have already staked out a lucrative share of the sex trade, Vietnam can pass laws outlawing outside interference in the development of its sex industry.

By viewing sex work as exactly what it is—namely, work—the government of Vietnam is in a position to recognize the contribution of prostitutes to the economy. Like any other job that requires training, prostitutes entering the industry should be educated about safe sex practices. Peer education has already proven to be important in this regard. English (the current language of international tourism) classes could also be an effective strategy to assist sex workers to negotiate safe sex with foreign clients, as has been found by Empower, a prostitutes' support group in Thailand.

Further, by recognizing support groups already involved in peer education and training in the sex industry, such as the SCF, Vietnam can assist in generating an exemplary development model for this industry. We would caution, however, that groups working with prostitutes should be responsible to the people involved in the sex industry, rather than to the government and its bureaucracies, including the police.

Should this alternative model come to pass, then foreign dominance and manipulation of the local sex trade need not occur and the concern of governments and the WTO about the organized sex trade need not be borne out in the Vietnamese context. And, by establishing laws and infrastructures that promote sex worker control, Vietnam can break the cycle of power and control that typifies organized sex tourism in other countries. Through cooperative efforts, education, training, and support, Vietnam has an opportunity to support the development of a local sex industry founded on the principle of worker control. And that is something of which Rosa Luxemburg would approve.

Chapter 16

Who Exploits Whom and Who Benefits?

Martin Oppermann

Sex tourism is a very intricate and far-reaching concept once one leaves the narrow confines of tourism for commercial sex purposes. The farther one moves towards the fringes of what could rightfully be considered sex tourism, the more ambiguous the term sex tourism becomes and the more confusing the situation as to who actually is the prostitute and who is the tourist becomes. Undoubtedly, sex is a major component of tourism, whether that be its use in tourism marketing, as an attraction, or as an activity. Sex tourism, in its fullest meaning, is a reality of tourism around the world, accounting for a sizeable portion of all tourism. Although some countries may be more renowned for their availability of commercial sex, sex tourism exists everywhere—in Europe, North America, the Caribbean, Latin America, Asia, Africa, Australia, or Oceania (e.g., Ashworth et al., 1988; Crush & Wellings, 1983; Launer, 1993; Naibavu & Schutz, 1974; Senftleben, 1986). And no form of societal or political suppression has been able to eradicate commercial sex activities anywhere, and that would cover only part of the whole sex tourism concept as discussed in Chapter 1. However, what appears quite obvious from the literature is that the greater the legal and societal suppression is, the greater the potential for the prostitutes to be exploited or, in other words, the greater the number of middle persons and parasites who benefit from this illegality.

Often, the state attempts to reduce the visibility of prostitution whereby acceptable levels "are determined by the existing moral climate, available resources and the behavior of those who define the immoral landscape" (Symanski, 1981, p. 2). A good example of that is provided by Iverson and Dierking in Chapter 8.

Symanski (1981) also provided an overview of the level of exploitation and other factors with respect to the type of prostitution. Table 16.1 shows some of these correlations. It indicates the inverse relationship between the number of dependency linkages and the exploitation level and the direct relationship between visibility and exploitation.

Table 16.1. Type of Prostitute and Interaction With Society

Type of Prostitute	Visibility	Exploitation	Dependency Linkages	Prices Charged	Social Esteem	Place
Call girl	low	low	few	high	high	hotel, apartment
Brothel, massage parlor	low	moderate to high	few	lower than call girls	variable	brothel, massage parlor
Street walker	high	very high	many	moderate to low	usually low	street, hotel, car, park

Power and Politics

International and Feminist Perspectives

By focusing on specific aspects of the whole sex tourism industry, many authors have successfully placed sex tourism into the context of exploitation of developing countries (e.g., Graburn, 1983; Latza, 1987; Maurer, 1991; O'Grady, 1992; Reinhardt, 1989; Schöning-Kalendar, 1989). For example, Graburn (1983) suggested that "at a psychological level these nations [Third World countries] are forced into the 'female' role of servitude, of being 'penetrated' for money, often against their will; whereas the outgoing, pleasure seeking, 'penetrating' tourists of powerful nations are cast in the 'male' role" (p. 441). "A new wave of colonialism appears to overrun developing countries. . . . The women in the periphery become the last 'unspoilt resource'—a good that can be traded unscrupulous" (Reinhardt, 1989, p. 90).

The problem with most of these approaches is that they really only scrutinize one particular part of the whole world sex tourism industry, namely tourists from the developed to developing countries who engage in sexual activities with commercial sex workers. As was discussed by Oppermann (Chapter 1), however, this represent an important albeit minor part of what should be considered sex tourism. Even in the infamous sex tourism destination countries Thailand and the Philippines, domestic demand for commercial sex workers exceeds international demand, just like international tourist demand is usually the minor partner of domestic tourist demand in most developing countries (Oppermann & Chon, 1997). In addition, many of the above-cited studies loose credibility by using data that are so obviously exaggerated.

What is interesting in the more feminist perspectives of sex tourism is the notion that the difference between commercial prostitution and marriage is minor: marriage is considered a life-term prostitution as the woman provides access to her body to one man in return for economic security, except the wages tend to be lower and the independence smaller (e.g., Dietrich, 1989; Graburn, 1983; Schöning-Kalendar, 1989). This line of thought is by no means new; around the turn of the century, August Bebel already asked the question "if not many women prostitute themselves by marrying" (Dietrich, 1989) and the radical part of the women movement in Germany at that time rejected marriage as well as the existing moral values. They asked for more independence from husband or father, better educational opportunities, equal rights, and voting rights (Dietrich, 1989). "Prostitution is a problem of society with its values and objectives, which in turn is influenced by history, religion, moral values, and politics" (Renschler, 1987c).

Double Moral Standards and Stigmatization of Sex Workers

> Indeed, it is a profound perversity of the male-oriented world that at one level prostitution is accepted with the wink of an eye, yet at another prostitution is universally treated as a deviation from the social–sexual norm. Laws have always condemned prostitutes (although usually not their clients), rendering them perpetually furtive and always open to exploitation at all levels. (Cottingham, 1981, p. 16)

N. Roberts (1994) provided a brief overview of how the stigmatization of prostitutes came about. She attributed it largely to the dominance of the patriarchate from around 2000 BC and the dominance of patriarchal religions such as Christianity and Islam.

Today, as Suren and Stiefvater (Chapter 11) vividly report, sex workers are still stigmatized, even if it is something as casual as topless dancing. Madden (1996) mentioned that phone sex workers can "hide" their real job duties quite well from their children or family, especially when they work usual office hours and can wear casual clothes. This also indicates the need to "hide" the true nature of the job, which obviously is a reaction to the, at least perceived, stigmatization of sex workers.

The double moral standard of society is also well expressed in Symanski's (1981) account of the stratagems used to "hide" places of prostitution:.

> As long as a disapproved activity is covert many people seem willing to ignore it, or at least attenuate their judgements about it. For such institutions as massage parlors, club hostesses and escort services the meaning of visibility would seem to reside as much in the social acceptability of a word or way of stating something as in the true nature of things. Disguises produce a social irony. So long as some segments of the population believe that massage parlors, escort services or similar operations are more or less what they claim to be, then such businesses will cater to innocent expectations. (p. 215)

Who Benefits?

Cottingham (1981) reported that only a mere fraction (10–15%) of what Japanese sex tourists spend on Filipino women ends up in the hands of the women. The sex club owner, tour operators, local guide, and Japanese guides all take their cuts. Similar accounts have been offered by Renschler (1987c), who suggested that "the greatest benefit from modern slavery and sex tourism is drawn by the whole chain of women traders, pimps, brothel owners, owners of bars and night clubs, taxi drivers, police, hoteliers and all those who stand behind them" (p. 33). However, she also mentioned that even in developing countries there is an increasing number of women who view prostitution as a desirable side income, a point mentioned by several other commentators (e.g., AGISRA, 1990; Häusler, 1994; Senftleben, 1986). Women in that category are commonly from the middle or upper class who can earn a multiple of what they could earn as workers, teachers, or executives. In those cases, it appears more a question of consumerism rather than the need for survival.

Thompson and Harred (1992) provided accounts of topless dancers who choose that job to support their studies or their family. In many instances, the money they could earn that way during limited and convenient working hours was the major attraction for entering that profession (Chapter 11 and Chapter 12). "Women become prostitutes because they decide to go for the best deal—for the amount of time they put in the money is good. It's right up there with being a lawyer" (Scott, 1994, p. 7). Similarly, Madden (1996) remarked that phone sex is a lucrative job.

The level of earnings and especially the share retained by the prostitutes themselves is apparently dependent on the level of the prostitute (see Chapter 1), if it is at the high-class end of the spectrum or more towards the poor end. The number of people and institutions taking their cut in prostitution is large and very diverse, but they all share one characteristic: they are people or institutions in power largely because of the stigmatization and illegalization of prostitution. "Even in so-called democratic countries the list of mundane abuses against prostitutes carried out by authorities will include raids, rapes, beatings, extortion, 'confiscation' of property and compulsory medical intervention" (Overs, 1994, p. 26). The more visible the prostitution, the more vulnerable are sex workers to harassment and exploitation.

Naibavu and Schutz (1974) took a more mercenary role in their appraisal of sex tourism for the national economy. In the case of Fiji, they suggested that

> Prostitution meets the criteria laid down in the Government's Development Plan more fully than almost any other industry. . . . Prostitution is a fully localised industry which gives employment to unskilled female workers for most of whom no other jobs are available. It requires no investment of foreign capital, yet it brings in large amounts of foreign exchange with a minimum of leakage back overseas. (p. 65)

The beneficiary role of the state is also mentioned by AGISRA (1990), who related that a large share of the registered prostitutes' earnings is taxed. Furthermore, those countries who "export" prostitutes to other countries generally benefit from the monetary transfers of those workers to their families at home. Senftleben

(1986) reported that legalized forms of entertainment in Taiwan bring substantial amounts of revenue to the local governments. Despite the official stigmatization of prostitutes by society and especially churches and governments, the same institutions have been traditionally among those benefitting the most from it. In the Middle Ages, brothels were owned by the city councils and in several instances by the bishop of the community (Dietrich, 1989; N. Roberts, 1994). Symanski (1981) refered to the state as a pimp, indicating the beneficiary and often innovative role of the state and leading social institutions (e.g., churches) have in prostitution and sex tourism.

Who Exploits Whom?

"Who exploits whom in a customer–prostitute relationship?" is an interesting question. Obviously, prostitutes are usually placed in the position of the exploited whose body is bought for the pleasure of men. However, some authors have questioned whether men actually get what they wanted. "Prostitution in the Australian context is often appraised by clients as deficient, in that prostitutes are criticized for being emotionally and sexually cold and for making little effort to please, or to disguise the commercial nature of the interaction" (Kruhse-MountBurton, 1995, p. 193). This would point to the fact that men want more than just the simple physical release, which indeed they might as well do through masturbation and for a lot less money. Men also look for "love" in a customer-prostitute relationship—thus their "disappointment" at the commercial approach to prostitution in Western societies. After all, perhaps this is one reason for some men to engage in sex tourism with planned sexual behavior with prostitutes in developing countries where their money supposedly can buy not only more sex, but also more tenderness on the side of the prostitute. The fact that few sex tourists in Kleiber and Wilke's (1995) study had also entered a customer–prostitute relationship at home during the preceeding 12 months would point in that direction too. The interesting phenomenon of open-ended prostitution where a prostitute may have several relationships to men (or women) overseas who send also money between their visits is yet another area where one might think that the customer has been had. The illegality of prostitution and the resulting provision of fronts and services such as massage parlors, topless and bottomless bars, strippers, and escort agencies has also provided an ideal ground for sexual ruses.

Marriage and the Prostitution Trade

Another aspect of the international trade in sex and in women is the marriage trade, which in turn often serves as a front for trading prostitutes, or better to press women into prostitution, as a number of different authors have described (e.g., Dietrich, 1989; Schöning-Kalendar, 1989). It existed in the Roman and Greek Empires and the royal brothels in Egypt, which were supplied with Indian women (Schöning-Kalendar, 1989). The white slavery trade seemed to have been especially prevalent in the latter half of the 19th century and there are many accounts of women who were traded around the world to end up either in marriage or prostitution or both (e.g., Chapter 5; Ackermann & Filter, 1994; AGISRA, 1990; Dietrich, 1989; Launer, 1991; Renschler, 1987a; Schöning-Kalendar, 1989). For example, Dietrich (1989) reported that about 8,000–10,000 women from Galizia were traded to South America alone. Today, there are virtually hundreds of agencies specializing in arranging international marriages or meetings with partners from overseas. Although many of those may indeed adhere to a sense of ethics, there are others that abuse the system and that are simply fronts for pressing women into prostitution. Reinhardt and Koss (1989) reported that several agencies in Germany offer women for a trial period and return guarantee. Hence, men can try out several women until they are satisfied with one (Ackermann & Filter, 1994); however, the women have little choice as their tourist visa runs out after 3 months. Other tactics of women traders are to offer well-paid jobs that never materialize once the women have arrived in the country and they are forced into prostitution to pay off their incurred debts (Ackermann & Filter, 1994), a practice that has been around for at least a century (see Chapter 5; Dietrich, 1989). Ackermann and Filter (1994) also reported that an estimated 15,000–20,000 women from Eastern Europe have been brought to Germany, one way or the other, and forced into prostitution since the end of the Cold War. And according to the same authors, the trade in Eastern European women now accounts for about 80% of the turnover in the women trade worldwide.

Two common factors emerge from the accounts of marriage and prostitution trade spanning several centuries. First, it appears to be a flow from the poor to the relatively affluent countries. The powerful and wealthy nations demand the services of women in the less powerful and poor nations, whether that be through physically conquering those countries, offering enough money to attract women to take the risk and move to another country, or by making use of the price differential for commercial sex and traveling to those countries. Indeed, Graburn (1983) argued that there exists a close connection between war, prostitution, and tourism.

Second, its roots can be found in the patriarcharical system and its inherent economic and political suppression of women (Reinhardt, 1989). Women tend to be less economically independent. The dependence on the men, usually in the role of the sole breadwinner of the family, has been and still is exploited by the men. Yet, over the last few decades, the traditional male role as the sole breadwinner has come increasingly under pressure with women becoming more autonomous due to better education and more better paid jobs. Kruhse-MountBurton (1995) illustrated how, in the case of Australia, this changing gender relation places enormous stress and pressure on the males (with resulting high suicide rates and other health problems). As a way out, men are led to believe that women in developing countries and especially Asia are more of the domicile and serving type (Bühler, 1989) that boost male egos and reaffirm their masculine identity (Kruhse-MountBurton, 1995). Marriage trade upholds the unequal gender relationship in the patriarchate (Klink, 1989; Reinhardt, 1989).

Final Thoughts

To reiterate, sex tourism is a reality of tourism around the world, accounting for a sizeable portion of all tourism, whether that be in Europe, North America, the Caribbean, Latin America, Asia, Africa, Australia, or Oceania. And it is time that other tourism researchers recognize its full importance. This book, with its wide range of different aspects of sex tourism and prostitution, has provided a glimpse of the intricate issues of sex tourism and prostitution. For example, Günther's (Chapter 7) report on the self-reasoning process of a sex tourist indicates the sociological and psychological complexities of what constitutes sex tourism and sex tourists. Few authors, however, have addressed the customers' perspective and even accounts on the prostitutes are rare. Similarly, issues such as the prostitute as the tourist or female demand for male and female prostitutes have hardly been dealt with at all. The data situation in this particular field of sex tourism is more deficient than in tourism in general, largely due to the illegality of prostitution and the social stigma attached to both prostitutes and sex tourists.

Contributors

Christine Beddoe was previously the National Director of ECPAT Australia and is now a consultant working with ECPAT to focus on prevention of child sex tourism in the South Pacific region. She has also worked at the ECPAT secretariat in Bangkok and has interests in tourism and human rights, the anthropology of tourism, and tourism ethics.

Kye-Sung (Kaye) Chon is Professor of Tourism and Marketing in the Conrad N. Hilton College of Hotel and Restaurant Management, University of Houston. A former hotel manager and industry consultant, Professor Chon's research interests include strategic marketing and consumer behavior in the tourism and hospitality industry.

Malcolm Cooper is Principal, University of Southern Queensland–Wide Bay Campus. He received his Ph.D. from the University of Birmingham (UK). He is an environmental planner/lawyer and tourism analyst and his current research interests include tourism planning, cultural tourism, the impact of tourism on coastal environments, and Asian tourism.

Heidi Dahles is teaching in the Department of Leisure Studies, Tilburg University, The Netherlands. She obtained her Ph.D. from Niymegen University, The Netherlands. She is a cultural anthropologist and her current research is focusing on tourism developments in Indonesia, in particular small entrepreneurship in tourism, the politics and policies of tourism, processes of regionalization, and heritage tourism.

Graham Dann is professor of Tourism in the Department of Tourism and Leisure, University of Luton, UK. He received his Ph.D. from the University of Surrey (UK). Within the sociology of tourism his research focuses on the areas of motivation, promotion, and semiotics.

John C. Dierking is an attorney who has practiced law on Guam for over 20 years. He serves as an Associate Professor in the Criminal Justice program of the College of Business and Public Administration at the University of Guam. His research interests include community planning issues and social control of industry.

Jon Griffin Donlon is a leisure behavior specialist. He focuses on controversial leisure and has published articles in this field in an array of academic and popular press publications. Currently, Dr. Donlon is Director of the Neoteric Center for the Study of Controversial Leisure, in Baton Rouge, LA. His area of work includes commercial sex, cock fighting, sport hunting, rec drug use, dangerous travel, etc.

Armin Günther is lecturer in Psychology at the University of Augsburg, Germany, where he also received his Ph.D. He is a psychologist and his current research interests include tourism and culture, new forms of touristic experience, risk perception, and methods of psychological research.

C. Michael Hall is based at the Centre for Tourism, University of Otago, Dunedin, New Zealand. He also holds positions at the New Zealand Natural Heritage Foundation, Palmerston North and the School of Leisure and Food Management, Sheffield Hallam University, Sheffield (UK). He has varied research interests in the tourism, recreation, heritage management, and environmental history fields.

Jody Hanson, who has a Ph.D. in adult education, is a freelance writer and sex industry researcher who has conducted field work in eight countries. She is currently working on a comparative study of the sex industries in New Zealand and Canada.

Vincent Heung is an Assistant Professor of Marketing in the Department of Hotel and Tourism Management at the Hong Kong Polytechnic University. His research interests include service quality in tourism, tourist behavior, and tourism trends.

J. S. Perry Hobson is Senior Lecturer in the School of Tourism & Hospitality Management, Southern Cross University, Australia. His main research interests are virtual reality and tourism, youth tourism, and tourism in the Asia–Pacific region.

Thomas J. Iverson is the Executive Director of the Sustainable Development Institute and Professor of Economics at the University of Guam. He received his Ph.D. from the University of Texas. His current research interests include tourism forecasting, psychographic market segmentation, and all aspects of sustainable development.

Rachel Kinder completed her studies in business with a major in tourism at Massey University (New Zealand) in 1995. Since that date she has been working as a consultant with Anderson Consulting in Wellington and Auckland, New Zealand.

Steven Kohm is an M.A. candidate in the Department of Geography at the University of Toronto, Canada. His current research interests include tourism and the prostitution trade, neighborhood politics and prostitution, and the regulation of sex on the Internet.

Shawna McKinley completed her B.A. in Tourism at Waiariki Polytechnic, Rotorua, New Zealand. Since then she has returned to British Columbia, Canada.

Helen Murphy was a student at Massey University, New Zealand. On completion of her studies in business studies with a major in tourism in 1996 she commenced work with a major hotel chain in New Zealand.

Martin Oppermann is Senior Lecturer in Tourism at Griffith University–Gold Coast, Queensland, Australia. He received his Ph.D. from Universität Tübingen (Germany). Martin is Editor-in-Chief of *Pacific Tourism Review* and Interim Co-Editor of *Journal of Travel & Tourism Marketing*. With over 100 scholarly research publications, he has published widely on issues such as tourism in developing countries, travel life cycle, and regional development. He is a tourism geographer and his current research interests include Pacific Rim tourism issues, tourist flows, lifelong travel patterns, destination loyalty, destination marketing, and sex tourism.

Joan Phillip is currently working towards her Ph.D. in the Department of Tourism and Leisure, University of Luton, UK. She received her B.Sc. And M.Phil. from the University of the West Indies, Barbados. With a training in sociology, her research interests include sex tourism and the sociocultural impacts of tourism in developing countries.

Chris Ryan, Ph.D., has recently joined the School of Management at the University of Waikato, New Zealand. He is Editor of *Tourism Management*. His research interests lie in tourism behaviors, economic impacts, and research methodologies.

John Selwood is a Professor of Geography at the University of Winnipeg, Canada. He obtained his Ph.D. from the University of Western Australia. He has a diverse range of interests that include geographical aspects of the sex trade, studies of urban and regional settlement, vacation homes, and domestic holiday-making.

Robert Stiefvater is an Assistant Professor at North Carolina Central University. He received his Doctorate from Indiana University. His research interstes are deviant recreation, qualitative inquiry, and leisure theory.

Asuncion Suren is an Assistant Professor at Indiana University in the Department of Recreation and Parks Administration. She earned her Ed.D. in Recreation Administration from Temple University in Philadelphia. Her main research interests are social deviance and youth at risk.

Bibliography

Abate, T. (1996, June 18). Boss may be watching you surf the Internet. *Winnipeg Free Press*.

Abramson, P. R., & Pinkerton, S. F. (1995). *Sexual nature, sexual culture*. Chicago: University of Chicago Press.

Ackermann, L., & Filter, C. (1994). *Die Frau nach Katalog*. Freiburg: Herder.

Adams, C. (1992). *Adjusting privatisation: Case studies from developing countries*. New York: Heinemann.

Adams, P. C. (1995). A reconsideration of personal boundaries in space-time. *Annals of the Association of American Geographers, 85*, 267-285.

AGISRA. (1990). *Frauenhandel und Prostitutionstourismus*. Muenchen: Trickster.

Alexander, M. W., & Judd, B. (1979). Do nudes in ads enhance brand recall. *Journal of Advertising Research, 18*(1), 47-50.

Almeida, A. (1989). Goa—Tourismus und Prostitution. In C. Euler (Ed.), *Eingeborene— ausgebucht: Ökologische Zerstörung durch Tourismus* (pp. 104-111). Giessen: Focus Verlag.

Anonymous. (1992). Facing up to AIDS: Thailand's example. *Far Eastern Economic Review, 155*(6), 28-35.

Anonymous. (1995). A soulless society. *Asiaweek, 21*(7), 24-28

Anonymous. (1996). Growing income inequality. *Hong Kong Business, 15*(165), 23.

Ansley, G. (1993, June 9). Nations combine in child prostitution crackdown. *New Zealand Herald*, p. 9.

Aparicio, M. (1993). Palmen, Strand und schöne Menschen. *ila, 167*, 16-18.

Ashworth, G., White, P., & Winchester, H. (1988). The red-light districts in the West European City: A neglected aspect of the urban landscape. *Geoforum, 19*, 201-212.

Attorney General's Department. (1994, June 8). *Government Response to the House of Representatives Committee on Constitutional and Legal Affairs Report on the Crimes (Child Sex Tourism) Amendment Bill 1994*. Attorney General's Department, Criminal Law Division, Canberra.

Beckmann, G., & Elzer, B. (1995). Frauensextourismus am Beispiel Kenias. *Vehement, 1*, 14-18.

Bell, E. (Ed.). (1980). *War on the white slave trade*. Toronto: Coles.

Berger, P. L., & Luckmann, T. (1966). *The social construction of reality*. Garden City: Doubleday.

Black, M. (1994). Home truths. *New Internationalist, 252*, 11-13.

Board of Investment. (1993). *Sri Lanka—annual report 1993*. Colombo: Author.

Bond, T. (1980). *Boy prostitution in Sri Lanka: The problems, effects and suggested remedies*. Colombo: Terres des Hommes.

Boorstin, D. J. (1985). *The image: A guide to pseudo-events in America*. New York: Athenaeum.

Booth, A. (1990). The tourist boom in Indonesia. *Bulletin of Indonesian Economic Studies, 26*(3), 45-73.

Britton, R. A. (1979). The image of the Third World in tourism marketing. *Annals of Tourism Research, 6*, 318-329.

Britton, S. (1991). Tourism, capital, and place: Towards a critical geography of tourism. *Environment and Planning D, 9*(4), 451-478.

Brothel took $1.4 m a year court told. (1996, June 11). *Dominion*.

Brown, N. (1992). Beach boys as culture brokers in Bakau Town, Gambia. *Community Devel-

opment Journal, 27, 361-370.

Bruyn, S. T. (1966). *The human perspective in sociology.* Englewood Cliffs: Prentice Hall.

Bühler, S. (1989). Ehe-Ideologie und Heiratshandel. In: Tübinger Projektgruppe Frauenhandel (Ed.), *Frauenhandel in Deutschland* (pp. 106-114). Bonn: J. H. W. Dietz Nachfahren.

Bugnicourt, J. (1977). Sex, Sonne, Strand. Tourismus überschwemmt Entwicklungsländer und hinterlässt Probleme. *Forum Vereinte Nationen, 5*, 1-2.

Butler, R. W. (1980). The concept of a tourism area cycle of evolution. Implications for the management of resources. *Canadian Geographer, 24*, 5-12.

Butler, R. W. (1990). The influence of the media in shaping international tourist patterns. *Tourism Recreation Research, 15*(2), 46-53.

Butler, R. W. (1991). West Edmonton Mall as a tourist attraction. *Canadian Geographer, 35*, 287-295.

Caplan, G. M. (1984). The facts of life about teenage prostitution. *Crime and Delinquency, 30*(1), 69-74.

Carroll, J., Broadhead, R., & Cassel, D. (1996). *1996 Canadian Internet handbook: Educational edition.* Scarborough: Prentice-Hall Canada.

Case studies from the concubine village. (1995, July 31). *Ming Pao Daily News*, p. 8.

Cassou. J. (1967). Du voyage au tourisme. *Communications, 10*, 25-34.

Cater, E. A. (1987). Tourism in the least developed countries. *Annals of Tourism Research, 14*, 202-226.

Chan, S. C., & Tsui, S. W. (1993). Female workers in special economic zones. *Next, 178*, 38-41.

Chen, S. X., & Choi, S. (1993). Desirable men. *Next, 178*, 42-46.

Cheuk, Y. H., & Chon, T. W. (1995, June 30). The yellow bus. *Next*, 66-72.

Chon, K.-S. (1990). The role of destination image in tourism: A review and discussion. *Tourist Review, 45*(2), 2-9.

Cohen, E. (1971). Arab boys and tourist girls in a mixed Jewish–Arab community. *International Journal of Comparative Sociology, 12*, 217-233.

Cohen, E. (1982). Thai girls and farang men: The edge of ambiguity. *Annals of Tourism Research, 9*, 403-428.

Cohen, E. (1985a). The tourist guide: The origins, structure and dynamics of a role. *Annals of Tourism Research, 12*, 5-29.

Cohen, E. (1985b). Tourism as play. *Religion, 15*, 291-304.

Cohen, E. (1986). Lovelorn farangs: The correspondence between foreign men and Thai girls. *Anthropological Quarterly, 59*(3), 115-127.

Cohen, E. (1988a). Traditions in the qualitative sociology of tourism. *Annals of Tourism Research, 15*, 29-46.

Cohen, E. (1988b). Authenticity and commoditization in tourism. *Annals of Tourism Research, 15*, 371-386.

Cohen, E. (1988c). Tourism and AIDS in Thailand. *Annals of Tourism Research, 15*, 467-486.

Cohen, E. (1993). Open-ended prostitution as a skilful game of luck: Opportunities, risk and security among tourist-oriented prostitutes in a Bangkok Soi. In M. Hitchcock, V. T. King, & M. J. G. Parnwell (Eds.), *Tourism in South-East Asia* (pp. 155-178). London: Routledge.

Commonwealth of Australia. (1995, December). *Australia's First Report Under Article 44(1)(a) of the United Nations Convention on the Rights of the Child.* Canberra: Author.

Cooper, D. (1994). Portraits of paradise: Themes and images of the tourist industry. *Southeast Asian Journal of Social Science, 22*, 144-159.

Cottingham, J. (1981). Sex included. *Development Forum, 9*(5), 16.

Crackdown on concubine keepers. (1995, March 27). *South China Morning Post.*

Crang, M. (1996). Magic kingdom or a quixotic quest for authenticity? *Annals of Tourism Research, 23*, 415-431.

Crick, M. (1989). Representations of international tourism in the social sciences: Sun, sex, sights, savings, and servility. *Annual Review of Anthropology, 18,* 307-344.

Crick, M. (1992). Life in the informal sector: Street guides in Kandy, Sri Lanka. In D. Harrison (Ed.), *Tourism and the less developed countries* (pp. 135-147). London: Belhaven Press.

Crompton, J. L. (1979). An assessment of the image of Mexico as a vacation destination and the influence of geographical location upon that image. *Journal of Travel Research, 17*(4), 18-23.

Crossley, J. C., & Jamieson, L. M. (1993). *Introduction to commercial and entrepreneurial recreation.* Champaign, IL: Sagamore Publishing.

Crush, J. S., & Wellings, P. A. (1983). The Southern African pleasure periphery, 1966-1983. *Journal of Modern African Studies, 21,* 673-698.

DaGrossa, P. S. (1989). Kampaeng Din: A study of prostitution in the all-Thai brothels of Chiang Mai City. *Crossroads, 4*(2), 1-8.

Dann, G. (1996). *The language of tourism.* London: CAB International.

Davis, D., & Harrell, S. (1993). *Chinese families in the post-Mao era.* Berkeley: University of California Press.

de Gallo, M.T., & Alzate, H. (1976). Brothel prostitution in Columbia. *Archives of Sexual Behavior, 5*(1), 1-7.

Department Pariwisata, Pos dan Telekomunikasi. (1995). *Derah Istimewa Yoygakarta Tahun 1995.* Yoygakarta: Author.

De Schryver, A., & Meheus, A. (1989). International travel and sexually transmitted diseases. *World Health Statistics Quarterly, 42*(2), 90-99.

del Rosario, V. O. (1994). Tourism and women: The perspective from feminist political economy. *Rethinking Tourism Conference,* Bali, August 3-6.

Department of Public Health & Social Services. (1984, May 18). *Rules and regulations to sanitary operation of massage parlors* (Document No. 0571). Mangilao: Author.

Dierking, J. C. (1989). *Rest and relaxation in Micronesia: Guam's sex oriented business—darkness or light?* Mangilao: University of Guam.

Dietrich, A. (1989). Mädchenhandel: Geschichte oder Vergangenheit?. In Tübinger Projektgruppe Frauenhandel (Ed.), *Frauenhandel in Deutschland* (pp. 18-40). Bonn: J. H. W. Dietz Nachfahren.

Dilley, R. S. (1986). Tourist brochures and tourist images. *Canadian Geographer, 30,* 59-65.

Din, K. H. (1989). Towards an integrated approach to tourism development: Observations from Malaysia. In T. V. Singh, H. L. Theuns, & F. M. Go (Ed.), *Towards appropriate tourism: The case of developing countries* (pp. 181-204). Frankfurt: Peter Lang.

Douglas, M. (1966). *Purity and danger: Analysis of the concepts of pollution and taboo.* New York: Routledge.

Durkin, K. F., & Bryant, C. D. (1995). "Log on to sex": Some notes on the carnal computer and erotic cyberspace as an emerging research frontier. *Deviant Behaviour, 16,* 179-200.

Easton, B. (1980). *Social policy and the welfare state in New Zealand.* Sydney: Allen & Unwin.

Ech, T., & Rosenblum, I. (1975). *Tourism in developing countries: Trick or treat? A report from The Gambia.* Uppsala: Scandinavian Institute of African Studies.

Echtner, C. M., & Ritchie, J. R. B. (1993). The measurement of destination image: An empirical assessment. *Journal of Travel Research, 31*(4), 3-13.

ECPAT Australia. (1996a, October). Update: Arrests and convictions. *ECPAT Australia, 35,* 6.

ECPAT Australia. (1996b, February). Legal updates. *ECPAT Australia, 28,* 1.

ECPAT Australia. (1996c, April). Minister of Foreign Affairs orders a "ruthless" inquiry into allegations of child sex abuse and Australian diplomatic staff. *ECPAT Australia, 30,* 1.

ECPAT Australia. (1996d, April). The N.S.W. Royal Commission continues to shock Australia and rock institutions. *ECPAT Australia, 30,* 3.

Elliott, D. (1996a). Empty riches. *Newsweek, 127*(9), 8–12.

Elliott, D. (1996b). Where Hong Kong men get treated like gods. In concubine village, redis-covering the past. *Newsweek, 127*(9), 10.

Ending the sex tours. (1995, June 23). *Sydney Morning Herald*, p. 17.

Evans, N. (1976). Tourism and cross cultural communication. *Annals of Tourism Research, 3,* 189–198.

Extra-marital affairs. (1995, October 25). *Ming Pao Daily News*, p. 7.

Fine, G. A. (1991). Justifying fun: Why we do not teach exotic dance in high school. *Play & Culture, 4,* 87–99.

Fish, M. (1984). Deterring sex sales to international tourists. *International Journal of Com-parative and Applied Justice, 8,* 175–186.

Foote, N. N. (1954). Sex as play. *Social Problems, 1,* 159–163.

Ford, J. B., LaTour, M. S., & Lundstrom, W. J. (1991). Contemporary women's evaluation of female role portrayals in advertising. *Journal of Consumer Marketing, 8*(1), 15–28.

Gartner, W. C. (1993). Image formation process. *Journal of Travel & Tourism Marketing, 2*(2/3), 191–216.

Geertz, C. (1963). *Peddlers and princes: Social development and economic change in two Indonesian towns.* Chicago: University of Chicago Press.

George, D. M. (1996, February). Sex sells. *Latte Magazine*, 38–43.

Gerlach, J. (1989). Spring break at Padre Island: A new kind of tourism. *Focus, 39*(1), 13–16, 29.

Gibson-Ainyette, I., Templer, D. I., Brown, R., & Veaco, L. (1988). Adolescent female prostitutes. *Archives of Sexual Behavior, 15,* 431–438.

Gilley, B. (1996). Irresistible force. *Far Eastern Economic Review, 159*(14), 18–24.

Gilley, M. C. (1988). Sex roles in advertising: A comparison of television advertisements in Australia, Mexico, and the United States. *Journal of Marketing, 52,* 75–85.

Goffman, E. (1974). *Frame analysis: An essay on the organization of experience.* New York: Harper.

Goldman, E. (1970). *The traffic in women and other essays on feminism.* Washington: Times Change Press.

Goughlin, R. J. (1950). *The position of women in Vietnam.* New Haven: Yale University Press.

Gould, J. (1992, September). Topless bars uncovered. *Redbook*, 119–121, 144–148.

Gould, S. J. (1995). Sexualized aspects of consumer behavior: An empirical investigation of consumer lovemaps. *Psychology & Marketing, 12,* 395–413.

Graburn, N. H. H. (1983). Tourism and prostitution. *Annals of Tourism Research, 10,* 437–442.

Graburn, N. H. H. (1989). Tourism: The sacred journey. In V. L. Smith (Ed.), *Hosts and guests: The anthropology of tourism.* Philadelphia: University of Pennsylvania Press.

Gunn, C. A. (1988). *Vacationscape.* New York: Van Nostrand Reinhold.

Günther, A. (1992). ". . . mit freundlichen Grüssen vom planeten TMA 1." Eine rahmenanalytische Etüde. In H. A. Gartman & R. Haubl (Eds.), *Bilderflut und Sprachmagie. Fallstudien zur Kultur der Werbung* (pp. 191–213). Opladen: Westdeutscher Verlag.

Hail, J. (1980). Scant options, little action. *Business Times Week, 2*(2), 11–16.

Hall, C. M. (1992). Sex tourism in Southeast Asia. In D. Harrison (Ed.), *Tourism and the less developed countries* (pp. 65–74). London: Belhaven Press.

Hall, C. M. (1994a). *Tourism and politics: Policy, power and place.* Chichester: John Wiley & Sons.

Hall, C. M. (1994b). Gender and economic interests in tourism prostitution: The nature, devel-opment and implications of sex tourism in South-East Asia. In V. Kinnaird & D. Hall (Ed.), *Tourism: A gender analysis* (pp. 142–163). Chichester: John Wiley & Sons.

Hall, C. M., & Jenkins, J. M. (1995). *Tourism and public policy.* London: Routledge.

Hang Seng Bank. (1996, April/May). The expanding role of Hong Kong as a service centre. *Hang Seng Economic Monthly*, 1.

Hanna, J. (1988). *Dance, sex, and gender.* Chicago: University of Chicago Press.

Hanson, J. (1996a). Transcripts of the interview at the Sex Worker Outreach Project, Ho Chi Minh City. Fieldnotes.

Hanson, J. (1996b). Learning to be a prostitute. *Women's Studies Journal, 12*(2), 77–85.

Hanson, J. (in process). Transcripts of interviews with sex-industry workers.

Haralambopoulus, N., & Pizam, A. (1996). Perceived impacts of tourism: The case of Samos. *Annals of Tourism Research, 23*, 503–526.

Harrell-Bond, B. E. (1978). *A window on the outside world: Tourism and development in The Gambia.* American University Field Staff Report 19.

Harris, M. (1996, June). Hong Kong: The great divide. *Marie Claire Australia, 10*, 10–20.

Hastings, J. (1993, May). Stripping yarns. *Mayfair*, 18–19.

Häusler, N. (1993). Die Schlange im Paradies? Tourismus und Akkulturation in Goa. In N. Häusler, C. Kamp, P. Müller-Rockstroh, W. Scholz, & B. E. Schulz (Eds.), *Unterwegs in Sachen Reisen: Tourismusprojekte und Projekttourismus in Afrika, Asien und Lateinamerika* (pp. 23–52). Saarbrücken: Verlag für Entwicklungspolitik Breitenbach.

Heatwole, C. A. (1989). Body shots: Woman in tourism-related advertisements. *Focus, 39*(4), 7–11.

Henriques, F. (1963). *Prostitution in Europe and the New World.* London: Magibon & Kee.

Heyl, B. (1977). The madam as entrepreneur. *Sociological Spectrum, 11*, 545–555.

Hobson, J. S. P., & Dietrich, U. C. (1994). Tourism, health and quality of life: Challenging the responsibility of using the traditional tenets of sun, sea, sand, and sex in tourism marketing. *Journal of Travel & Tourism Marketing, 3*(4), 21–38.

Hobson, J. S. P., & Ko, G. (1994). Tourism and politics: The implications of the change in sovereignty on the future development of Hong Kong's tourism industry. *Journal of Travel Research, 32*(4), 2–8.

Hobson, J. S. P., & Williams, A. P. (1995). Virtual reality: A new horizon for the tourism industry. *Journal of Vacation Marketing, 1*(2), 125–135.

Holcomb, B., & Luongo, M. (1996). Gay tourism in the United States. *Annals of Tourism Research, 23*, 711–713.

Hong Kong Census and Statistics Department. (1991). *Population census report.* Hong Kong: Author.

Hong Kong Census and Statistics Department. (1995). *Annual digest of statistics.* Hong Kong: Author.

Hooper, J. (1990). *Beneath the visiting moon: Images of combat in Southern Africa.* Lexington: Lexington Books.

Hopkins, J. (1990). West Edmonton Mall: Landscape of myths and elsewhereness. *Canadian Geographer, 34*, 2–17.

House of Representatives. (1994a, May 4). Crimes (Child Sex Tourism) Amendment Bill, 1994, second reading. *Hansard.*

House of Representatives. (1994b, June 29). Crimes (Child Sex Tourism) Amendment Bill, 1994, second reading. Representatives Main Committee. *Hansard.*

House of Representatives Standing Committee on Legal and Constitutional Affairs. (1994). *Crimes (Child Sex Tourism) Amendment Bill 1994 Advisory Report.* House of Representatives Standing Committee on Legal and Constitutional Affairs, Parliament of the Commonwealth of Australia, Canberra.

Huang, T. (1989). Development of China's SEZs. *Beijing Review, 32*(12), 21.

Hubner, J. (1992). *Bottom feeders: From free love to hard core.* New York: Bantam Publishing.

Huggs, K. (1992, August 5). What's my line? *The Times of Acadiana*, 33–36.

Humphreys, L. (1970). *Impersonal sex in public places*. Chicago: Aldine.

Hunt, J. D. (1975). Image as a factor in tourism development. *Journal of Travel Research, 13*, 1–7.

Huxley, A. (1964). *Brave new world*. London: Chatto & Windus.

Inquiry into pederast Fisk's Thai trips. (1996, October 18). *The Australian*.

Ireland, K. (1993). *Wish you weren't here. The sexual exploitation of children and the connection with tourism and international travel*. London: Save the Children.

Jackman, S. (1993). *Child poverty in Aotearoa/New Zealand*. Wellington: Council of Christian Social Services.

Jafari, J. (1987). Tourism models: The sociocultural aspects. *Tourism Management, 8*, 151–159.

Jayawardena, L., Maaslans, A., & Radhakrishnan, P. N. (1988). *Stabilization and adjustment policies and programs in Sri Lanka*. Helsinki: University of Finland.

Jenkins, W. I. (1978). *Policy analysis: A political and organizational perspective*. New York: St. Martin's Press.

Jenness, V. (1990). From sex to sin as work. *Social Problems, 37*, 403–420.

Jensen, I. (1990, August 16). Thailand's war on AIDS. *The Nation*, 38.

Jordan, J. (1991). *Women in the New Zealand sex industry talk to Jan Jordan*. Auckland: Penguin.

Joseph, W. B. (1982). The credibility of physically attractive communicators: A review. *Journal of Advertising, 11*(3), 15–24.

Kando, T. M. (1975). *Leisure and popular culture in transition*. Sacramento: The C. V. Mosby Company.

Karsh, C. A., & Dann, G. (1981). Close encounters of the Third World. *Human Relations, 34*, 249–268.

Kelly, F. (1990, May 12). Asian flesh trade now big business . . . and growing. *New Zealand Herald*, pp. 2, 4.

Kerin, R. A., Lundstrom, W. J., & Sciglimpaglia, D. (1979). Women in advertisements: Retrospect and prospect. *Journal of Advertising, 8*, 37–42.

Kerr, D. (1994). *Crimes (Child Sex Tourism) Amendment Bill 1994, Second Reading Speech*. House of Representatives, Parliament of the Commonwealth of Australia, Canberra.

Keyes, C. F. (1984). Mother or mistress but never a monk. *American Ethnologist, 11*, 223–241.

Khin Titsa (1980). *Providence and prostitution: Image and reality for women in Buddhist Thailand*. London: Allen & Unwin.

Kirsch, A. T. (1975). Economy, policy and religion in Thailand. In G. W. Skinner & A. T. Kirsch (Eds.), *Change and persistence in Thai society* (pp. 172–196). Ithaca: Cornell University Press.

Kleiber, D., & Velten, D. (1994). *Prostitutionskunden: Eine Untersuchung über soziale und psychologische Charakteristika von Besuchern weiblicher Prostituierter in Zeiten von AIDS*. Baden-Baden: Nomos-Verlagsgesellschaft.

Kleiber, D., & Wilke, M. (1995). *Aids, Sex und Tourismus: Ergebnisse einer Befragung deutscher Urlauber und Sextouristen*. Baden-Baden: Nomos-Verlagsgesellschaft.

Klink, S. (1989). Vom Marsch des Patriarchats durch die menschliche Intimsphäre. In Tübinger Projektgruppe Frauenhandel (Ed.), *Frauenhandel in Deutschland* (pp. 93–105). Bonn: J. H. W. Dietz Nachfahren.

Kohm, S., & Selwood, J. (1997). Controlling the crimogenic place: The evolution of Winnipeg's sex trade. In B. Thraves, A. H. Paul & R. Widdis (Eds.), *The Estevan papers* (Regina Geographical Studies No. 6). Regina: University of Regina.

Kotler, P., & Turner, R. E. (1993). *Marketing management*. Scarborough: Prentice-Hall Canada.

Kraus, R. (1990). *Recreation and leisure in modern society*. New York: Harper Collins Publishing.

Krippendorf, J. (1996). Interviewed for "The Tourist." BBC Television—transmitted in New Zealand on *BBC World Television*, July 10, 1996.

Kruhse-MountBurton, S. (1995). Sex tourism and traditional Australian male identity. In M. F. Lanfant, J. B. Allcock, & E. M. Bruner (Eds.), *International tourism—identity and change* (pp. 192-204). London: Sage.

Landers, A. (1996a, June 14). *Winnipeg Free Press*.

Landers, A. (1996b, June 25). *Winnipeg Free Press*.

Laskey, H. A., Seaton, B., & Nicholls, J. A. F. (1994). Effects of strategy and pictures in travel agency advertising. *Journal of Travel Research, 32*(4), 13-19.

Lasswell, H. D. (1936). *Politics: Who gets, what, when, how?* New York: McGraw-Hill.

LaTour, M. S., & Henthorne, T. L. (1993). Female nudity. Attitudes toward the ad and the brand, and implications for advertising strategy. *Journal of Consumer Marketing, 10*(3), 25-32.

Latza, B. (1987). *Sextourismus in Südostasien*. Frankfurt: Fischer.

Launer, E. (Ed.). (1991). *Frauenhandel*. Göttingen: Lamuv.

Launer, E. (1993). *Zum Beispiel Sextourismus*. Göttingen: Lamuv.

Lea, J. P. (1988). *Tourism and development in the Third World*. London/New York: Routledge.

Lee, W. (1991). Prostititution and tourism in South-East Asia. In N. Redclift & M. T. Sinclair (Eds.), *Working women: International perspectives on labour and gender ideology*. London: Routledge.

Legislation. (1994, July 20). *Commonwealth of Australia Gazette*, GN28, p. 1479.

Leheny, D. (1995). A political economy of Asian sex tourism. *Annals of Tourism Research, 22*, 367-384.

Lenz, I. (1978). *Prostitutional tourism in South East Asia*. Berlin: Freie Universität.

Leung, L.T. (1995, October 30). The cost of extra marital affairs. *Hong Kong Economic Journal*, p. 3.

Lew, A. A. (1987). A framework of tourist attraction research. *Annals of Tourism Research, 14*, 553-575.

Lindblom, C. E. (1959). The science of muddling through. *Public Administration Review, 19*, 79-88.

Linn, G. (1995). Manufacturing migration. *Hong Kong Business, 14*(160), 50-52.

Lowry, L. L. (1993). Sun, sand, sea & sex: A look at tourism advertising through the decoding and interpretation of four typical tourism advertisements. In K. S. Chon (Ed.), *Proceedings 1993 STTE Conference* (pp. 183-204). Miami.

Lubeigt, G. (1979). Economie, tourisme et environement en Thailande. *Cahiers d'Outre Mer, 32*, 371-399.

Lucas, E. (1994). Reinventing Atlantic City—again. *Association Meetings, 6*(5), 24-37.

Lukes, S. (1974). *Power: A radical view*. London: Macmillan.

Luxembourg, R. (1927). Stagnation and progress in Marxism. In D. Ryanzanov (Ed.), *Karl Marx: Man, thinker and revolutionist* (pp. 106-111). New York: International Publishers.

Mabbett, H. (1987). *In praise of Kuta. From slave port to fishing village to the most popular resort in Bali*. Wellington: January Books.

MacCannell, D. (1976). *The tourist: A new theory of the leisure class*. New York: Schrocken Books.

Mackie, V. (1992). Japan and South-East Asia: The international division of leisure. In D. Harrison (Ed.), *Tourism and the less developed countries* (pp. 75-84). London: Belhaven Press.

Maclean, J. R., Peterson, J. A., & Martin, W. D. (1985). *Recreation and leisure: The changing scene*. New York: Macmillan.

Madden, C. (1996, December). I do phone sex for a living. *She & More*, 29-30.

Man on first child sex tour charge. (1995, September 28). *Telegraph-Mirror*, p. 3.

Mannion, J., & Ridge, P. (1996). Sacrifical lambs. *More, 156*, 58-61.

Mano, K. (1993, March). A club on one's own. *Playboy*, 121-130.

Maurer, M. (1991). *Tourismus, Prostitution, Aids.* Zürich: Rotpunktverlag.

McClelland, D. (1961). *The achieving society.* New York: Free Press.

McCumber, D. (1992). *X-rated: The Mitchell brothers.* New York: Simon & Schuster.

McLeod, E. (1982). *Women working: Prostitution now.* Kent: Croom Helm.

Meisch, L. A. (1995). Gringas and Otavalenos: Changing tourist relations. *Annals of Tourism Research, 22,* 441-462.

Mendis, E. D. L. (1981). *The economic, social and cultural impact of tourism in Sri Lanka.* Colombo: Christian Workers Fellowship.

Middleton, S. (1993). *Educating feminists: Life histories and pedagogic issues.* New York: Teachers College Press.

Miller, R. (1991). Selling Mrs. Consumer: Advertising and the creation of suburban socio-spatial relations, 1910-1930. *Antipode, 23,* 263-301.

Mings, R. C., & Chulikpongse, S. (1994). Tourism in Far Southern Thailand: A geographical perspective. *Tourism Recreation Research, 19*(1), 25-31.

Mitchell, A. A. (1986). The effect of verbal and visual components of advertisements on brand attitudes and attitude toward the advertisement. *Journal of Consumer Research, 13,* 12-23.

Mosel, J. N. (1966). Fatalism in Thai bureaucratic decision making. *Anthropological Quarterly, 39,* 190-199.

Muecke, N. (1992). Mother sold food, daughter sells her body. *Social Science Medical, 35*(7), 891-901.

Mulder, N. (1994). *Inside Indonesian society. An interpretation of cultural change in Java.* Bangkok: Editions Duang Kamol.

Mulhall, B. P., Hu, M., Thompson, M., Lin, F., Lupton, D., Mills, D., Maund, M., Cass, R., & Millar, D. (1993). Planned sexual behaviour of young Australian visitors to Thailand. *The Medical Journal of Australia, 158,* 530-535.

Mull, R. F., Bayless, K. G., & Ross, C. M. (1987). *Recreational sports programming.* North Palm Beach: The Athlectic Institute.

Muntarbhorn, V. (1993, February 9). *Sale of Children: Report Submitted by the Special Rapporteur Appointed in Accordance with the Commission on Human Rights Resolution 1992/76.* E/CN.4/1993/67/Add.1.

Muntarbhorn, V. (1996, October). Report from the World Congress Against the Commercial Sexual Exploitation of Children, Sweden August 27-31. *ECPAT Australia, 35,* 1-2.

Murphy, J. F., Williams, J. G., Niepoth, E. W., & Brown, P. D. (1973). *Leisure service delivery system: A modern perspective.* London: Henry Kimpton.

Murphy, P. E. (1985). *Tourism: A community approach.* New York/London: Methuen.

Naibavu, T., & Schutz, B. (1974). Prostitution: Problem or profitable industry? *Pacific Perspective, 3,* 59-68.

Nash, D. (1981). Tourism as an anthropological subject. *Current Anthropology, 22*(5), 461-481.

New Zealand Prostitute's Collective. (1989). *Submission to the Parliamentary Select Committee on Justice and Law Reform Regarding the Crimes Bill 1989.* Wellington: Author.

Nunez, T. (1989). Touristic studies in anthropological perspective. In V. L. Smith (Ed.), *Hosts and guests: The anthropology of tourism.* Philadelphia: University of Pennsylvania Press.

Odzer, C. (1990). *Patpong prostitution: Its relation to, and effect on, the position of Thai women in Thai society.* Ph.D. dissertation, New School for Social Research.

Odzer, C. (1994). *Patpong sisters: An American woman's view of the Bangkok sex world.* New York: Arcade Publishing & Blue Moon Books.

O'Grady, R. (1981). *Third World stopover.* Geneva: World Council of Churches.

O'Grady, R. (1992). *Gebrochene Rosen: Kinderprostitution und Tourismus in Asien*. Bad Honnef: Horlemann.

O'Malley, J. (1988). Sex tourism and women's status in Thailand. *Society and Leisure, 11,* 99-114.

Oppermann, M. (1992). Intranational tourist flows in Malaysia. *Annals of Tourism Research, 19,* 482-500.

Oppermann, M. (1996). Sex tourism and prostitution: Issues and questions. In M. Oppermann (Ed.), *Pacific Rim tourism 2000: Issues, interrelations, inhibitors* (pp. 274-280). Rotorua: Waiariki Polytechnic.

Oppermann, M., & Chon, K. S. (1997). *Tourism in developing countries*. London: International Thompson Press.

Overs, C. (1994, February). Unfair cop. *New Internationalist, 252,* 26-28.

Pat, Y. H. & Chan, P. K. (1994, June 24). The threat from concubines. *Next,* 58-67.

Parish, W., & Whyte, M. (1978). *Village and family in contemporary China.* Chicago: University of Chicago Press.

Parliamentary Joint Committee on the National Crime Authority. (1995). *Organised Criminal Paedophile Activity.* A report by the Parliamentary Joint Committee on the National Crime Authority, Parliament of the Commonwealth of Australia, Canberra.

Peck, J. G., & Lepie, A. S. (1989). Tourism and development in three North Carolina coastal towns. In V. L. Smith (Ed.), *Hosts and guests: The anthropology of tourism* (pp. 203-222). Philadelphia: University of Pennsylvania Press.

Perera, L. (1978). *Case study: Hiddakawu.* Seminar: The Role of Tourism in Social and Economic Development, Colombo, Sri Lanka.

Peterson, R. A., & Kerin, R. A. (1977). The female role in advertisements: Some experimental evidence. *Journal of Marketing, 41,* 59-63.

Phongpaichit, P. (1982). *From peasant girls to Bangkok masseusses.* Geneva: International Labour Organisation.

Pihichyn, P. (1996, June 25). Net provides link up to Polish Imahe. *Winnipeg Free Press.*

Pocock, D. (1980). *Humanistic geography and literature: Essays on the experience of place.* London: Croom Helm.

Pocock, D. (1982). Writers who knew their places. *Geographical Magazine, 54*(1), 40-43.

Pollay, R. W. (1986). The distorted mirror: Reflections on the unintended consequences of advertising. *Journal of Marketing, 50,* 18-36.

Posner, R. A. (1992). *Sex and reason.* Cambridge, MA: Harvard University Press.

Pruitt, S., & LaFont, S. (1995). For love and money: Romance tourism in Jamaica. *Annals of Tourism Research, 22,* 422-440.

Reinhardt, S. (1989). Sexualität: Suche nach einer neuen Sichtweise. In Tübinger Projektgruppe Frauenhandel (Ed.), *Frauenhandel in Deutschland* (pp. 88-92). Bonn: J. H. W. Dietz Nachfahren.

Reinhardt, S., & Koss, T. (1989). Liebe im Sonderangebot—der Heiratsmarkt. In Tübinger Projektgruppe Frauenhandel (Ed.), *Frauenhandel in Deutschland* (pp. 115-134). Bonn: J. H. W. Dietz Nachfahren.

Relph, E. (1976). *Place and placelessness.* London: Pion.

Relph, E. (1987). *The modern urban landscape.* Baltimore: John Hopkins University Press.

Renschler, R., (Ed.). (1987a). *Ware Liebe—Sextourismus, Prostitution und Frauenhandel.* Wuppertal: Peter Hammer Verlag.

Renschler, R. (1987b). Ein Internationales Problem. In R. Renschler (Ed.), *Ware Liebe: Sextourismus, Prostitution, Frauenhandel* (pp. 19-62). Wuppertal: Peter Hammer Verlag.

Renschler, R. (1987c). Prostitution und Frauenhandel am Beispiel Thailand. In R. Renschler (Ed.), *Ware Liebe: Sextourismus, Prostitution, Frauenhandel* (pp. 103-129). Wuppertal: Peter Hammer Verlag.

Richins, M. L. (1991). Social comparison and the idealized images of advertising. *Journal of Consumer Research, 18,* 71-83.

Richter, L. K. (1989). *The politics of tourism in Asia.* Honolulu: University of Hawaii Press.

Richter, L. K. (1992). Political instability and tourism in the Third World. In D. Harrison (Ed.), *Tourism and the less developed countries* (pp. 35-46). London: Belhaven Press.

Richter, L. K. (1993). Tourism policy-making in South-East Asia. In M. Hitchcock, V. T. King, & M. J. G. Parnwell (Eds.), *Tourism in South-East Asia* (pp. 179-199). London: Routledge.

Rimm, M. (1995). Marketing pornography on the information superhighway. *Georgetwon Law Journal, 83,* 1849-1915.

Roberts, J. (1988, August 15). Kiwi spearheads child rescue mission. *New Zealand Women's Weekly,* 22-24.

Roberts, N. (1994, February). The whore, her stigma, the punter and his wife. *New Internationalist, 252,* 8-9.

Roebuck, J., & McNamara, P. (1973). Ficheras and free-lancers: Prostitution in a Mexican border city. *Archives of Sexual Behavior, 2*(3), 231-244.

Rose, C., & Thomas, D. (1995). *Net.sex.* Indianapolis: Sams Publishing.

Rosenblum, K. E. (1975). Female deviance and female sex role: A preliminary investigation. *British Journal of Sociology, 26,* 169-185.

Ross, M. (1977). Football and baseball in America. In P. Rose (Ed.), *Sport and society: An anthology* (pp. 102-112). Boston: Little Brown.

Rossman, J. R. (1995). *Recreation programming: Designing leisure experiences.* Champaign, IL: Sagamore Publishing.

Rowbottom, J. (1991). Risks taken by Australian men having sex in South East Asia. *Venereology, 4*(2), 56-59.

Russell, R. V. (1996). *Pastimes: The context of contemporary leisure.* Madison: Brown & Benchmark Publishers.

Ryan, C., & Kinder, R. (1994). The deviant tourist and the crimogenic place—the case of the tourist and the New Zealand prostitute. In J. Cheyne & C. Ryan (Eds.), *Tourism downunder: A tourism research conference* (pp. 55-71). Palmerston North: Massey University.

Ryan, C., & Kinder, R. (1996a). The deviant tourist and the crimogenic place—the case of the tourist and the New Zealand prostitute. In A. Pizam & Y. Mansfeld (Eds.), *Crime and international security issues* (pp. 23-35). Chichester: Wiley and Sons.

Ryan, C., & Kinder, R. (1996b). Sex, tourism, and sex tourism—the thresholds and margins of interactions between tourist and prostitute. *Tourism Management, 17,* 507-518

Sack, R. (1988). The consumer's world: Place as context. *Annals of the Association of American Geographers, 78,* 642-664.

Samarasuriya, S. (1982). *Who needs tourism? Employment of women in the holiday-industry of Sudugama, Sri Lanka.* Colombo/Leiden: Unpublished Research Report.

Save the Children Fund. (1995). *The HIV/AIDS prevention and management programme.* Ho Chi Minh City: Author.

Schmitz, A. (1987a). Aspekte des Frauenhandels in der Schweiz. In R. Renschler (Ed.), *Ware Liebe: Sextourismus, Prostitution, Frauenhandel* (pp. 83-100). Wuppertal: Peter Hammer Verlag.

Schmitz, A. (1987b). Prostitution und Frauenhandel am Beispiel Dominikanische Republik. In R. Renschler (Ed.), *Ware Liebe: Sextourismus, Prostitution, Frauenhandel* (pp. 130-154). Wuppertal: Peter Hammer Verlag.

Schöning-Kalendar, C. (1989). Dem Thema auf der Spur. In Tübinger Projektgruppe Frauenhandel (Ed.), *Frauenhandel in Deutschland* (pp. 9-16). Bonn: J. H. W. Dietz Nachfahren.

Scott, V. (1994, February). The professional. *New Internationalist, 252,* 7.

Sekhar, K., (Ed.). (1995). A window to the street. *NETWORK of Saskatchewan Women, 10*(1).

Senate. (1994, June 3). Crimes (Child Sex Tourism) Amendment Bill, 1994, second reading. *Hansard.*

Seneviratne, M. (1994). *Evil under the sun—child prostitution in Sri Lanka.* Colombo: Swastika Publications.

Senftleben, W. (1986). Tourism, hot springs, resorts and sexual entertainment: Observations from Northern Taiwan—a study in social geography. *Philippine Geographical Journal, 30,* 21-41.

Sex tourists targeted. (1993, November 5). *Canberra Times,* p. 16.

Shaw, G., & Williams, A. M. (1994). *Critical issues in tourism: A geographical perspective.* Oxford: Blackwell.

Shen, Y. (1993). *China's tourism: Industry, policies and coordinate development.* Beijing: Tourism Education Press.

Sijuwade, P. O. (1995). Counterfeit intimacy: A dramaturgical analysis of an erotic performance. *Social Behavior and Personality, 23,* 366-376.

Silver, R. (1993). *The girl in scarlet heels.* London: Century.

Silverman, J. (1993). Topless dancing: Why I like it, why I do it. *Glamour,* 242-243, 279-281.

Simmons, R., Davis, B. W., Chapman, R. J. K., & Sager, D. D. (1974). Policy flow analysis: A conceptual model for comparative public policy research. *Western Political Quarterly, 27,* 457-468.

Sinclair, M. T., & Vokes, R. W. A. (1993). The economics of tourism in Asia and the Pacific. In M. Hitchcock, V. T. King, & M. J. G. Parnwell (Eds.), *Tourism in South-East Asia* (pp. 200-213). London: Routledge.

Smith, S. L. J. (1983). *Recreation geography.* London: Longman.

Smithies, M. (1986). *Yoygakarta. Cultural heart of Indonesia.* Oxford: Oxford University Press.

Soedarso, S. (1992). *The role of visual arts in cultural tourism development in central Java and the special district of Yogyakarta.* Jakarta: Regional Office for Science and Technology for SE Asia.

Soedjarwo, A. (1991). *Social aspects of the special province of Yogyakarta.* Second country seminar on regional development, September 3-6, Yoygakarta, Indonesia.

Soley, L. C., & Reid, L. N. (1988). Taking it off: Are models in magazine ads wearing less? *Journalism Quarterly, 65*(4), 960-966.

Sorkin, M. (1995). See you in Disneyland. In M. Sorkin (Ed.), *Variations on a theme park: The new American city and the end of public space* (pp. 205-232). New York: Hill and Wang.

Spender, D. (1983). *There's always been a women's movement this century.* London: Pandora Press.

Squire, S. J. (1988). Wordsworth and lake district tourism: A study of romantic reshaping of landscape. *Canadian Geographer, 32,* 237-247.

Squire, S. J. (1994). The cultural values of literacy tourism. *Annals of Tourism Research, 21,* 103-120.

Steadman, M. (1969). How sexy illustrations affect brand recall. *Journal of Advertising Research, 9*(1), 15-19.

Stiefvater, R. E. (1996). *The social construction of leisure for illegal recreational drug users.* Ph.D. dissertation, Indiana University.

Stol, A. (1980). *Charter Naar Bangkok.* Rotterdam: Ordeman.

Suthaporn, S. (1983, July 1). VD and prostitution: An inseparable problem. *Bangkok Post,* p. 12.

Symanski, R. (1981). *The immoral landscape: Female prostitution in Western societies.* Toronto: Butterworth.

Tamosaitis, N. (1995). *Penthouse guide to cybersex: The sexiest underground guide to electronic erotica.* New York: Penthouse International.

Tantiwiramanond, D., & Pandey, S. (1987). The status and role of Thai woman in the pre-modern period. *Sojourn, 2,* 155-159.

Thiemann, H. (1989). Reisende Maenner: Sextourismus als spezielle Form der ökologischen Zerstoerung—Das Beispiel Thailand. In C. Euler (Ed.), *Eingeborene—ausgebucht: Ökologische Zerstörung durch Tourismus* (pp. 91-103). Giessen: Focus Verlag.

Thomas, W. I., & Thomas, D. S. (1928). *The child in America.* New York: Alfred A. Knopf.

Thompson, J. (1994, July 25). Ashamed to be a Kiwi. *New Zealand Women's Weekly,* 52-53.

Thompson, W. E., & Harred, J. L. (1992). Topless dancers: Managing stigma in a deviant occupation. *Deviant Behaviour, 13,* 291-311.

Tinsley, H., & Tinsley, D. (1982). *Psychological and health benefits of the leisure experience.* Carbondale: Southern Illinois University.

Tisdell, C., & Wen, J. (1991). Foreign tourism as an element in PR China's economic development strategy. *Tourism Management, 12,* 55-67.

Tjokrosudarmo, S. (1991). *A brief outline of the approach to tourism development.* Second country seminar on regional development, September 3-6, Yogyakarta, Indonesia.

Toufexis, A. (1996, February 19). Romancing the computer: A cyberadultery suit shows the risk of looking for love online. *Time.*

Truong, T. (1983). The dynamics of sex tourism: The case of Southeast Asia. *Development and Change, 14*(4), 533-553.

Truong, T. (1990). *Sex, money and morality: Prostitution and tourism in Southeast Asia.* London: Zed Books.

Tübinger Projektgruppe Frauenhandel (Ed.). (1989). *Frauenhandel in Deutschland.* Bonn: J. H. W. Dietz Nachfahren.

Turner, V. (1974). *The ritual process.* Harmondsworth: Penguin.

Unger, L. S., & Kernan, J. R. (1983). On the meaning of leisure: An investigation of some determinants of the subjective experience. *Journal of Consumer Research, 9,* 381-392.

Urry, J. (1990). *The tourist gaze.* London: Sage.

Uzzell, D. (1984). An alternative structuralist approach to the psychology of tourism marketing. *Annals of Tourism Research, 11,* 79-99.

Van Schaardenburgh, A. M. (1996). *Local participation in tourism development. A study in Cahuita, Costa Rica.* M.A. thesis, Tilburg University.

Vietnamese National Administration of Tourism. (1995). *Summary report of the tourism development plan to the year 2010.* Hanoi: Author.

von Krause, J. (1993). "Kinder sind kein Gemüse, das man einfach kaufen und konsumieren kann." Tourismus und Kinderprostitution in Thailand. In N. Häusler, C. Kamp, P. Müller-Rockstroh, W. Scholz, & B. E. Schulz (Eds.), *Unterwegs in Sachen Reisen: Tourismusprojekte und Projekttourismus in Afrika, Asien und Lateinamerika* (pp. 333-354). Saarbrücken: Verlag für Entwicklungspolitik Breitenbach.

Wagner, U. (1977). Out of time and place—mass tourism and charter trips. *Ethnos, 42,* 38-52.

Walker, D., & Ehrlich, R. S. (1992). *"Hello my big-big honey." Love letters to Bangkok bar girls and their revealing interviews.* Bangkok: Dragon Dance Publications.

Walton, J. (1993). Tourism and economic development in ASEAN. In M. Hitchcock, V. T. King, & M. J. G. Parnwell (Eds.), *Tourism in South-East Asia* (pp. 214-257). London: Routledge.

Wane, J. (1996, November). Male order sex. *She & More,* 60-65.

Weeramunda, A. J. (1993). *Report on the pilot survey of child prostitution in a selected area of Kalutara district.* Colombo: University of Colombo.

Wilkinson, P., & Pratiwi, W. (1995). Gender and tourism in an Indonesian village. *Annals of Tourism Research, 22,* 283-299.

Williams, A. P., & Hobson, J. S. P. (1994). Tourism—the next generation: Virtual reality and surrogate travel, is it the future of the tourism industry? In A. V. Seaton (Ed.), *Tourism: The state of the art* (pp. 283-290). Chichester: John Wiley & Sons.

Williams, A. P., & Hobson, J. S. P. (1995). Virtual reality and tourism: Fact or fantasy? *Tourism Management, 16,* 423-428.

Wolf, Y. (1993, June). The world of the Kuta cowboy. A growing subculture of sex, drugs and alcohol is evident among male youth in the tourist areas of Bali and Lombok as they seek an alternative to poverty. *Inside Indonesia,* 15-17.

Woodside, A. G., & Lysonski, S. (1989). A general model of traveler destination choice. *Journal of Travel Research, 27*(4), 8-14.

World Tourism Organization. (1994). *WTO news January/February.* Madrid: Author.

Yacoumis, J. (1989). South Pacific tourism promotion: A regional approach. *Tourism Management, 10,* 15-28.

Yan, M. W., Chen, M., & Lee, C. H. (1996). Jail sentance for Hong Kong man and his Chinese concubine. *Next, 320,* 46-53.

Yik, F. (1995). Bars with prostitutes. *East Magazine, 161,* 84-87.

Yiu, Y. (1994, September 2). It's the fashion to have a concubine. *Next,* 72-73.

Zaring, J. (1977). The romantic face of wales. *Annals of the Association of American Geographers, 67,* 397-418.

Index